A PRACTICAL GUIDE TO
JAPANESE GARDENING

A PRACTICAL GUIDE TO JAPANESE GARDENING

From design options and materials to planting techniques and decorative features

Advice and step-by-step projects, with over 700 illustrations, plans and photographs

Charles Chesshire

Special photography by Alex Ramsay

LORENZ BOOKS

This edition is published by Lorenz Books, an imprint of
Anness Publishing Ltd, Hermes House,
88–89 Blackfriars Road, London SE1 8HA
tel. 020 7401 2077; fax 020 7633 9499
www.lorenzbooks.com; www.annesspublishing.com

If you like the images in this book and would like to
investigate using them for publishing, promotions or
advertising, please visit our website
www.practicalpictures.com for more information.

UK agent: The Manning Partnership Ltd;
tel. 01225 478444; fax 01225 478440;
sales@manning-partnership.co.uk
UK distributor: Grantham Book Services Ltd;
tel. 01476 541080; fax 01476 541061;
orders@gbs.tbs-ltd.co.uk
North American agent/distributor: National Book Network;
tel. 301 459 3366; fax 301 429 5746;
www.nbnbooks.com
Australian agent/distributor: Pan Macmillan Australia;
tel. 1300 135 113; fax 1300 135 103;
customer.service@macmillan.com.au
New Zealand agent/distributor: David Bateman Ltd;
tel. (09) 415 7664; fax (09) 415 8892

Publisher **Joanna Lorenz**
Editorial Director **Helen Sudell**
Project Editor **Emma Clegg**
Copy Editors **Catherine Best** and **Alison Bolus**
Designers **Simon Daley** and **Mike Morey**
Jacket design **Anthony Cohen** and **Balley Design**
Additional materials and equipment text **Jenny Hendy**
Illustrators **Anna Laflin** and **Anna Koska**
Special photography (locations and steps)
  Alex Ramsay
Special photography (materials and equipment)
  Peter Anderson
Production Controller **Claire Rae**

All rights reserved. No part of this publication may be
reproduced, stored in a retrieval system, or transmitted in
any way or by any means, electronic, mechanical,
photocopying, recording or otherwise, without the prior
written permission of the copyright holder.

© Anness Publishing Ltd 2009

A CIP catalogue record is available from the British Library.

PUBLISHER'S NOTE
Although the advice and information in this book are
believed to be accurate and true at the time of going to
press, neither the authors nor the publisher can accept
any legal responsibility or liability for any errors or
omissions that may be made.

Previously published, in part, as *Japanese Gardening*.

Page 1: *The dry garden at Ryogen-in, Kyoto*
Page 2: *The Japanese maple in autumn*
Page 3, from left: *Syoko-ho-en, near Kyoto; digging a
mound in a courtyard garden; stepping stone path, water
basin, lantern and bamboo gate in a tea garden*
Page 4, from top: *The Golden Pavilion, Kyoto; a pair of
sand cones in the Shinto shrine of Kamigano, Kyoto; a
stroll garden path leading to a gateway; Secateurs and
pruning shears; a shelter in the stroll garden of Karaku-en
in Okayama*
Page 5, from top: *Boxwood clipped into rounded shapes;
placing rocks as part of a dry waterfall; raked gravel
patterns; placing elements in a mixed stone path; the moon
bridge at the Huntington Botanical Gardens in Los Angeles.*

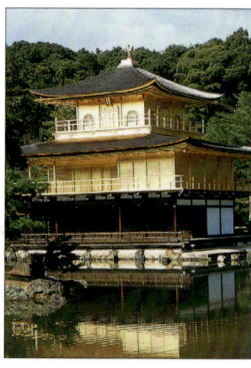

Contents

Introduction	6
A HISTORY OF JAPANESE GARDENING	8
The evolution of the garden	10
Waves of Chinese influence	12
Modern & Western influences	16
INSPIRATIONS	18
The natural landscape	20
The influence of Zen	26
Architectural elements	30
Understanding the Japanese garden	34
Translating the style	37
CLASSIC GARDEN STYLES	40
Pond gardens	42
Dry gardens	46
Tea gardens	50
Stroll gardens	54
Courtyard gardens	58
NATURAL MATERIALS	62
Rocks & boulders	64
Choosing rocks & boulders	68
Moving rocks & boulders	70
Paving & stepping stones	72
Cobbles, pebbles & paddlestones	74
Sand, grit, gravel & slate	76
Dry water	80
Making a dry waterfall & stream	82
Plants & planting	84
Topiary	88
WATER FEATURES	92
Streams, waterfalls & ponds	94
Preparing the watercourse	98
Building a meandering stream	100

Pond liners, pumps & filters	102
Creating edges for a pond	104
Tsukubai & shishi-odoshi	106
Making a *sui-kinkutsu*	111
Constructing a reservoir	112

CREATIVE CONSTRUCTS 114
Paths	116
Path styles	120
Tea houses & other buildings	122
Boundaries	124
Making a tea-path gate	130
Bridges	132
Making a *yatsuhashi* bridge	134
Decorative artefacts	136
Lighting	138

CREATING A GARDEN 142
Making a plan	144
The pond garden style	146
Garden plan: a pond garden	148
How to make a pond garden	150
Making a pond with a soil liner	152
Making a pine island	154
Building a waterfall	156
The dry garden style	158
Garden plan: a dry garden	160
How to make a dry garden	162
Positioning rocks	164
Placing edging stones	166
Improving drainage	168
The tea garden style	170
Garden plan: a tea garden	172
How to make a tea garden	174
Arranging a *tsukubai*	176
Setting a lantern	178
Laying stepping stones	180

The stroll garden style	182
Garden plan: a stroll garden	184
How to make a stroll garden	186
Making a pond with a flexible liner	188
Making a gravel path	190
Making a wisteria arbour	192
The courtyard garden style	194
Garden plan: a courtyard garden	196
How to make a courtyard garden	198
Building a bamboo screen fence	200
Laying a paving-stone path	202
Building a mound	204

PLANT DIRECTORY 206
How plants are named	208
How to use the plant directory	209
Spring trees & shrubs	210
Spring blossom	212
Late spring & summer trees, shrubs & climbers	215
Summer flowers	218
Autumn foliage	220
Autumn flowers	223
Evergreen shrubs	225
Evergreen trees & conifers	229
Ferns	233
Bamboo	234
Palms	235
Other plants of interest	236

Care & maintenance	238
Glossary	246
Useful addresses	248
Index	250
Acknowledgements	255
Plant hardiness	256

Introduction

"Visualize the famous landscapes of our country and come to understand their most interesting points. Recreate the essence of these scenes in the garden, but do so interpretatively, not strictly."

From the *Sakuteiki*, the earliest known book of Japanese garden design, written in the 11th century.

Left: *Water plays a crucial role in Japanese gardens. This waterfall at St Mawgan, in Cornwall, England, is designed to look naturally formed. The source of the water is well hidden amongst the lush foliage of bamboo.*

The Japanese garden has captured the imagination of Western gardeners ever since they discovered its delights in the 19th century. Japan, isolated from the rest of the world from the 1630s to over 200 years later, had been nurturing extraordinary and unique styles of architecture, poetry, painting, flower arranging and gardening. When artists, architects and designers in the West were finally exposed to these Japanese arts in the late 19th century, they were astonished by what they found.

The strong influence of Japanese arts is still being felt today. Of these arts, Japanese garden design, in particular, exerts a powerful and mystical grip. Steeped in significance and refinement, the Japanese garden has enormous appeal, especially for garden designers seeking both a deeper meaning and a more contemporary edge for their own gardens.

THE STYLES OF JAPANESE GARDENS

Japanese landscape gardens can be broken down into five main styles – pond gardens, dry gardens, tea gardens, stroll gardens and courtyard gardens – and each of these has a long and intimate relationship with the history of Japan. Even a modest knowledge of Japanese history, especially the country's relationship with China and Buddhism, will go a long way towards helping us to understand the art of the Japanese garden, and thereby enabling us to reproduce it.

It was the dynamic, creative energies of Zen monks and painters of the medieval period that set the stage for the development of the exceptional art form that is the Japanese garden. These ancient gardens, especially those constructed of stone and sand (some of which survive even from the 15th century), have become the benchmark of abstract garden art throughout the world.

THE SIGNIFICANCE OF PLANTS

Plants are fundamental to all but a few Japanese gardens. Most of the plants used possess symbolic significance, including the twisted pine, scattered cherry blossom, pendulous wisteria, the lotus ('purity rising out of the mud') and fiery Japanese maple. These plants are always placed with restraint and care, and gardeners celebrate the seasons through their fleeting beauty. Everything in the garden – plants, rocks, lanterns, water – serves a role in the creation of a unified, harmonious and poetic picture. This is an art in which the whole is far greater than the sum of its parts.

Right: *A patchwork of different species of moss in the dappled sunshine at Sanzen-in, Ohara, near Kyoto. The soft velvet carpets of moss under Japanese cedars (*Cryptomeria*) produce a magical effect.*

THE SIGNIFICANCE OF WATER AND ROCKS

Water is one of the most important elements in the Japanese garden. It can often be found in the form of a pond, a stream or a simple small water basin. Even when water is absent, its presence is often suggested through areas of sand and gravel, or dry streams. Rocks are equally important and are regarded as possessing a kind of spiritual and living essence that needs to be respected if they are to be placed successfully.

A real understanding of the two elements of rock and water, through careful observation in nature, will help to form a good basis for creating Japanese-style gardens. The more the natural law of these elements is understood, the easier it becomes to treat them in abstract ways.

It is this abstraction of nature that is most difficult to reproduce successfully. But don't be put off: it is perfectly possible to assimilate some of the simple beauty of Japanese gardens without delving into the often esoteric meaning behind them.

HOW TO USE THIS BOOK

This book shows you exactly how to create a beautiful and individual Japanese garden. The first two chapters take you through the history of the gardening style, and the environmental and cultural elements that have inspired and influenced it, in particular Zen, and attitudes and beliefs concerning the natural world. This section also describes ways in which the principles have been interpreted over the years, and suggests how you might continue this tradition by adapting them. The five main garden styles (pond, dry, tea, stroll and courtyard) are then outlined in their traditional forms so you can think about which ones most appeal. Chapters on Natural Materials and Creative Constructs introduce essential elements, supported by practical explanations of how to achieve them, and a section on Water Features shows how to plan all the water-based items. Creating a Garden looks at each style more closely, with each one presenting a detailed garden plan and showing how to combine three key practical elements to create part of a garden. The plant directory gives a selection of plants, followed by advice on care and maintenance.

Left: *Statues of the Buddha are not common in Japanese gardens, but this one makes up part of an entrancing collection assembled in a forest of bamboo by the early 20th-century artist Hashimoto Kansetsu.*

A HISTORY OF JAPANESE GARDENING

The story of this gardening tradition is both long and fascinating. Understanding its history and learning about the people who were involved in its development gives an insight into the philosophy that inspires the Japanese garden. With such knowledge, we can plan and create gardens in this style with confidence and conviction. Although the essential style of Japanese gardens can be imitated simply by copying their outward form and appearance, reproducing their spirit requires a much deeper understanding.

The following chapter leads us through the main Japanese historical periods, made distinct by wave after wave of Chinese and Buddhist influences. These have combined with the Japanese people's strong sense of self, and their glorious landscape and native religion, to produce the uniquely curious and beautiful art form that is the Japanese garden. It is remarkable that garden styles from over 1,000 years ago still inform today's gardens. Even in the most avant-garde modern gardens you can often find motifs from Heian romanticism, the dry gardens of the Muromachi period or the tea gardens of the Momoyama period.

Above: *A chequerboard of stone squares sunk into a sea of moss.*
Left: *A tea house at Saiho-ji Moss Temple in Kyoto.*

The evolution of the garden

There are six important periods in the history of the Japanese garden, most of them coinciding with dramatic changes in Japan's history. The division into six is an oversimplification, but it helps to explain the evolution of some of the distinct styles of these gardens. Each period is defined not only by the practicalities and customs of contemporary Japanese life, but also by the conflicts and changes brought by religion, culture, politics and warfare. Chinese artistic influence was strong, and Buddhism brought a sense of spirituality to Japanese garden design.

Above: *A garden of clipped shrubs, which are known as* o-karikomi, *at Sanzen-in, a garden from the Edo period.*

THE DIFFERENT PERIODS
As recently as the 1970s, a garden from the 9th century was excavated in Nara. The history of the Japanese garden really starts at that time, now known as the Nara period. It continues through the five subsequent periods – the 11th-century Heian period, the 13th-century Kamakura period, the 15th-century Muromachi period, the 16th-century Momoyama period (which all centred around the old capital of Kyoto), and lastly the 18th- and 19th-century Edo period (after the capital moved to Tokyo). The gardens of the 20th century are more complex in their style and are dealt with later under "Modern and Western influences".

NARA PERIOD (710–94)
A period of pond and stream gardens, and gardens for ceremonies (Chinese Tang dynasty, 618–906)
Built in 710, Nara, which lies some 48km (30 miles) south of Kyoto, was the last of the ancient capitals of Japan. Excavations in 1974 found vestiges of an ornamental garden on the site of an old palace. They revealed a winding stream, edged in gravel and pebbles in a naturalistic style, with unique, sophisticated rock arrangements. These gardens were almost certainly used for ceremonial purposes, and were quite similar to those that were constructed in China during the same period.

HEIAN PERIOD (794–1185)
The first wave of Chinese influence and Pure Land Paradise gardens (Chinese Tang dynasty, 618–906; Five Dynasties, 906–60; Chinese Song dynasty, 960–1279)
This, the most romantic period in Japanese cultural history, saw a great many refinements, and also showed a new sensitivity to detail and a focus on the seasons and rituals, all of which evolved under imperial rule in Kyoto. One of the key features was the creation of pond and island gardens that reproduced the Mystic Isles of the immortals and the Pure Land Paradise garden of Buddha Amida, into which the souls of the pure could be reborn after death.

Another new feature was the garden design that enabled court ceremonies, music and poetry readings to be performed in courtyards, on boats and by the side of streams. The *Sakuteiki*, possibly the world's first great garden treatise, was written during this period in the 11th century.

Left: *This woodblock print by Katsushika Hokusai (1760–1849) shows a group of ladies visiting the wisteria gardens at Edo-period Kameido. Traditional Japanese garden design was closely linked to formal social etiquette.*

KAMAKURA PERIOD (1185–1392)

The second wave of Chinese influence with the arrival of Zen (Chinese Song dynasty, 960–1279; Yuan or Mongol dynasty, 1279–1368; Chinese Ming dynasty, 1368–1644) Minamoto was the first *shogun* (military dictator) in Japan, and his government, based in Kamakura, took little interest in the arts until Buddhist monks began returning from China bringing tea, paintings of the Song dynasty and early artefacts of the Ming dynasty. They were also influenced by the Zen Buddhism of China. The imperial family in Kyoto continued with the same traditions as in the Heian period. Around 1339, the Saiho-ji and Tenryu-ji gardens were created in Kyoto, inspired by scenes from Song-dynasty paintings. Zen monks started to make gardens, and rocks became an important element.

MUROMACHI PERIOD (1393–1568)

The era of the devastating Onin wars and the refining influence of Zen on garden-making (Chinese Ming dynasty, 1368–1644)

The mingling of the warrior classes with the imperial classes in Kyoto led to an extraordinary flowering of the arts. This period saw the building of the Golden Pavilion in the 1390s and the Silver Pavilion in the 1470s by Ashikaga shoguns, whose pond-filled stroll gardens were a departure from the earlier preference for boating lakes. The most important innovation of this period was the creation of "dry water" gardens (*kare-sansui*) that used rocks set in gravel or sand to symbolize water. The designs of these gardens were influenced by Zen Buddhism and the black and white ink landscape paintings. The most famous of these gardens are the Daisen-in (made in about 1513) and the Ryoan-ji (1499).

Right: *The Golden Pavilion in Kyoto, which is covered in gold leaf, was built in the 1390s by the first of the Ashikaga shoguns, marking the beginning of the Muromachi period.*

MOMOYAMA PERIOD (1568–1603)

The era of the unifiers who would build Japan as a single nation and the rise of the tea masters and the merchant class (Chinese Ming dynasty, 1368–1644)

Three successive military unifiers built gardens using far larger rocks than before, designed as an expression of power, but this excess was also tempered by the modesty of an important new feature: the tea house and garden. The famous tea-ceremony ritual was initially popularized by a merchant called Rikyu, who was one of the most influential figures in Japan.

Above: *The gardens around Nijo Castle, in Kyoto, were constructed at the beginning of the Edo period. These gardens used larger rocks than ever before and in greater numbers.*

EDO PERIOD (1603–1867)

The era of National Isolation and the private stroll gardens (Chinese Qing dynasty, 1644–1911)

In 1603, the Tokugawa shogunate moved to the eastern capital, Edo (now Tokyo), where strict social structures were enforced. The gardens of this period are characterized by stroll gardens, the most famous being the Katsura Detached Palace, in Kyoto. With its many pond-side tea houses and buildings, and exquisite framed views, it might represent the last great peak in large-scale Japanese garden art.

Meanwhile, wealthy city merchants and samurai developed the small courtyard garden, incorporating motifs from the dry gardens and the tea gardens of earlier ages. In time, gardens became more ostentatious, losing the creative edge and philosophical depth of their predecessors. Since 1867, however, when Japan reopened its borders to the West, gardens have explored the minimalism of Zen and more avant-garde and naturalistic styles, although still incorporating traditional motifs such as the Mystic Isles.

Waves of Chinese influence

Before AD 607, Japan was a primitive culture that had received only a trickle of Chinese cultural influence through Korea. After 607, a whole host of influences were suddenly accessible to the Japanese people through their contact with China. When the first Japanese ambassador to China arrived in Ji, the Chinese capital, in 607, he would have seen vast lake-and-island gardens, encircled by pavilions, surrounding the imperial palaces. China must have been a revelation to the Japanese, and this was the beginning of many centuries of cultural exchange.

Above: *The gardens of Tenryu-ji are situated in Kyoto. Created in the 1300s, some parts were later adapted to fit with changing tastes.*

THE CHINESE STYLE

In Chinese gardens, islands were often used to represent the Mystic Isles, the mythical abode of the immortals. The Chinese Emperor Han Wu had built his own lake and a fantastical island garden in the hope of enticing the immortals down to part with the secret elixir for eternal youth. The Mystic Isles were believed to float on the backs of turtles, while the immortals were carried around on the backs of cranes. These myths had a huge impact on the Japanese imagination and, to this day, the Mystic Isles, cranes and turtles still feature prominently, usually in the form of carefully composed rock groupings. Rocks not only represented islands, however, but also came to symbolize Mount Shimusen, the central mountain in Buddhist mythology and an important mountain-water image that arrived in Japan from China.

BUDDHIST INFLUENCE

A major force in Japan, Buddhism gained particular importance from the mid-6th century onwards, incorporating additional Chinese influences. Even though the emperor of Japan placed the country under the protection of the Buddha, the indigenous Shinto gods, or kami, retained a strong influence, closely associated with the emperor and with the general well-being of society.

Ponds were central to the Buddhist concept of paradise and became as essential to Japanese gardens as they had been in China. The Amida Buddha's Land of Paradise garden was described as being planted with gem-laden trees, while golden sands edged lily-filled lakes. On these lakes, heavenly hosts waited for devout souls to give them new birth on a lotus blossom in the realm of bliss. The great Amida garden of lakes and islands became the image for Nara- and Heian-style gardens.

THE ONSET OF THE JAPANESE STYLE

In 794, when the capital was moved to what is now Kyoto (Heian Kyo), the pond-and-winding-stream garden was the pre-eminent garden design.

Left: *Ancient Chinese gardens displayed trees and fantastic rocks in their courtyards. The Japanese, although heavily influenced by the Chinese, had a preference for a more naturalistic approach to garden design.*

Above: The Chinese myths of the Mystic Isles still inspire designers today. In the dry garden of Ryogen-in, created in the 1980s, stands the central mountainous island of Horai.

Left: A landscape of mountains and a river by Japanese painter and Zen priest Toya Sesshu (1420–1506). His Zen-inspired landscapes were influential within both the painting and garden design styles of Japan.

Above: A turtle island at Konchi-in where the head and flippers can be picked out from among rocks and clipped shrubs.

Gradually, during the Heian period, fuelled by the cultured society of Kyoto, a true Japanese garden style began to emerge. This style slowly and indiscernibly blended Buddhism, the Mystic Isles and Shinto's sacred groves into the distinctive art form that is so recognizable today.

GEOMANCY

Meaning the Chinese science of divination, geomancy affected the design of palaces, towns and gardens by its insistence that buildings, plants and rocks must be placed in a very precise manner according to certain forces or lines of energy, to ensure that they were in balance and in tune with the natural order. If a placement was wrong, trouble and ill health could descend on an individual, a whole household or even the nation. In fact, the choice of the site of the new city of Kyoto, modelled on the Chinese city of Chang'an and its palaces and gardens, followed Chinese geomantic principles.

Each of the elements is linked to a direction: earth at the centre, water in the north, fire to the south, wood in the east and metal in the west. Other Chinese approaches to the elements maintained that each direction could also represent colours, planets, seasons and guardian gods.

The principles of yin and yang also form part of the science of geomancy, but they are not always regarded as precise opposites and may be seen as complementary forces. Most phenomena contain an element of both yin and yang, because bringing them together produces harmonious conditions. For example, combining water (yin) with the sun or fire (yang) creates the right conditions to enable seeds to germinate.

PAINTINGS

The next wave of influences on the Japanese garden also came from China, in part through its painters. The Chinese artists of the Tang and Song dynasties painted mountains, pine trees beside waterfalls, streams falling into lakes, and paths weaving through rocks. These artists, more than all of the great Chinese imperial parks, influenced the Japanese garden. Meanwhile, Japanese monks and artists who visited China saw temples of great beauty, as well as hermit monks and artists living a simple life in huts and caves, and they returned home with a desire to emulate the Chinese lifestyle and the arts that they had encountered there.

ZEN BUDDHISM

Japanese monks were eager to practise a purer version of Buddhism without esoteric practices such as the worship of Buddha Amida. They found in China practitioners of Chan (or Zen, as it is known in Japan), a word derived from the Sanskrit *dyana*, which means meditation. Zen Buddhism places much more focus on the individual and on his or her efforts to control the mind, especially through meditation, and the experience of "no-ness".

By the late 1500s, Japanese Zen masters had become the next great garden-makers, once again inspired by Chinese and Japanese paintings featuring dry gardens of sand and rocks. Their gardens became increasingly abstract, often carrying hidden messages of Zen symbolism.

TEA GARDENS AND CEREMONIES

The paintings, poetry and spiritual writings of the Chinese literati were not the only sources of inspiration for Japanese painters and Zen monks. The design of the Japanese tea house was also inspired by the rustic hermitages of the Chinese literati and artists residing in their mountain retreats. As a result, the merchants and monks would develop a completely new style of garden, which included a path (known as a *roji*) that led to a tea house.

By the early 16th century, this new style had evolved into the influential form of the tea garden, and Japanese garden design took a brand new imaginative direction. The Japanese tea garden is one that is very familiar to Western eyes, with its key features such as a tea house, lanterns, water basins and wells.

Top right: *This two-fold screen by Kano Eitoku (1543–90) shows a romantic depiction of birds and a waterfall.*

Right: *In the garden at Konchi-in, various symbolic forms are depicted with rocks and pines, with fine white gravel spread around them to represent the sea.*

WAVES OF CHINESE INFLUENCE 15

Modern & Western influences

From 1633, when shogun Iemitsu declared the Japanese borders closed, until the Americans arrived to reopen them by force in 1852, Japan was a hidden, secret country. Very few links with the West survived during this period, and even the Chinese had little contact with their neighbours. While the country developed in isolation during the major part of the Edo period (1603–1867), Japanese artists continued to express themselves in painting, literature and design, making use of a strong internal cultural tradition in which artistic endeavour could flourish.

THE AMERICAN ATTACK

Until 1852, when the Black Ships of the American Navy fired their first few warning salvos at the Tokugawa shogunate to force the Japanese to open their ports and begin trading with foreigners, the influence of the modern Western world had been limited. Once these trading and communication channels opened, the West's influence made a mark in technical and artistic terms. This was a two-way interaction, as the impact of Japanese culture in the West was also significant.

The Japanese regime in 1852 was in a sad state of decline. However, after the American attack, the impoverished imperial family replaced the shogunate that had held power for 250 years, and enjoyed a new ascendancy.

Above: *The roof garden of the Canadian Embassy in Tokyo, designed by the Buddhist monk Shunmyo Masuno in the 1990s, and inspired by the Rocky Mountains.*

Below: *Mirei Shigemori, an artist and garden maker, redesigned the garden of Tofuku-ji in Kyoto, in the 1930s. He was the first to see the potential of the Japanese garden to become a vehicle for contemporary expression. He was also influenced by the Western art forms of the time.*

16 A HISTORY OF JAPANESE GARDENING

JAPANESE ARTS REACH THE WEST

From the mid-19th century onwards Japan's influence on the West made itself felt, with Japanese prints and artefacts flooding Western markets, invigorating the art world and inspiring the Impressionists, among others. Great architects, such as Frank Lloyd Wright (1869–1959) and Charles Rennie Mackintosh (1868–1928), found a raw simplicity in Japanese gardens and architecture. They also admired the beauty of natural materials, which they used in conjunction with their own modern materials: glass, concrete and steel.

In gardening terms, what particularly appealed to Western eyes was the style of extraordinary gardens such as the Ryoan-ji, in Kyoto, whose brooding mystery affects people as much now as it did when it was built in the 1490s. This Zen-style garden influenced many Western designers who, although perhaps unfamiliar with the concepts of Zen Buddhism, found in the garden an art form that gave expression to their own minimalist, atonal and avant-garde creations.

WESTERN ARTS REACH JAPAN

While the West was absorbing Eastern influences, the Japanese showed an extraordinary capacity to assimilate other traditions, both digesting and also reinventing them. There was (and still is), for example, a hunger for English-style gardens, which were initially copied, as Chinese gardens had been, before being integrated into the Japanese mainstream and given an Eastern slant.

MODERN JAPANESE DESIGN

By the 1930s, however, the design of more traditional Japanese gardens had become rather stale and clichéd, and this situation prompted one or two designers to re-evaluate the use of established materials and motifs. The greatest of these was Mirei Shigemori (1896–1975), who made private and temple gardens from the 1930s to the 1950s. He gave his gardens a modern twist but, interestingly, continued to employ traditional motifs and natural materials alongside the contemporary use of concrete.

Since the 1950s, many newly created gardens have replaced natural rocks and boulders with raw, blasted, quarried materials, plastics and metals, in much the same way as 17th-century gardens blended the artificial with the natural. This incorporation of new materials, while retaining the pure simplicity of Zen gardens, is still the hallmark of contemporary Japanese garden design.

One of the latest movements in the evolution of the Japanese garden is towards a more natural style of garden design, featuring a combination of both native plantings and naturalistic streams. However, what also stands out with these contemporary Japanese gardens is that Japan cannot entirely shed its cultural and historical past and that, even now, the most up-to-date garden designs still hark back through the ages to the 11th-century Heian gardens in their use of natural materials, as was laid down in the oldest surviving work on Japanese gardening – the *Sakuteiki*.

Above: *A Japanese tea garden, designed by Maureen Busby for the 2004 RHS Chelsea Flower Show in London. The main feature of a tea garden is a stepping-stone path that passes through a "wilderness".*

INSPIRATIONS

The Japanese garden possesses a style quite unlike any other. This unique character can be attributed to three factors: the outstanding natural landscape and the spirit of Zen, which both inspired it, and the importance of architectural features within the garden.

Japan is an archipelago of rugged coastlines and has a volcanic mountainous landscape, with steep rocky streams that tumble through forests. This wonderful natural topography and native flora inspired gardeners to recreate in their own gardens what they saw around them. The ancient Japanese also believed that the trees, rocks, mountains and water had power over the gods of their Shinto religion.

The pared-down, minimalist way of interpreting and recreating the natural landscape around them within the garden originated in the spirit of Zen, with the careful use of space and understatement.

A final factor to consider is the spiritual significance of architectural features in the Japanese garden, including the tea houses, and the technique of *shakkei*, whereby views both within and beyond the garden are framed by manmade or natural elements.

This chapter looks at the features that make the character of the Japanese garden distinct, and explains how this style can be understood and interpreted in the West.

Above: *Plum blossom is associated with the start of spring.*
Left: *In the garden of Hosen-in in the mountains north of Kyoto, a clipped hedge frames the natural landscape and draws it in through the stems of bamboo.*

The natural landscape

Looking out over an expanse of sand raked into perfect lines, set in a perfect rectangular courtyard with one or two rocks, and an azalea or two clipped so much that they barely flower, you might be forgiven for thinking that Japanese gardeners are more inclined to fly in the face of nature than sympathize with it. Yet Japan's own natural landscape of mountains, windswept pines, waterfalls and islands directly inspires and informs their garden designs, resulting in a spiritual style that gives inspiration to gardeners all over the world.

Above: *Under certain conditions, snow will stick to pine needles. In Japan these attractive white baubles are commonly known as "snow flowers".*

AN INSPIRING STYLE

Japanese garden design was initially influenced by the Chinese. However, the natural mountainous and coastal landscapes of Japan, coupled with the people's spiritual reverence for rocks and trees, derived from their native Shinto religion, together created a second powerful influence. By incorporating a careful selection of indigenous plants and imitating the natural features of the countryside, albeit in a restrained, stylized form, Japanese garden designers have developed a unique style.

THE TOPOGRAPHY OF JAPAN

A mountainous archipelago of four main islands, Japan also has hundreds of small rocky islets. The mountains – over 50 of which are volcanic – are steep and wooded and scored with rocky streams, hot springs and rivers. In fact, most are still wooded up to their peaks because, until recently, Buddhism was the official religion and the eating of meat and fish was prohibited. This meant that, unlike in other parts of the world, their hills and mountains have not been stripped of vegetation by sheep, goats and cattle. To this day, natural features such as mountains, rocks and streams continue to inspire Japanese garden designers and are recurring features of the Japanese garden.

THE MOUNTAIN MOTIF

Mountains are a uniquely powerful influence over the imagination and gardens of the Chinese and the Japanese. Through myth and religion, mountains stand as the central feature of many of their garden designs. The Mystic Isles myth (which developed off the Chinese coast) is a typical example. There were five islands, one of which was called P'eng-lai, which later became Horai in Japan. These Mystic Isles, like the real islands of Japan, were large and mountainous, towering thousands of feet high, their sides steep and precipitous, reaching up to high plateaux rich in greenery. Here were misty blue valleys where all the beasts and birds were white, trees bore pearls, the flowers were fragrant and the fruits brought immortality to those who ate them. Along the shores of the islands lived blissfully happy immortal beings in golden, silver and jade pleasure pavilions. The immortals were not gods, but men who suffered no sickness or death, and developed supernatural powers, being able to float through the air. Sometimes they were carried on the backs of giant cranes, another key feature of Japanese design.

Originally, the myth says, the Mystic Isles floated about and were not fixed to the ocean floor. Then, the Supreme Ruler of the Universe commanded the islands to be secured by 15 enormous turtles, but one day a giant cast a net and caught six of the turtles.

Right: *Vermilion Torii gates originate in Shinto religion and symbolize sacred ground. They make a bold feature in the Karlsruhe Japanese garden in Germany.*

SYMBOL OF SHINTO: THE *TORII* GATE

The typical vermilion-painted gateway to Shinto shrines may be found at the entrance to many Buddhist temples as well. The gateway marks the progress of the worshipper from the day-to-day world outside to the sacred world inside, and passing under it is part of the cleansing ritual common to Shinto and Buddhist worship. *Torii* gates are usually made of wood, metal or stone, with two upright supports and two crossbars over the top. The word *torii* is thought to derive from a resting perch for birds; the birds will bring good luck to the temple, as they are considered to be messengers from the gods in the Shinto religion. These days, wealthy visitors to a Shinto shrine may donate a new *Torii* gate to thank the gods for their success in business.

Some others drifted away and were lost, leaving just three. The early Japanese might well have believed that they already lived on these Mystic Isles. Whatever the case, the island of Horai, the crane and the turtle became themes embedded in their gardens, even being reproduced in Mirei Shigemori's garden at the Tofukuji, as recently as 1938.

When you add to this ancient myth the divinities of Shinto (see below), the natural landscape of Japan, the influence of the distantly revered and idealized landscapes of China, and the Lands of Paradise promised by some Buddhist sects, the whole concoction becomes an inspirational mix for the development of a very special and beautiful style of gardening.

THE INFLUENCE OF SHINTO

Shinto – the religion of Japanese settlers who arrived by sea, possibly from Korea, in the 3rd or 4th centuries – means "way of the gods". It involved animistic and pagan-style rituals, and centred around rocks, trees and plants. It was believed that these objects possessed spiritual aspects that could draw the gods down to earth. There were two kinds of gods, or *kami*: those that descended from above, and those that lived across the sea and gave birth to the main islands of Japan. These two sets of gods were symbolized by sacred rocks and sacred ponds. These rock and pond motifs occur again and again in Japanese gardens, both past and present.

The Shintoists believed that certain places in the wild were inhabited by

Above: *Although boldly abstract, the design of the Site of Reversible Destiny in Gifu, Japan, incorporates the mountain motif while also echoing the form of the distant landscape.*

the gods. To this day, you will still find trees wrapped in ropes near shrines, as well as old trees and rocks that have become shrines in their own right. *Shime*, the binding of objects or even people with rice straw ropes, may originally have been used to designate territory, while the bound artefacts symbolize land or islands. It is interesting to note that the word *shima*, meaning "garden", comes from shime.

Go-shintai ("the home of the gods") and *iwa-kura* ("seats of the gods") can also still be found throughout Japan. They have been purified and covered with layers of sand and gravel to become *shiki-no-himorogi*, or "sacred precincts". Some special rocks may even have been added.

Such rituals and sacred spaces had an important influence on the use of rocks in gardens and dry landscape gardens. The interplay between the flat expanse of the sea (symbolized by sand or gravel) and the rugged immensity of rocks and old trees provided a kind of aesthetic that inspired the leap from the purely spiritual space of Shinto to the secular space of the garden. This aesthetic

Left: *Detail from a screen (c.1600–1640) illustrating episodes from* The Tale of Genji. *This classic of ancient Japanese literature is interwoven with symbolic references to nature.*

Right: *At the end of the 19th century, the designer Ogawa created gardens inspired by nature. This recalled the early gardens of the 10th century, such as this one at Syoko-ho-en, near Kyoto.*

may also explain why the Chinese style of garden was not copied "religiously". Shinto and the natural landscape of Japan provided a fertile influence that adapted the Chinese style into something new.

INTERPRETATIONS OF NATURE

The natural world has been a constant feature of Japanese gardens from the early days of the Heian period (794–1185), when inspiration came straight from the landscape and natural surroundings, right up to the present, when abstract and contemporary gardens still demonstrate a profound understanding of nature. The Italian garden aims to express an intellectual and philosophical vision of nature; the English garden is mainly based on the idealized world of the pastoral idyll; but the Japanese garden uses nature in a highly symbolic way.

More specifically, in the 15th and 16th centuries, Japanese designers turned increasingly to their great landscape painters for artistic inspiration, just as the late 18th-century English picturesque garden was inspired by the paintings of Claude Lorrain and Nicolas Poussin. Along with nature, painting has been a common starting point for many gardening movements.

THE *SAKUTEIKI*

The earliest known treatise on gardening, the *Sakuteiki* – the subtitle of which was "Setting of Stones" – was written in the mid-11th century. It was more of a technical journal for the select few, but many of its rules are still adhered to today as elemental precepts. Stones are said to have "desires", and the book recommends ways of listening to them, vital if they are to be placed correctly in the Japanese garden, as if they were in the wild.

The chapter headed "Nature" describes the remarkable and vivid use of the imagery of coastlines, streams, rocks, islands and waterfalls in garden design, and details a range of features with specific instructions. For example, stones can be used in different ways – perhaps placed in streams in order to modulate the flow of water, used as bottom or solitary stones, or as diffused stones to interrupt and divert the flow. Furthermore, garden streams (*yarimizu*) can be created in various styles, for example as if they are flowing through a valley, or as if they are broad rivers, or mountain torrents. There are also descriptions of, and instructions for creating, different kinds of waterfall, all of which are relevant to the Japanese gardener today.

Garden streams often pour down a waterfall into a lake or pond. These ponds represent lakes or the sea, and are dotted with islands, their shorelines punctuated by promontories made of white sand to evoke the beaches of distant landscapes. Miniature windswept ocean beaches, coves and undulating shorelines are planted with soft grasses. Islands also come in different guises, with rocky shores, for example, or in forest, meadow and wetland styles.

The earliest Japanese gardens, from the Heian period when the *Sakuteiki* was written, still have an important influence on modern garden designers who look to nature for inspiration. These gardens emphasize that we should observe but not slavishly copy nature, consulting the "genius of the place" before transforming it into art. As the *Sakuteiki* suggests, "Visualize the famous landscapes of our country and come to understand their most interesting points. Recreate the essence of these scenes in the garden, but do so interpretatively, not strictly."

HEIAN CULTURE AND DESIGN

In the culture of the Heian period, as distinct from the later austere Zen and Muromachi periods, the aristocracy that had settled around the Emperor in Kyoto enjoyed years of peaceful luxury. They spent much of their time writing poetry, and became more and more detached from the business of running the country. A kind of melancholy pervaded their lives. They believed that they were living in the *Mappo*, the Buddha's period of Ending Law, with declining social and religious mores. They hoped to be transported to his Western Paradise, depicted in their gardens as lakes and islands, for an afterlife of eternal bliss. This life was seen as a fleeting interlude, a dream between two realities.

The Heian aristocracy closely observed nature, noting every whim and expression as a sign and symbol to compare with love, death, honour and the great range of human emotions. These emotions were often symbolized by plants, and the early Heian gardens used many flowering shrubs, such as kerria, deutzia, lespedeza, azalea and osmanthus, as well as cherries, maples, wild roses and irises. In the two great novels of the time, *The Pillow Book* (995) by Sei Shonagon and *The Tale of Genji* (early 11th century) by Murasaki Shikibu, trees and flowers, as well as the weather, were used to symbolize human thoughts and desires.

THE SEASONS AND THEIR PLANTS

Around Kyoto, the seasons are fairly predictable, right down to the first rumblings of thunder over the mountains that herald the beginning of the rainy season in midsummer. By then, the cherry blossom, wisteria and azalea will have long dropped their last blooms and the hydrangeas started to colour. At the same time, it will be sweltering in the sub-tropical south in Kyushu, while in northern Honshu and Hokkaido, trees growing below the melting snows on the mountainsides have not yet come into leaf. Apart from the northern reaches, most of Japan endures uncomfortably hot and rainy summers. This is why the Heian elite in Kyoto placed such a strong emphasis on the two main garden seasons – spring (the most important) and autumn – an emphasis that still exists today. The seasons were also considered to be part of the geomantic system, with flowers used to depict the cardinal lines of energy; good planting and design helped to protect the household from misfortune.

In modern Japan, the plum and peach blossoms are the fanfare for spring, followed shortly by the cherry blossom.

Top: *The cherry blossom heralds the height of spring and is the most popular season for viewing gardens in Japan.*

Above: *The mop-headed* Hydrangea macrophylla, *growing profusely in a shaded woodland, is a classic summer flower.*

Top: *Trees are planted extensively in Japanese gardens for their autumn colour, such as this katsura tree in the Tully garden in Ireland.*

Above: *The vivid colour of a traditional Japanese Torii gate stands out dramatically in a snow-covered garden.*

> ## THE FOUR SEASONS IN JAPANESE GARDENS
>
> **Spring**
> *Weather*: mild and pleasant – the best growing season and the best time to visit Japan.
> *Plants*: plum, peach and cherry blossom, azalea, wisteria, camellia.
> *Festivals*: many festivals linked with spring flowers, including Golden Week (April/May) to celebrate the abundant cherry blossom.
>
> **Summer**
> *Weather*: hot, humid and rainy with thunderstorms, oppressive heat day and night.
> *Plants*: iris, hydrangea, lotus blossom.
> *Festivals*: iris festival in late May. Bon, a Buddhist festival honouring the ancestors. Many Japanese people leave the cities and visit the cooler mountain areas of the north.
>
> **Autumn**
> *Weather*: mild, less humid with sunshine and cold nights. Season of typhoons.
> *Plants*: *Acer palmatum* and *Enkianthus*.
> *Festivals*: local festivals (*matsuri*) linked with rice harvest.
>
> **Winter**
> *Weather*: very cold, often snowy, but some clear days with winter sun.
> *Plants*: bamboo, pine, cedar and other evergreen trees and bushes.
> *Festivals*: New Year festivals (*Omisoka*) when the whole country takes time off and all businesses are shut.

Then come the native camellias, azaleas and floribunda wisterias, while, in early summer, iris festivals are celebrated up and down the country. The lotus, the enduring symbol of Buddhism, also flowers in summer. The autumn is marked by the Japanese maples (*Acer palmatum*) which grow in Japan's forests, as does *Enkianthus*, which sets ablaze the hillsides and hillside temples at this time. Chrysanthemums, symbols of the imperial family, long life and good fortune, are grown especially for festivals in late autumn. In winter, the pine, cedar and bamboo are celebrated.

The Japanese use some native plants, such as cherries, azaleas, pines and bamboos, within their gardens, but tend to ignore a vast range of their native flora. This indicates restraint rather than a limited palette. So a hedge may be made up of a number of evergreen shrubs but will not blend masses of bright-coloured foliage. In this way, the final effect is restrained even when a large number of plants have been used.

The influence of Zen

Zen Buddhism was introduced to Japan from China by monks in the 13th century. Once established, it provided a consistent influence for all aspects of Japanese culture and arts. The "no-ness" of Zen philosophy, in particular, prompted some important developments in garden design – the dry gardens surrounding many Buddhist temples were a rich source of inspiration for Japanese garden designers and the influence of this simple, restrained style, with its symbolic use of raked effects in gravel and the subtle placing of rocks, has been felt from East to West.

Above: *Natural rocks have been replaced by slabs of blasted quarry stone and assembled with fragments of the rock. The mountain image and empty space are typical features of the Zen garden.*

THE ARRIVAL OF ZEN BUDDHISM

The pioneer monks who introduced Zen to Japan initially met with a bleak response from the rather philistine military government based in Kamakura, south of present-day Kyoto. Two or three generations later, however, Zen found new patrons among the rival warlords and the imperial family so that, by the early 1300s, there were some 300 Zen monasteries in Kamakura and Kyoto. These temples, part of what was called the Five Mountain Network, promoted studies in a range of Chinese arts and philosophies. Apart from studying neo-Confucian metaphysics, the monks were also highly skilled in poetry, painting, calligraphy, ceramics, architecture and garden design.

A less erudite group of rural monks, who were known as Rinka (meaning "forest"), practised in another network of Zen temples and devoted themselves strictly to Zazen, or sitting Zen (meditation), as well as *koan* (the writing of riddles). Their self-discipline and loyalty to their masters appealed to the rising warrior class, the samurai, to whom the Rinka monks preached stern moralizing sermons. This philosophy was shared by other followers of Zen, whose teachers or masters also transmitted their values to their disciples. There were no written scriptures, though, and none of the trappings of esoteric Buddhism, such as mandalas, chanting and the reciting of scriptures, which had dominated Japanese life for the previous 500 years.

ZEN AND THE DRY GARDEN

Dogan (1200–53), a monk who lived during the Kamakura period, was well known for emphasizing the "no-ness" of all things (emptiness, void or non-substantiality). This aspect of Zen meant finding what might be called the "perfect expression of pure mind". Garden designers expressed this "no-ness" in the empty space of sand in dry gardens. Sand had already been used within Shinto sacred precincts, then in front of palaces for court

Left: *The stump of an enormous Japanese cedar bound and housed as a shrine in its own right. The Shinto belief that trees, rocks and other natural objects possessed spirits was incorporated into Zen garden design.*

Above: *Rocks in a "sea" of gravel represent the Mystic Isles, from the ancient myth adopted by the Zen tradition.*

Right: *Zen monks were drawn to the world of the Chinese scholar-hermit. They created tea houses, such as this one at Toji-in Temple, and tea paths imbued with the spirit of Zen.*

ceremonies, before evolving into a representation of the sea or a white canvas for painter-gardeners. Under the auspices of Zen practitioners, the empty stretch of sand came to represent a meditative spiritual space. Sometimes these gardens look like familiar landscapes, or brush paintings, and if contemplated for long enough, they induce a sense of calm.

It was mostly the Zen monks who designed the extraordinary spaces known as *kare-sansui* (dry landscapes), which have become synonymous with Japanese gardening, most notably at the famous dry gardens of Ryoan-ji and Daisen-in. Zen exercised a strong influence over Japanese gardening (and still does), and it also gave greater precision and discipline to the art of garden design. Even if you are not steeped in the mysteries of Zen, you can appreciate the extraordinary beauty and sense of style and the pared-down, abstract visions of nature to be found in these gardens.

Right: *At the Canadian embassy in Tokyo, a dry garden with natural rocks and sand pays homage to the past while also displaying the brave cutting edge of modernity.*

ZEN AND THE TEA GARDEN

The evolution of the tea garden had strong links to the Zen monks. Used originally by them as an aid to wakefulness during long periods of meditation, tea soon became an essential part of Buddhist rituals. It was only a short step for Zen monks, as garden makers and tea drinkers, to bring these two arts together. So the tea garden, at first just a simple rustic path to the tea house, became associated with important traditions.

ZEN AND MODERN GARDEN STYLE

When creating a Zen-style dry garden, consider the influences that created them. Many contemporary gardens are made up of a few rocks, a layer of sand or gravel and a bamboo plant or pine tree, and are glibly described as being very Japanese or, worse, very Zen. That is only true, however, if there is no hint of the superfluous. Nor should any one feature dominate. Zen-style dry gardens, or tea gardens, should be imbued with purity and restraint.

Above: *The Zen garden of Tenju-an, in Kyoto, dating from the late 14th century, is a superb example of the interplay between geometric, manmade and irregular natural forms.*

THE ESSENCE OF THE ZEN GARDEN

While the first Japanese gardens of the 11th century were poetic readings of nature and 15th-century gardens were inspired readings of the master landscape painters, the gardens of both periods were disciplined attempts to understand the self and the universe. What this meant in practical terms was that there was an avoidance of the trite, the obvious and the emphatic. Unnecessary distractions and the use of excessive colour or form were also avoided. The prime ingredients were those that in the 13th century became defined as the seven aspects of Zen:

- asymmetry
- simplicity
- austere sublimity
- naturalness
- tranquillity
- subtle profundity
- freedom from attachment

These qualities were also applied to other art forms in a Zen style, such as calligraphy and poetry.

Even people with no experience of meditation or of Zen Buddhism can appreciate the calming beauty of a Zen garden. If you want to imbue your garden with the spirit of Zen, you should try to make your garden reflect a quiet, contemplative world and avoid the kind of deliberate gestures that come from a busy, overactive mind. The art is to avoid over-stimulating the senses in the way that you might experience in a Western garden.

A Zen garden will avoid carefully contrived colour schemes, rocks with strange shapes, gushing fountains or brightly painted buildings. For example, the red-painted Chinese bridges that you see in some Japanese gardens would not be seen in a Zen garden because such features were seen to divert the eye and stimulate the mind instead of calming it.

It is the approach to the Zen arts that is important, whether it be in garden design, painting or the martial arts. The spirit of Zen, the "emptiness" conveyed by an area of raked gravel in a dry garden, should be as much in the mind of the man with the rake as in the clean sweep of the gravel. Although Zen is a state of mind that takes years to perfect, the garden designer can still plan a garden with the spirit of Zen in mind, making calmness and tranquillity a central feature, avoiding bright colours and ensuring that the landscaping and planting are kept to an absolute minimum.

Zen garden with raked waves

This dry garden in Ryongen-in, Kyoto, was redesigned and constructed in 1980 on the site of an old garden. The "canvas" of this painterly garden is a rectangle of a sea with parallel raked waves. Maintained in a more exaggerated form than older gardens of this style, the essential elements are the same as those of the 15th century. The parallel lines of raked gravel change to deep concentric waves as they lap around the main features in the dry sea. Towards the back is the tallest group of rocks, which represent Mount Horai (*Horai-san*), the foremost of the Mystic Isles. These isles were said to be carried on the backs of turtles, so the main mossy island is designed as a turtle island (*kame-shima*). The immortals lived on these isles, holding the secret elixir for eternal youth and immortality. They travelled around on the backs of cranes, and the third rock arrangement is a crane island (*tsuru-shima*).

The rectangular frame is made from a combination of edging stones and roof tiles. On two sides a border of moss is contained between the edging and the wall, while in the foreground the temple veranda and garden are divided by a border of pebbles. Pine trees have also been planted into the border.

The garden can be read as an artistic impression, with the bolder shapes and the deeper waves creating a dramatic effect on the viewer. Nevertheless, the simplicity of the design and the significance of the main features give a sense of permanence.

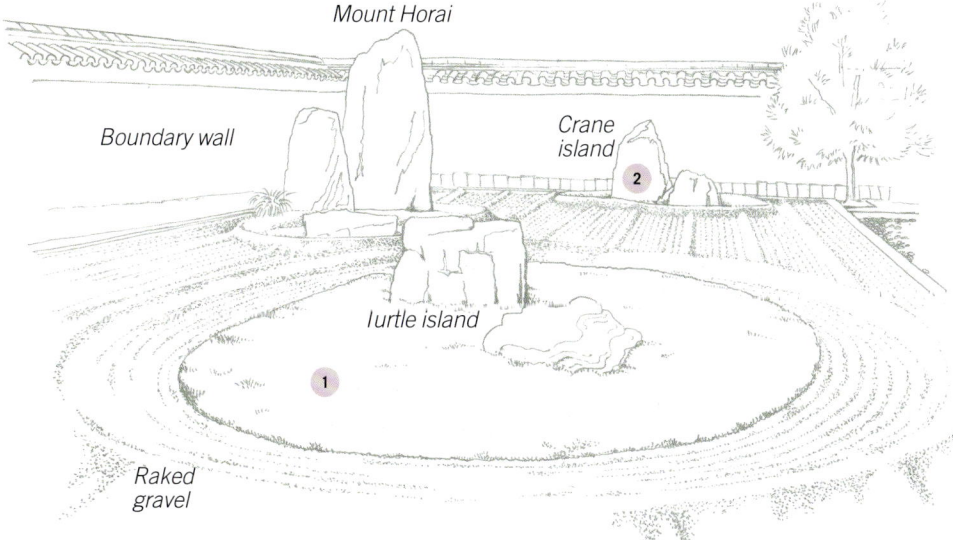

Right: *In the dry garden at Ryogen-in, the three main symbols of the Mystic Isles are laid out in a sea of sand. In the foreground is a turtle island; back left is Mount Horai, the tallest of the Mystic Isles; with a crane island at the rear.*

THE INFLUENCE OF ZEN 29

Architectural elements

Up to the Edo period (1603–1867), all major garden styles evolved in towns and were defined by the layout of the main buildings, courtyards, entrances and boundaries. Later, large gardens were laid out in more rural locations, where small buildings such as arbours, pavilions and tea houses were often placed to keep the human focus, so maintaining the relationship between architecture and garden. Another role for architecture was in the technique of *shakkei*, where buildings, trees or shrubs would frame a view of the landscape beyond the garden.

ARCHITECTURAL INTERACTION

The relationship between a Japanese garden and the architecture of the main house, temple or garden buildings is quite unlike that of the formal Western garden. In the West, the details and forms of the architecture tend to influence the design of formal gardens, but by contrast the formal Japanese garden enjoys the interplay between the angularity of the architecture and the curve of natural forms. Although dry and courtyard gardens are often contained within the rectilinear confines of garden walls, the forms of the gardens themselves are more like paintings held within a picture frame.

Above: *In the dry garden at the Tofuku-ji, the architectural line of the* hojo *abbot's quarters, the surrounding walls and the lines of raked sand make it hard to define exactly where the building ends and the garden begins.*

Below: *The view from the temple veranda overlooking the garden at Shoden-ji reveals not only the garden but also the distant sacred Mount Hiei. This capturing of a view was part of the garden design device known as* shakkei.

Right: *This contemporary design by Maureen Busby shows a strong interplay between the buildings and the gardens that surround them.*

In other styles of Japanese garden, the natural forms of stepping stones, rocks, pine boughs and bamboos are brought very close to the buildings. Sometimes camellias or azaleas may be clipped into geometric forms to accentuate or even imitate the architecture, but asymmetry and dynamic natural forms within the design are usually preferred.

CHINESE INFLUENCES

The Japanese buildings of the Nara (710–94) and Heian (794–1185) periods, like their gardens, were more or less copies of the Chinese. But differences began to develop during the Heian period: the Japanese already showed a preference for the natural finish of timber, rather than the more flamboyant painted buildings common in China at the time, and roofs were also less sweeping and curved than their Chinese counterparts.

> ### GARDEN BUILDINGS
>
> Japanese garden buildings and structures have particular characteristics that mark them as different from most Western styles:
>
> • the preferred materials are natural, such as bamboo, reed, and sawn or raw timber (sometimes with the bark on);
>
> • materials are not painted, but left to look as natural as possible;
>
> • at times when the Chinese influence was strong, especially the very early Nara period (early 8th century) and the later Edo period (early- to mid-19th century), buildings and structures, such as bridges, were sometimes painted bright red-orange, in dramatic contrast to the typically muted look apparent in the rest of the garden.

The principal style of Heian aristocratic homes was known as *shinden* (literally, "sleeping hall"). This main hall, or *shinden*, was set at the centre of a square building, with two adjacent wings to the sides for concubines and wives. From these two wings, two corridors (the east and the west) led south to the main garden. In the space between these two corridors was an open, sand-covered courtyard, which was reserved for ceremonies and entertainment. Through part of this courtyard, a stream might meander and feed into the main pond beyond.

At the end of the east and west corridors were pavilions, usually named after their primary function – for instance, the fishing pavilion was often built on stilts over the main pond, but was just as likely to have been used by musicians. Another pavilion may have covered the well or the spring that fed the pond.

Over the next 200 years, Japanese architecture evolved into smaller and more refined urban residences. By the Muromachi period, monks and samurai showed a marked preference for the *shoin* style. *Shoin* was a term that referred to the alcove that was set within one of the outer walls of the main building. This alcove had papered walls in order to allow natural light to illuminate a specially designed shelf or a desk for reading and writing. The *shoin* was a kind of library or study that, for the warriors and abbots, symbolized their arrival as members of the intelligentsia or literati. This new architectural style was found in many temples and houses, which also had verandas and sliding panels that opened up to reveal their gardens.

The tea house also employed some aspects of the *shoin* style, especially the alcove, but the general style of tea-house architecture was more rustic. The Japanese tea house, which was originally known as the "mountain place in the city", combined the rustic charm of the thatched hut (*soan*) with the sophistication of a more literary and urban style of architecture (*shoin*). This hybrid style was, and still is, most popular for building tea houses and garden buildings.

The alcove of the tea house, known as the *tokonoma*, was a place in which to display works of art, especially calligraphy scrolls and poems, alongside simple country-style flower arrangements.

SHAKKEI

Many old houses and temples have verandas with pillars that support the roofs. These pillars also frame a view of the garden. The view of the garden from indoors can be regarded as if you are looking at a painting. The art of framing is even more important when a spectacular distant view can be captured – for example, the sight of Mount Fuji, near Tokyo, or Mount Hiei, near Kyoto. This technique is called *shakkei*, or "borrowed scenery", but was once known by the more evocative term *ikedori*, meaning "captured alive". It was an important device that involved more than simply having a "nice view" from your house. *Shakkei* meant that prominent distant features could, in effect, be drawn into the garden itself and so become an intrinsic part of its overall composition.

Although most Westerners wishing to reproduce a Japanese garden will not own a Japanese-style home, they may have verandas, picture windows or other forms of framing that can be used to capture their garden, and perhaps also a more distant view. In this way, architecture can be used to make the garden part of the house.

Above: *The pillars that support the verandas of temples and tea houses can frame the garden beyond them in the same way as the frame of a landscape painting. This design accentuates the contrast between the architecture and the natural form.*

Below: *Sliding rice paper panel doors (*shoji*) open up a view from a tatami-matted tea room at Isui-en, Nara. The square opening interacts with the weaving stems of Japanese maples.*

> ### FRAMING THE VIEW
>
> If you are creating a Japanese garden around a Western-style house, think of how a Japanese house would interface with the garden. You should aim to:
>
> • create key viewing points, where the garden and the distant view are framed as a complete composition;
>
> • use large picture windows to frame the view of the garden and beyond;
>
> • use the supporting pillars of a veranda or an arbour to frame a focal point;
>
> • take extra care to frame the view of a dry garden.

Toji-in tea houses

Yoshimasa, the shogun of the late 15th century who inspired a great flowering of the arts of Japan, is said to have designed this thatched tea house in the garden of Toji-in. The garden is unusual in that it has two tea houses set side by side, and this helps to illustrate the design principles of the tea house. The style is derived from a combination of an older style of *shoin* architecture, including sliding panels, rice paper windows and a place to study, with the *soan* style of rustic huts of mountain farmers. The thatched roof is constructed in the same way as a farmer's house or barn, often including ventilation for silk worms, which were kept in the attic space. The rustic charm alludes to the Taoist hermit monks who lived in such buildings.

Traditional tea houses such as this often combine raw materials. Pillars made from tree trunks with the bark still on might feature, alongside strips of split bamboo and screens of natural plaster. There might also be finely carved shelves and surrounds to the *tokonoma*, the alcove inside the tea house where decorative objects were placed as a focus for the tea ceremony. The floor is laid out with tatami reed mats around a hearth set in the floor to heat the hot water for tea. While simple and appearing to be rustic, tea houses can be quite complicated and elaborate. The Toji-in tea house commands a view over the garden, but tea houses can also be placed in more secluded spots within a garden.

Shingle-covered canopy
Old tree
Typical thatched roof ridge
Traditional tiled roof
Rustic wooden pillars
Split bamboo strips bound with wire
Shoe stone
Wooden screen bound with jute and backed with rice paper

Right: *Two hermitage-style tea houses, built using contrasting materials, are set side by side in the gardens of Tojo-in, Kyoto. The simple architecture and thatched roof are modelled on those of rustic farm buildings.*

ARCHITECTURAL ELEMENTS

Understanding the Japanese garden

Despite the complexity of different kinds of Japanese garden, the common Western impression is of a small, carefully cultivated, stylized space, filled with clipped shrubs, rocks and stone artefacts such as lanterns, pagodas and Buddhas. In reality, the finest Japanese gardens are larger than many Western city gardens, and the artefacts are quite superfluous to their design. What counts is the spirit of the garden, and how the different elements are balanced. A sensitively styled Japanese garden should include the following principles.

Above: *Monochromatic ink paintings with their simple brushwork were frequently imitated by the creators of Zen dry gardens.*

NATURE AND RELIGIOUS SPIRIT

The beauty of many of the great Japanese gardens lies in their sublime vision of nature. The pleasure people took in the poetic beauty of flowers and cherry blossom that was so evident in the 11th century still lingers on in the celebratory cherry blossom festivals of today. The Japanese also held great reverence for their landscape gods and recognized the power of *yugen* ("hidden depth"), describing the feeling of awe that nature can evoke. This reverence has always been an important influence in the garden designs of Japan, inspiring the recreation of, for example, an open ocean, the way a river flows, and how a mountain range is encircled by mist.

ROCKS AND WATER

The standard elements of rocks and water are designed and placed to imitate as far as possible the way they occur in the natural landscape. So ponds should be created with naturalistic outlines, with inlets and gravel beaches just as if nature had shaped them. Rocks should not be positioned as individual, monolithic pieces, as they are in Chinese gardens, or admired in isolation as one would a piece of sculpture on a pedestal. They are also presented as part of the natural landscape.

NATURAL AND MANMADE ELEMENTS

Although water and rocks are the foundation of the garden, the design of any artefacts and buildings follows a carefully observed and orchestrated relationship between the natural and the manmade. The finely polished wooden panels of the tea house might be in-filled with rough plaster, while the wooden support posts might still have their bark on. The concept of *wabi-sabi* is equally important. This was a poetic term adopted by the tea masters to describe a quality of raw simple beauty, touched with the patina of age.

ASSYMMETRY AND BALANCE

Symmetry is rarely found in Japanese gardens, where the elements are characteristically arranged in odd numbers to bring to mind the asymmetry that characterizes nature.

Below: *The flat expanse of gravel, the horizontal lines of the hedge and some of the rocks in the Karlsruhe Japanese garden are balanced by several vertical rocks and the distant* torii *gate.*

Right: *There is no symmetry to this view, but all the elements are perfectly balanced. The large pond, crossed by a stepping-stone path, leads the eye to the trees, and the background is crowned by the Great Buddha Temple of Nara.*

Occasionally, an entranceway will have straight paths bordered by a pair of hedges or a view might be framed by rugged pine trees, but symmetry is generally seen by Japanese gardeners as something that restricts the imagination.

Instead of a symmetrical format, you need to create a design that feels natural, yet has a balanced composition, as well as a good sense of proportion between open and enclosed areas, enough empty space to allow the imagination to roam, and an easy transition from one section of the garden to another. The need for free-flowing movement applies not only to the observer's passage from area to area but also to specific elements. So paths and streams must meander and wander as they do in the wild, and ponds must appear to have naturally formed outlines.

ADDITIONAL NATURAL FEATURES

It can be useful to adopt the approach of the master painters when planning a Japanese garden, starting by dividing the site up into different layers:

• the foreground can be sand, gravel, moss or grass, featuring a water basin, rock or plant;

• the middle section can include a pond, island groups of rocks, and a weathered pine tree or clipped shrub;

• in the background, leave more open space with just the occasional rock, and use any distant view;

• frame the garden with an informal band of evergreens, walls or bamboo fencing.

CREATING LAYERS OF INTEREST

In the past, Japanese garden designers were inspired by old Japanese paintings. Composed with layers of interest and the artful play of light and shade, they helped them create a landscape's essence, framing it and dividing it into foreground, middle and distance.

Every element of a Japanese garden is there as part of the whole, whether a beautiful cherry tree or a millstone placed on a stepping-stone path.

Below: *The warm effect of the azaleas in this garden in Ito Shizuoka, Japan, shows how to integrate colour sensitively within the landscape.*

THE IMPORTANCE OF COLOUR

Although all the elements in a Japanese garden are subservient to the whole, this does not mean that the bright beauty of plum or cherry blossom or the autumn leaves of a maple are harmful to the design; they should be carefully considered for the part they play in celebrating the seasons. At the same time, plant colours should never be allowed to overwhelm a design, so showy, variegated, gold or purple foliage plants should in general be excluded. A good guide is that Japanese maples provide colour in the autumn and azaleas in the spring.

Interpreting a garden

The garden around the temple of Raikyu-ji, in Takahashi, was created by the 17th-century master gardener and tea-master Kobori Enshu. The central island set in a sea of gravel symbolizes Mount Horai and the Mystic Isles, and is wrapped in artistically clipped azaleas. The rounded shapes of the clipped shrubs that hug the main island emphasize the forms around them, either the rocks or the hilly landscapes that lie outside the garden. The effect is highly abstract, quite playful but also very sophisticated.

Each layer of the garden builds on the one before it. The foreground of raked sand, the rocks, the rolling "hills" of azaleas, the background evergreens, the spreading canopies of maples, all build up to the outline of Mount Atago in the distance.

Although essentially asymmetrical, this garden could be considered as very formal, and requires careful maintenance. The topiary, especially, needs a trained eye and a skilled hand to keep the shapes uniform. Each aspect of the design needs to be considered as part of the whole.

Also included are elements of the tea garden. A stepping-stone path starts at the temple and curls across the sea of gravel, behind the Mystic Isles and on around the garden into the shady depths of the trees. Here, a lantern has been carefully placed to light the path and to form another part of the overall composition.

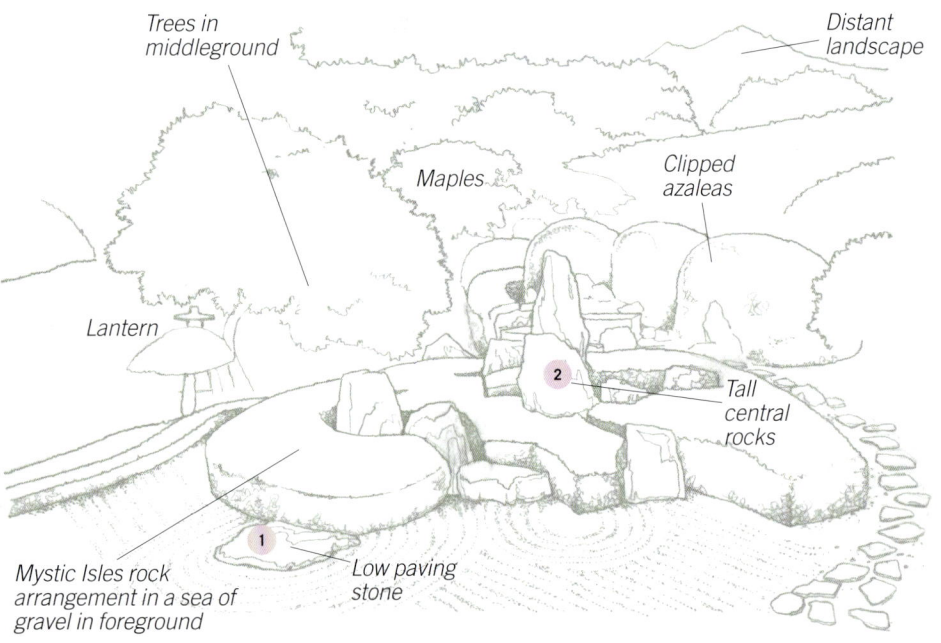

Right: *The garden of Raikyu-ji, one of the masterpieces of Kobori Enshu (1579–1647). The gardens of this designer incorporate many of the essential elements of Japanese gardens in an elegant and balanced manner.*

Translating the style

Garden design in Japan is an ancient art form, and therefore one that is in tune with the country's culture and history. Indeed, Japanese gardens have often inspired other historic Japanese artworks, such as paintings on silk or parchment, porcelain decoration and poetry. The classic heritage of this gardening style is still preserved and valued within Japan and beyond, but it is also open to modern adaptation. There follows an evaluation of 19th- and 20th-century interpretations, and the challenges of using this established style and its traditional elements within modern gardens.

Above: *Although cobbles are often carefully set to imitate the flow of water, in this garden they have been placed with an emphasis that produces a more artistic effect.*

EARLY INTERPRETATIONS

When European and American gardeners became exposed to Japanese gardens in the late 1800s, most of them were only able to "read" them in the context of their own culture or of contemporary Japanese fashions. Japan had by then lost touch with its garden history. Zen was not properly understood at this stage, and it was only in the late 20th century that the true heart of the Japanese garden began to be more accurately interpreted.

Those early imitations of Japanese gardens created by Western gardeners in the late 19th and early 20th centuries included many of the artefacts found in authentic Japanese gardens, such as lanterns and pagodas, but these tended to be placed around ponds that were surrounded by the lush plantings so popular in Europe at the time. Many English "Japanese-style" gardens of this time were quite beautiful, with their blossoming rhododendrons and magnolias, but they were far from authentically Japanese.

These gardens are important for the way in which they illustrate the style of the times in which they were made, with the Japanese Garden at Tatton Park in Cheshire perhaps the best example. While English Victorian and Edwardian gardens in the Japanese style can be appreciated for their own beauty, their creators had little understanding of the principles behind Japanese garden design, and they should not be used as models by those wishing to follow in the Japanese tradition.

MINIMALISM AND ARTISTRY

As an abstract concept, the Japanese garden has become a springboard for modern designers. Minimalist gardens claim to owe much of their inspiration to Zen and its philosophy of "nothingness". While this may be partly true, these gardens often fail to capture the essence of a Japanese Zen garden. They tend to rely on manmade rather than natural materials, and lack the fine sense of proportion and balance so essential to the spirit of the Japanese garden.

Left: *In the precincts of the Shinto shrine of Kamigano, Kyoto, sits this pair of sand cones. Pairs of cones in a sea of sand are also found in some Zen gardens, as symbols of purification.*

GARDEN MATERIALS

One of the problems facing those keen to make Japanese gardens can be finding the right materials. It can be quite tricky and sometimes very expensive to buy some of the exact materials that you might find in a genuine Japanese garden. Rocks of the best kind may not be available in your area, and transport costs may be prohibitive. So you might ask yourself whether rocks are an essential element to your design, and consider the possibility that clipped plants such as azaleas would achieve an acceptable alternative, albeit creating an altogether different result.

The same is true for gravel. The search for the perfect gravel for a dry garden, of the right colour, size and texture, may not always be successful, and if you do use very fine gravel or sand it will require regular and careful maintenance.

To solve this problem you need to ask yourself some basic questions. If you want to avoid the trouble of raking and re-raking the gravel on a regular basis, a more ordinary gravel would be satisfactory and you could then use a simpler design that is easier to maintain.

Below: *Mirei Shigemori was the first Japanese garden designer to break with traditional design. This dry garden dates from the mid-1900s.*

Above: *This contemporary garden in Tofuku-ji interprets traditional brushwood fencing and rock representations with great inventiveness.*

Certainly, the Japanese have used gravel and rocks to such a peak of artistry that any garden design with a spread of gravel and artfully placed rocks will have a clear Japanese influence.

Any style of garden created away from its natural context will require an interpretation that suits your local conditions, your local resources, your budget and the space available. These constraints may in fact help to focus your creativity and inspire you to design a Japanese garden that is truly individual.

MODERN INTERPRETATIONS

There are examples of Japanese-style gardens being built on rooftops, using lightweight but realistic fibreglass rocks, and where the classic profile of the Japanese pine tree has been carved in metal. Similarly, concrete, stainless steel and fibreglass have all been used in contemporary Japanese gardens and are quite acceptable as part of a modern garden scheme. This approach is a different interpretation of the traditional style, but the essence of the Japanese garden is still clearly evident.

In the André Citroën gardens in Paris, the French garden designer Gilles Clément created a riverbed garden using gravel and dwarf willows bordered by silver-leafed shrubs. As in a Japanese Zen design, the garden is framed in a rectangle. He also placed stepping stones in the gravel, but instead of random stone he used raised square wooden blocks to cross over the "dry water" of the riverbed. The design is inspired by Japan in the use of gravel, stepping stones and the rectangular frame, but the whole is no longer identifiable as Japanese. It has transformed into something entirely original and unique.

The dry garden, a model that the Gilles Clément garden in Paris translates with such imagination, is an accessible one to emulate. It can be small, requires a minimum of planting and the basic materials of gravel or sand and rocks. The tea garden, with its reflections of journeys taken along paths through mountain wildernesses, finally arriving at a hermitage, is a concept that is wide open to contemporary interpretation.

Traditionally, pond and stroll gardens contain many artefacts, such as lanterns and pagodas, and these can appear excessive to Western tastes. A modern interpretation could, however, use the principle of a garden based around a pond but achieve this in a minimalist way without artefacts. The courtyard garden has perhaps the greatest potential in a modern garden as it is so intrinsically part of city culture and needs only a small space. This style of garden corresponds as closely with city gardens today as when they evolved in the Edo period in Japan.

Above: *Japanese black pines in the Huntington Botanical Gardens have been pruned to give a windswept look and combined with a rugged scree and bold rocks.*

Below: *The Jardin Argenté at Parc André Citroën in Paris is a modern and original design vision that has the clear spirit of the Japanese garden at its heart.*

TRANSLATING THE STYLE 39

CLASSIC GARDEN STYLES

When you start to think about choosing one of the five main styles of Japanese garden design – pond gardens, dry gardens, tea gardens, stroll gardens or courtyard gardens – you should understand that these are an over-simplification of a much more complex art form. But these categories do provide a good initial approach, and having made your choice, you can then add elements from other styles.

The first consideration will be what style will suit your garden or site best. A pond garden will need a fairly large area of at least a quarter of a hectare (roughly half an acre). A dry garden can be laid out in a very small space but ideally a flat one. A tea garden is more of a lifestyle decision than one dependent on the size or quality of the site. Tea gardens while traditionally complex and led by rituals, can in practice be small or extensive; paths can be long or short, undulating or flat; while the tea house can be secluded or prominent. Stroll gardens generally need a fair amount of space and a reliable source of water; they are best on uneven sites, where small hills can be raised and paths can wander around them. Finally, a courtyard garden can be as small as a few square metres (yards). This overview of the traditional styles will help you make your choice before you start to design your garden.

Above: *This rock evokes a Chinese junk floating in a bay.*
Left: *Symmetrical layout contrasts with the natural forms of Japanese maples in the dry garden at Tenju-an, Kyoto.*

Pond gardens

Ponds, lakes and streams have always been central to the Japanese garden, instilling a sense of tranquillity, joy and calm. Water features, such as ponds and streams, always appear totally natural within the surrounding landscape, even if they are constructed artificially, and obvious manmade features, such as fountains, are avoided. You do not need a particularly large garden to include an expanse of water, although the results will obviously be much more dramatic if you are able to construct a feature of some size and presence.

Above: *A turtle island carrying Mount Horai, from the myth of the Isles of the Immortals, in the Heian period garden of Motsu-ji.*

THE HISTORY OF POND GARDENS

There is a general nostalgia in Japan for a romantic period in Japan's history, exemplified by the stories in the *Tales of Genji* by Murasaki Shikibu. Although written in the 11th century, this is still a very popular novel. In it you will find references to many kinds of plants and to boating parties. Both in the 17th century, at the Katsura Palace, and in the 19th century, after the restoration of the emperor as the head of state, gardens were created to reawaken the spirit of those times. So although this style of garden is very old, it still has a place in the hearts of the Japanese today. The naturalistic aesthetic makes it all the more relevant in times when nature is so much under threat, especially in Japan.

THE POND GARDEN OF MOTSU-JI

We can gain some inspiration for the design of present-day pond gardens by looking briefly at a famous example from Japan's past, Motsu-ji, in Hiraizumi, Iwate, which is one of the very few surviving pond and island gardens from the 12th century. Today, you can still see Motsu-ji's great lake, which is bordered by formal iris beds and dramatic rock arrangements. Nothing remains of the palace and temple complexes, but remarkably there are sufficient vestiges of this garden to conjure up images of how it might have been used. These glimpses into the past are intriguing. Guests at great "winding-water" banquets would sit by streams that wove through meadows before entering the lake. Resplendent garden parties were held in which painted dragon barges, filled with musicians dressed in elaborate costumes, were rowed and punted around the lake. At special ceremonies, people might pray for rain to fall in

Above: *The garden of the Moss Temple at Saiho-ji was a 12th-century pond garden, with islands linked by wooden bridges. It has now become famous for its velvet carpets of moss.*

Left: *An ambitious waterfall scheme in the Rheinaue Garden, Germany, creates drama through well-observed rock arrangements and in the ways that the water spills over the rocks.*

order to water the rice fields, or they might evoke Amida Buddha in his Paradise garden.

The lakes of early pond gardens such as Motsu-ji were broad and well-lit, glimmering under the sun, moon and stars, while weeping willows swayed and shaded their banks. Birds and fish would have added movement and colour to this intoxicating scene. The lakes had a pebbled bottom or were edged with beaches of silver sand and backed by low hills planted with trees and shrubs. This style of pond garden differs from the later stroll gardens in having none of the more familiar tea houses, lanterns or water basins. Instead, the pond contained islands, often linked by bridges.

LATER POND GARDENS

Pond gardens remained popular in Japan, but as they became smaller, their outline became increasingly complex and indented and the rock arrangements more artistic and painterly. The sumptuous gowns of the ladies of the Heian period would have made it impossible for them to stroll around large lakeside gardens, and so in the Kamakura and Muromachi periods, ponds became smaller, and formed part of the first

Above left: *Recycled materials, such as these millstones, make beautiful stepping stones. Old temple pillar bases and sections are also popular in Japan.*

Above: *The gardens of the Heian shrine, in Kyoto, were created in the late 19th century to recreate the spirit of the 10th- and 11th-century gardens of the Heian period.*

KEY CONSIDERATIONS

Location	Choose the lowest part of the garden to make your pond, as this will look most natural and you will have a good view of the water.
Lining the pond	If you have room for a large pond, you can line it with clay and make it deep enough for boating. If your pond is small, line it with a butyl liner.
Surroundings	You will be able to use the soil dug out for the pond to make natural-looking small hills and undulating ground around the edges.
Edges	Use the natural contours of your pond to make beaches of cobbles or sand, caves or grottoes. A small sandy beach may be just the place to moor a small boat and launch it into the water.
Water flow	Ponds are usually filled by a natural or manmade stream. The water can be re-circulated using an electric pump. Different types of feeder stream will work well, from a flat meandering type to a steep waterfall.
Rocks	The placing of rocks in a feeder stream or waterfall and around the edges of a pond must be handled carefully. Try out the position of each rock until it looks perfectly natural in its setting, following the "request" or "desire" of the stone and bearing in mind which way the water will flow. Rocks can also be used as part of an island, particularly if you are making a crane or turtle shape, or as a bridge between the island and the mainland.
Extra features	Irises are the most common plants in Japanese ponds. You can also construct an island in your pond in an asymmetrical position, perhaps with a bridge linking it to the mainland.

Left: *Ponds, such as this one at Tenju-an, were used for boating parties, and were the central feature of all gardens until the appearance of dry gardens.*

TURTLE AND CRANE ISLANDS

Another common feature of the pond garden was the group of islands that represented the Isles of the Immortals. Some of these took the form of turtles and cranes. They can be included in today's gardens, although it is important to point out that Japanese representations of the crane or turtle are rarely naturalistic. The crane island is made up of a group of rocks, with one taller rock usually sitting up like a wing. In the groups of rocks representing turtles, the head and flippers are sometimes discernible, but more often the image is utterly abstract and only a trained eye can appreciate what is being depicted.

Turtle and crane motifs are not essential to a pond garden, but they can be included if they are treated with some sensitivity. To recreate a crane or turtle island, look at some famous examples. You will find that some are made entirely of groups of

real stroll gardens, a style of Japanese garden that we will look at later on. Most of these later pond and stream gardens were confined within walls, which meant that their size was fairly limited – a factor that makes it easier for us to envisage the practicalities of trying to create one in a smaller Western garden.

In trying to reproduce such a style, one has to imagine a far more poetic time, as well as one in which there was a far greater reverence for nature. While later gardens were influenced by painters and Zen philosophy, the Heian pond garden takes nature in its well-observed form as a principle feature in the design.

FOLLOWING NATURAL FORMS

The *Sakuteiki*, which was written in Heian times, names many forms of pond styles, islands, streams and waterfalls, and even notes the best techniques for planting trees. Even now, we can draw on this ancient work for inspiration when designing contemporary pond gardens. For example, when placing rocks or choosing the course of a stream, you need to follow the "desire" or "request" of the stone or water. Inanimate rocks were, and still are in Japan, thought to possess personalities that must be treated with respect. By doing this, you will achieve a balanced and harmonious design for your garden.

It is also important to remember that the design of a water garden should be asymmetrical, even though the adjoining architecture may be symmetrical. This interplay between the formality of the architecture and the informality of the garden is part of the genius of Japanese gardens. The design of the pond is key, and achieving a pleasing shape is vital to the success of the finished pond.

Below: *Winding streams emulate a natural type of stream, with the rocks positioned to modulate the flow.*

rocks, while others are islands of earth with rocks protruding into the lake, which can be seen as flippers, a tail or a head. You are not aiming to create literal reproductions of these animals.

PINE ISLANDS

A favourite for Japanese gardens is a pine island, which is evocative of the windswept pine-clad islands of Matsushima, a scenic site in northern Japan, famous throughout Japanese garden history. Large pond gardens may include several pine islands of varying sizes, but if there is just one island, this could be reached by a traditional Chinese red-painted bridge, the most popular style of bridge when the Matsushima garden was made.

Above: *Japanese koi carp, considered to be a symbol of prosperity and good luck, were developed from the basic black carp, or* Magoi.

PLANNING A POND GARDEN

The pond or lake is the central feature of this style of garden and should be large enough and deep enough for a small boat, which can be kept moored to a stone or on view in an open-sided, ornate Chinese-style boathouse. There should be at least one island in the pond, often two, linked by bridges. By the 14th century, when ponds became smaller, the curved Chinese bridges were replaced by bridges made from less ornate materials such as rocks or unpainted timber. Small islands can be planted with pine trees or grasses.

The outline of the pond can be indented with coves, beaches and grottoes. The land around the pond might be hilly, with the hills planted naturalistically with groups of trees. You can easily create a pond garden planted with iris beds and dotted with well-placed rock arrangements, possibly with a gently sloping sandy beach area. Imagine recreating those splendid outdoor celebrations with an *al fresco* pond-side supper for friends, perhaps lit with some paper lanterns.

READING AROUND THE SUBJECT

There is a range of useful background reading material to help the gardener to understand the roots of the pond garden style. Despite their age, the

Above: *Placing a lantern at the end of a gravel spit is still a popular recreation of the famous natural scenic site of the Amanoshidate Peninsula on the north coast of Honshu.*

following books still have a place in the hearts of the Japanese.
• The *Sakuteiki* contains a wealth of practical ideas to inspire gardeners, with descriptions of streams, waterfalls and the symbolism of rock forms.
• *The Tales of Genji* by Murasaki Shikibu, written around the same time as the *Sakuteiki*, provides another important source of garden styles.
• *The Pillow Book* by Shonagon, also a contemporary of the *Sakuteiki*, makes amusing observations on the culture and gardens of the period.

Above: *A pine island in the tranquil lake setting of the Heian shrine, in Kyoto.*

Dry gardens

Dry gardens are often referred to as *kare-sansui*, which literally means "dry mountain water". This is a style of garden in which water has been replaced by sand, gravel or pebbles. These gardens have also become synonymous with what we now often call a Zen garden. Dry gardens were conceived by the Japanese with abstract designs, often just consisting of gravel, and as deeply spiritual and symbolic landscapes. They can also be enjoyed by visitors as peaceful and restorative environments where they can be appreciated for their calm beauty.

Above: *An unusual treatment for a dry garden at Shisendo, Kyoto. The fine sand has been brushed with a besom around a tree stump.*

THE HISTORY OF DRY GARDENS

Dry gardens have inspired garden designers throughout the world. An understanding or, better still, an experience of Zen will help you to find their spiritual essence, but another way to look at dry gardens is to see them as minimalist landscape art.

Before looking at the main features of the dry garden and how it can be successfully created in the West, it will be helpful to consider some of the historical, artistic and religious principles behind this unique garden style. The precise origins of such dry gardens remain a little obscure. References to dry landscapes occur as early as the 11th century, but they refer to the natural placement of rocks in grass or moss, and not to dry representations of water.

It is possible that the early Shinto shrines were a starting point. The great shrines at Ise stand in vast rectangles of gravel. This gravel was replaced every 20 years as part of the rituals of renewal and cleansing, while rocks were (and still are) used to represent the Buddha and the Buddhist Trinity. The earliest dry rock arrangements that preceded the *kare-sansui* may have been at Joeji-in, near Yamaguchi, where a collection of rocks was laid in an area of moss between the temple and the pond. This garden, which was created in the mid-1400s, is attributed to Sesshu, the great Japanese painter who reproduced his angular brush strokes in the garden using flat-topped and angular rocks. Sesshu was a monk, and also a painter and gardener, therefore possessing a rare

Below: *The rocks in this area of the garden at Nanzen-ji in Kyoto are arranged to display the innate quality of the stones.*

Above: The Mystic Isles rock arrangement at Tofuku-ji has immense power. The designer, Mirei Shigemori, used much larger and darker rocks than in more traditional arrangements.

Above: This garden near Kyoto was created in a small, rectangular framework. Raked sand and a single maple in a mossy mound prove how little you need to create a perfect scene.

combination of talents. Looking at his paintings can be a source of inspiration even today.

These dry gardens were not created because of a natural absence of water. (Indeed, there is an abundance of water in many of the temple gardens around Kyoto. At the Ryoan-ji, for example, there is a large pond on the other side of the wall from the dry garden.) Instead, they were created for a mixture of artistic and philosophical reasons. The first reason was based on the example of Japanese painters, whose artistic work inspired gardeners to use a monochromatic treatment of the landscape, and the second was linked to the philosophy of Zen.

THE INFLUENCE OF ZEN

Most dry gardens appear in Zen temples and are therefore strongly associated with Zen Buddhism and meditation.

The dry gardens in Zen temples tend to be framed within rectangular courtyards close to the abbot's quarters (*hojo*). They can be viewed as paintings, illustrating distant and idealized landscapes "hung" within their rectangular frame. As garden style evolved throughout the 15th century, its influences shifted away from art as an inspiration for natural landscapes towards art as a means of teaching Zen tenets.

In Zen, one reaches one's true self by diverting one's gaze from the material to the spiritual world. Through meditation, one can experience what is known as the "void", a formless state of no-self, which Zen defines as the original human state. Time spent in this state is a form of spiritual renewal. This "meditative void" can be equated to those areas of unpainted whiteness in a picture and to the empty space of raked sand in a dry

Right: The garden of Tenju-an, in Kyoto, is a superb example of the interplay between geometric manmade and irregular natural forms.

Above: *At Nanzen-ji, in Kyoto, over two-thirds of the dry garden is composed of sand. The rest is dedicated to this group of rocks and shrubs.*

Below: *The raked circles of sand in the Ryoan-ji garden represent the rough seas and the rocks the sacred mountains of the Mystic Isles.*

garden. Whereas lay people might look at a Zen garden and see islands in an ocean or mountain tops circled in mist, Zen practitioners will simply see space, a reflection of the infinite space that lies deep within us. Many of the arts of Zen employ the use of space to encourage this kind of self-awareness. The act of raking gravel is a meditative practice for Zen monks, while some Zen gardens include arrangements of rocks that signify aspects of Buddhism, for monks to contemplate.

RYOAN-JI

The Ryoan-ji garden, in Kyoto, is a timeless example of the exceptional degree of artistry and the deep understanding of the painters, monks and garden-makers of the late 15th century, when it is thought that this garden was constructed. The Ryoan-ji is a rectangular courtyard bordered on three sides by a clay and oil wall and on the fourth side by the abbot's quarters, where a long veranda overlooks the garden from about 75cm (30in) above the level of the garden. The area is about the size of a tennis court, and is neatly edged in a frame of blue-grey tiles. The whole of the inner space is spread with a fine, silvery grey quartzite grit that is raked daily along its length in parallel lines. This "sea" of sand is the background canvas to 15 rocks in five groups of 5-2-3-2-3 (see page 66), fringed by moss. This pattern recurs throughout the Far East, even in the rhythm of music and the chanting of Buddhist texts. The parallel lines of raked gravel break their pattern and form circles around the groups of rocks like waves lapping against island shores.

The magical way that the rocks are grouped and spaced has gripped generations of visitors, and not just monks, artists, poets and gardeners. No one knows the exact meaning of these groupings. Some have described them as a tiger taking her cubs across a river, while others see them as mountains in the mist or as islands

Right: A simple dry garden using one bold and interestingly shaped rock and a small grove of carefully trimmed bamboo, in the grounds of Nijo castle, Kyoto.

surrounded by sea. One reason for this puzzle is that Zen practitioners probably started with an idea, but ended up focusing on universal truths and abstract, natural shapes. When creating your own arrangements, bear in mind that the setting of the stones should follow their own "desire". The stones or rocks need not be particularly exceptional in themselves and should not be set as individual pieces of sculpture.

DESIGNING A DRY GARDEN

In the intial stages of planning a dry garden, first imagine a distant misty mountain landscape, a stream with waterfalls or a rocky shoreline. Look at how streams and rivers flow, how waves lap against rocks, and you will learn how to use the inspiration of nature to make raked gravel patterns around rocks.

Once you have composed a picture in your mind, then let go of the superfluous and simply allow the essence of the composition to take over, and minimize it. Remember that an unfilled space is just as important as a space containing objects or plants. This "minimalism" has inspired many contemporary garden designers to reproduce the dry garden in modern urban environments. After all, dry gardens were often created in domestic courtyards, not just in Zen temples. A simple composition could be created with a rock or two, a stone lantern, a water basin and a section of bamboo fence set simply in a stretch of sand.

USING PLANTS IN THE DRY GARDEN

Dry gardens are not restricted to just sand, gravel and rocks – they also involve plants. At the garden of the Shoden-ji, in north-west Kyoto, rocks have been replaced by mounds of clipped azaleas in more or less the same kind of pattern as the rocks at the Ryoan-ji. The azaleas are clipped so much that they do not flower very well, but form is considered far more important than colour in this style of Japanese garden. If you liken these gardens to the monochrome paintings that inspired them, it is clear that colour is of little or no importance, while composition and space are paramount.

CONTEMPORARY INTERPRETATION

Dry gardens may appear to be quintessentially Japanese, but the appeal of their pared-down, minimalist style is both universal and contemporary. Once you have understood how and why the original 15th-century dry gardens were created, you may want to employ new, exciting methods of expressing the same principles, but in ways and with materials that are more relevant to your own culture and landscape.

Above: Dry rock arrangements are often centred around a main stone, which may have symbolized the Buddha, the sacred mountain of Shimusen or Mount Horai of the Mystic Isles.

Above: The dry "silver" garden created by Gilles Clément at the Parc André Citröen in Paris is Japanese-inspired and represents a dry river bed planted with silver shrubs.

DRY GARDENS 49

Tea gardens

Tea gardens were designed as places in which to appreciate *sado*, the tea-drinking ceremony. These spaces were seen to represent a break in a journey from a busy urban centre to a secluded country retreat. The design and philosophy of the tea garden can easily be adapted for the modern garden, and suits city life now as much as it did in the 16th century. Each element of a tea garden – for example, the stepping stones, lanterns, water basins and even the tea house itself – can easily be created using modern materials.

Above: *Every tea garden has a tsukubai arrangement – a low water basin filled with fresh water and accompanied by a lantern.*

THE HISTORY OF TEA GARDENS

Tea, imported from China, had been drunk at the imperial court since the 9th century, but its cultivation did not start in Japan until the 13th century. The Buddhist monk Eisai, returning from pilgrimages to China, is credited with introducing both Zen Buddhism and tea plants to Japan.

Tea was drunk by Buddhist monks as an aid to wakefulness during their long hours of meditation. It also became popular among the poets, intellectuals, samurai and merchants at the end of the 15th century. The monks and intellectuals brought the worlds of Zen Buddhism, poetry, fine porcelain and art appreciation together into the theatre of tea drinking, and created what is known as the "tea ceremony", drawing the simple act of drinking tea into the realm of high art. By the mid-16th century, tea ceremonies, tea houses and tea gardens were part of the culture of Japan.

The first great tea masters of the 16th century built their tea houses to imitate the mountainside hermitages of the Chinese sages. These sages were learned in the arts, philosophies and religions of their time. The Japanese also built their own style of hermitage that evolved into the tea house, not in the mountains, but right in their back gardens in cities such as Kyoto, Nara and the port of Sakai, near present-day Osaka. The gardens

Below: *Tea houses are most often constructed from natural materials that are allowed to weather. This tea house has a tiled roof, whereas many others are thatched.*

Below: *A bamboo panel tied with jute is framed between two branches. At the step, guests remove their shoes before entering the tea house.*

Right: *Not all tea ceremonies take place inside a tea house. A special lacquered table is prepared for an outdoor tea ceremony* (no-da-te), *often conducted in an informal style.*

around these "mountain places in the city", as they became known, were originally based on paths, symbolizing the routes taken by pilgrims on their way to meet sages in their hermitages. The tea garden, or *roji*, which means "dewy path" or "dewy ground", evokes those mountain paths and gradually evolved to include an elaborate set of sophisticated symbols.

The greatest tea master was the 16th-century Sen no Rikyu, who had a preference for the rustic and the rough. His successors, such as Furuta Oribe and Kobori Enshu, who created gardens in the early 17th century, were from the samurai class and had more of a taste for sophisticated manmade materials. By the 17th century, tea paths were often made of formal square paving and millstones. The tea houses also changed, becoming more refined, more open and less humble.

Later still, tea houses evolved into tea arbours, where tea might be drunk while looking out over the garden. The changing aesthetic from the Muromachi period through to the Edo period shows a slow evolution from *wabi-sabi* ("withered loneliness"), indicating a taste for the impoverished, to *asobi*, which is a more playful and artistic style.

THE TEA GARDEN RITUAL

After generally passing through a main gate, guests would enter the first half of the tea garden, known as the outer *roji*. They might then be asked to wait, often in a small shelter or booth, before being led deeper into the garden, then to the tea house. On the way, they might pass through a middle "stooping gate", perhaps with a lantern nearby, designed to force the guests to bow slightly – a moment of enforced humility to stimulate an awareness of the material world the guests were leaving behind and of the higher, purer realms of consciousness they would encounter in the tea house.

After passing under the stooping gate, the guests would enter the inner *roji* that surrounded the tea house. This part of the garden was the "wilderness", which represented the wild mountain landscape that might surround a Chinese hermitage. The guests would then wash their hands and mouths at a low basin called a *tsukubai* (or "stooping basin"). This a lower style of basin than the taller *chozubachi*, which is a water basin more frequently found near the veranda of the main house.

Below: *Planting in tea gardens is generally less tightly controlled and more suggestive of a wilderness.*

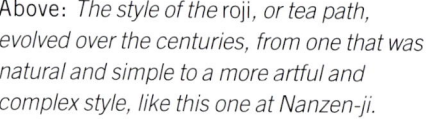

A lantern often accompanies the *tsukubai*, as many tea ceremonies took place in the evening.

After cleansing themselves, the guests would proceed to the tea house, remove their shoes and enter through a small hatch-like entrance, the *nigiriguchi*. This entrance was made too small for a samurai still wearing his sword to enter, so some tea houses had special racks built outside to hold swords. Once inside, the guests would admire a seasonal flower arrangement and a scroll hanging in an alcove, known as the *tokonoma*. The most important guest would sit with their back to the *tokonoma*. The tea ceremony would then begin.

Above: *The style of the* roji, *or tea path, evolved over the centuries, from one that was natural and simple to a more artful and complex style, like this one at Nanzen-ji.*

CONSTRUCTION OF THE TEA HOUSE

The tea house was often built to look like a rustic thatched hut, but it was always constructed with the finest planed timber. Elegant rush matting, called *tatami*, lined the floor. The rustic appearance of the tea house, combined with the refinement of domestic and temple architecture, created a whole new language in garden architecture – a discipline that is still studied today.

THE FEATURES OF A TEA GARDEN

A tea garden can include a range of decorative features, such as gates, water basins and lanterns, as well as following certain aesthetic rules,

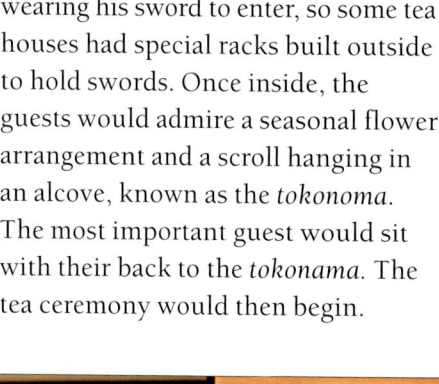

Left: *Inside the tea house or tea room is a specially designed alcove (*tokonoma*), decorated with a simple "country-style" flower arrangement and a calligraphy scroll.*

Right: *A waiting booth at Chikurin-in, a tea garden near Kyoto. This type of shelter is sited near the beginning of a tea path, as a place for guests to gather until invited to the tea house.*

such as an attention to detail and cleanliness, which are apparent in all Japanese gardens.

The tea house itself could be quite traditional in appearance, built with a thatched roof and sliding panels. One shogun even had a portable tea house built that was gilded throughout, as a symbol of his power. Thus, the basic principles of the tea garden could be adapted to suit the aspirations and taste of the owner.

TEA GARDENS IN MINIATURE

In small town gardens where space may not allow for a tea house, the Japanese will convert one room in the house into a tea room with a *tatami*-matted floor. For the tea garden they would still devise a path, or *roji*, that wanders through a "wilderness" of just a few paces from one door, then returning via a side door, perhaps with a *nigiriguchi*, into the tea room. The whole point is to be able to create an illusion of wandering through a wild mountainside. The onus is placed on the guests to comprehend that the journey they are taking is "real", but to help them, the garden designer will include pointers and hints as to the symbolic nature of each element.

If a whole *roji* is reduced to a few metres (yards) in length, it would still include a few stepping stones, a water basin, a lantern and one or two plants, such as a camellia or a bamboo, to suggest the wilderness. A rock might indicate a mountain, while a post might be enough to suggest a middle crawl-through gate (see page 172). That is the essence of the tea garden: creating a spiritual, rather than a literal, journey.

THE FLEXIBILITY OF THE TEA GARDEN

Once the significance of the tea garden has been grasped, you can be as creative as you want, just like the designers of the 16th century. While one tea master might have enjoyed a natural look, another might have preferred a creative mix of the manmade and the natural. Such adaptability is the main reason why tea houses and tea gardens never really died out, reappearing in stroll gardens and courtyard gardens to the present.

A tea garden does not have to be imbued with the tenets of Zen to be intriguing or even beautiful. Indeed, when Zen Buddhism went out of favour in Japan and Confucianism was in the ascendancy, the tea ceremony continued to thrive, but it evolved to express a more outward and cultured refinement than the deeper inner transformative power of Zen. This illustrates just how flexible the concept of the tea ceremony and garden can be, and that it can easily be reinterpreted to accommodate virtually any culture.

When you are creating a tea garden of your own, you could make a simple layout with just a few scattered rocks, bamboos, natural paving and bamboo gates, or a much more elaborate affair. You could build your own tea house, to whatever level of complexity and authenticity you want, or you could simply convert any garden building into a tea house, even with chairs and tables, although the space should be kept clean and treated with a certain degree of reverence, so that you can entertain guests in a quiet and respectful atmosphere. All you really need for a tea garden is a path.

Right: *A waiting booth (koshikake) in the inner tea garden, or* roji, *at Chishaku-in, Kyoto. This simple square construction has a thatched reed and bamboo roof and a pair of benches.*

Stroll gardens

A stroll garden is one in which the visitor is encouraged to amble slowly along paths that circle around a small pond or lake. Although there had been stroll gardens in Japan since the 14th century, they came to the fore in the Edo period of the 17th century and beyond. Unlike the earlier pond and stream gardens, where the emphasis was on the water, and boating was the main activity, the emphasis in a stroll garden was on the paths that wound among a new set of garden motifs. Classic examples are all large gardens, but, as long as there is room to wander, smaller ones are possible.

Above: *Most stroll gardens have a path that circles around a central pond, with specially contrived views at strategic points.*

THE HISTORY OF STROLL GARDENS

The stroll garden is one of the most familiar Japanese garden styles, partly because it incorporates so many aspects of other styles. You will find stepping-stone paths, lanterns, water basins and tea houses from the tea garden; expanses of sand with a rock or two, usually near the main building, from the dry garden; and the use of water in streams, waterfalls and ponds from the pond garden. Other elements might include bamboo fences and bridges of all kinds. The tea houses, tea arbours, lanterns, bridges and contrived views of scenes reproduced from historic or famous places around Japan or even China that could be found here were all carefully placed to entertain the stroller.

When the stroll garden was developed in the 17th century, the pervasive aesthetic of the times was not as "spiritual" as that of the earlier dry and tea gardens. There was more of a sense of playfulness (*asobi*) as well as a desire for the sumptuous and magnificent, and Japanese garden owners prided themselves on their connoisseurship of the arts.

Nevertheless, stroll gardens managed not to be overly ostentatious because they still employed the restraint and cultivated poverty of many of the aspects of the tea garden. This restraint in garden design was known as *shibumi* (meaning "astringent"), which underlined their markedly minimalist, unpretentious and subdued beauty. *Shibumi* is a term that can also be used to describe many contemporary Japanese gardens.

Although some of the gardens of the *daimyos* (land-owning lords) were somewhat grandiose, there were other, smaller gardens that were delightfully playful in their use of plants, water and architecture. A stroll garden could be as large as 20 hectares (50 acres) or be created in as little as 25sq m (about a sixteenth of an acre). Through the careful use of space and meandering paths, smaller areas can be made to look much larger than they actually are. One device that was commonly practised in stroll gardens was the "borrowing" of scenery, such as distant buildings and hills outside the bounds of the garden, as part of the garden plan – a technique known as *shakkei* (see page 30).

In the years following the fall of the Tokugawa shogunate at the end

Left: *Azaleas in flower in the small stroll garden at Shisendo, Kyoto. A simple garden, it has fine sand paths, rounded azaleas and a small pool with irises.*

of the Edo period and the emperor's restoration as the head of state (Meiji period), there was a return to more romantic ideals, as seen in the Heian period 1,000 years earlier. Some of these late-19th-century stroll gardens adopted a more naturalistic form, in which streams were designed to look like those found in wooded mountains. This style was more appealing to Western gardeners than the earlier very prim and trimmed stroll gardens.

ROCKS AND TOPIARY

In most stroll gardens, rocks played a far less prominent role than they had in the earlier Kamakura and Muromachi periods, partly because the Edo period was based on the new capital, Edo (Tokyo), where rocks were far scarcer than they had been around the previous capital, Kyoto. This scarcity led garden designers to rely more on clipped shrubs for dramatic form. This distinctive form of topiary, known as *o-karikomi*, is a fine art that is still practised extensively today. All kinds of plants were clipped: shrubs were trimmed into hedges or rounded forms like small hills, and sometimes huge evergreens were carved into abstract shapes. These mounds of clipped shrubs were mostly azaleas and

Above: *The 19th-century garden of Murin-an is full of illusions. A pair of wild-looking mountain streams appear almost like great rivers flowing through the "hills" of azalea.*

Left: *A mass of clipped azaleas is typical of the planting style in Edo-period stroll gardens. A few rocks are interspersed among them, but rocks feature less prominently than in earlier styles. This was because rocks were scarce around the then new capital of Edo, present-day Tokyo.*

Right: *An early Edo-period stroll garden in Kyoto. Here the rocks are dramatic and symbolic of the power of the shogun, Tokugawa Ieyasu, who built this garden at Nijo Castle, with the exaggerated masses as a statement of his own prestige.*

Left: *The 14th-century garden of the Tenryu-ji was one of the first pond-style gardens with strolling paths, but this was a period when the natural placement of rocks was the key feature.*

Below: *Larger stroll gardens often include groves of cherries, plums or peaches, whose blossoms are especially celebrated in spring.*

camellias, but any number of different evergreens might be employed and, occasionally, even deciduous shrubs such as enkianthus, whose leaves glow fiery red in the autumn.

When rocks were used in a stroll garden, they might be smaller stones strung like beads along the edge of ponds or used as stepping stones along paths or across inlets. Some of these stones were recycled architectural fragments such as temple pillar bases, old bridge supports or millstones. This practice of recycling materials was known as *mitate* ("to see anew").

VIEWING POINTS

Although stroll gardens are designed to be walked around, they are also meant to be viewed from the main house or from arbours in the garden. Traditional Japanese houses had verandas, raised above ground level, from which you look over an expanse of brushed or raked sand stretching as far as the pond. At the near edge of the pond you will find clipped azaleas and an occasional rock. Distant shores might be overhung by pines, their branches supported by posts.

STREAMS

At one end of the pond, a stream might enter, with a wide estuary traversed with stepping stones. These may be made from natural stone or formal slabs. Bridges that cross over streams or inlets can be a single slab of curved, carved granite, or a curved wooden bridge, sometimes painted red like a Chinese bridge. In more naturalistic settings, log bridges or natural stone can be used. The stream babbles over pebbles as it enters the pond. Further upstream, it is narrower, tumbling between rocks and over waterfalls, and hugged by ferns and sedges.

If you are blessed with a natural fall of land, you can create a stream that follows the slope of the ground.

Left: *A lantern sits on a promontory, playing the role of a lighthouse. Lanterns, in varied styles, are often strategically placed around the strolling paths, near gateways and at the base of hills.*

KEY CONSIDERATIONS

Ponds These are usually the main feature of the stroll garden, to which all paths eventually lead via a wandering route. Ponds can include small islands with bridges and may be fed by a stream or waterfall.

Paths The design of the main path is essentially to circle the pond, visiting or passing through various features, views and buildings on its way. Smaller paths may take off from this main path, leading to tea houses or to other main garden features.

Plants The designer can celebrate the seasons through many wonderful Japanese plants, such as cherries, azaleas, wisterias, maples, irises, hydrangeas, pines of all kinds and a host of herbaceous plants such as miscanthus and Japanese anemones. Cherries, plums and maples might be planted in groves for the greatest impact; irises grow well in the estuaries to the pond or in a stream; hydrangeas flourish in the wooded shade of cryptomerias or maples; while grasses, anemones and toad lilies might poke out from among rocks or by the water's edge.

If your garden is flat, you can still create the illusion of a mountain or hillside from which a stream might naturally flow. In most cases, you will need a pump to recycle and oxygenate the water, especially if your pond is stocked with fish such as koi and carp, but the water should be kept fairly shallow, only about 60cm (2ft) deep, so the fish can be easily seen. Deeper bays and shelters can be built to give the fish some shade and protection in the extreme heat or cold.

THE ROUTE TO THE TEA HOUSE

If you plan to make a tea house or arbour, your visitors will be drawn along paths of stepping stones, guided by bamboo fences and through gates, past lanterns and water basins, to the tea house itself. Tea arbours are more open than tea houses, as they were used for less formal occasions where the emphasis was on a commanding view of the garden. Other buildings might include a thatched umbrella shelter or a Chinese-style hexagonal summerhouse. Paths may pass through groves of cherries or maples, sometimes in an open grassy glade, or under-carpeted with moss where the shade is deeper.

DESIGNING A STROLL GARDEN

Although stroll gardens can include many elements, the individual components should not distract from the whole. The plan can simply include a path, a pond, a few clipped shrubs, a lantern and some trees, such as maples, pines or cherries. Decorative elements such as flowering plants or statues should be used with care and restraint.

Even though stroll gardens may lack the spirituality of other styles, they obey certain rules of balance, and look to nature or famous scenes for their inspiration. When planning a garden in this style, focus on a simple design that includes a well-shaped pond and an interesting path, rather than an assorted handful of Japanese artefacts.

Above: *Although generally they are more elaborate and impressive, stroll gardens often include features found in earlier pond gardens, such as the stone bridge here.*

Right: *The azaleas in the stroll garden of Murin-an are clipped into abstract shapes and dispersed quite randomly.*

Courtyard gardens

The history of the courtyard garden starts in the early 17th century, but for contemporary designers the small, enclosed space adjoining a building still offers fantastic design possibilities. The design is generally simple, sometimes planned as a light extension to the house with large windows and doors, sometimes as a usable outdoor space. Small courtyard gardens, designed to be viewed through glass panels or set within atriums open to the sky, are now being created everywhere from large museums and corporate headquarters to private homes.

Above: *Courtyard gardens in contemporary settings can give a designer the chance to experiment with new materials.*

THE FIRST COURTYARD GARDENS

In the Heian period, courtyard gardens, or *tsubos*, were simple, small, enclosed spaces, perhaps inhabited by a single plant. The rooms that overlooked them, and the courtyards themselves, were named after these plants: the Imperial Palace of Sento, in Kyoto, still has a Wisteria Court. Although the medieval residences of the samurai would have had *tsubos*, it was the rise of the merchant class in the late 16th century and throughout the Edo period that led to the refinement of the art of the courtyard garden (*tsubo-niwa*) in the early 17th century.

The small Edo courtyard gardens, like the much larger stroll gardens of the same period, were amalgams of preceding garden styles, but they often lacked the coherent principles and philosophies that lay behind their parent styles. For instance, when the inspiration was a tea garden, tea paths were rarely used, nor did religion play a role. Instead courtyard gardens appropriated the motifs and artefacts

Below: *Courtyard gardens borrow motifs from other styles, such as the rocks and sand of the dry garden and the stepping-stone path of the tea garden.*

of previous styles. Where it was not possible to build a tea house, a room in the house might be used. The journey to this room could be via a "path" (*roji*) that would lead guests on a detour through the "wilderness" in the garden to maintain the illusion that they were heading somewhere special.

As the Edo period progressed, the insularity of the shogun's policies made the landed nobility (*daimyo*) poorer, while the merchants accumulated great wealth. The merchants were afraid to show off their money, as they could have had it confiscated, despite their importance within the national economy. In those days, the merchants were considered to be the lowest class; this was to prevent them from using their money to exert too much influence. Consequently, they constructed modest shop fronts to conceal a complex world of deep rooms and small enclosures, passages and courtyard gardens (*machiya*) hidden from the public in a style that made incredibly economic use of space. Some of these original gardens can still be seen in cities throughout Japan, but more such small gardens are being built today, often owing to lack of space

Below: *This tiny garden at Sanzen-in is a welcome island of green in the centre of the building, where there is only just enough light for plants such as ferns, mosses and bamboos to grow.*

Above: *An entrance garden to the Silver Pavilion (Ginkaku-ji) in Kyoto illustrates the exceptional artistry of combining natural forms with the geometric.*

Below: *This Zen-style hotel courtyard has two shapes set in the sand: a grass circle and a grass gourd shape. These shapes are recognized symbols of hospitality.*

COURTYARD GARDENS

Left: *This lush garden is located in Okinawa. The rear courtyard is enclosed by the L-shaped building, and by the successive layers of garden against a steep slope.*

explored Japan in the mid-19th century were astonished by the stroll gardens, but were equally amazed by these beautiful small town gardens.

Temple complexes also had *tsubo-niwa* gardens, usually simple dry gardens with one or two rocks and a "pool" of raked gravel. So, too, did restaurants, where narrow passageways were made into elaborate gardens with stone paving bordered by lanterns and clipped evergreens such as azaleas, mahonias, nandinas and bamboos. These gardens were, and still are, invariably too shady and too small for most flowering shrubs or cherries, limiting the range of plants to glossy evergreen shrubs such as aucubas, fatsias and camellias, as well as shade-loving ferns, bamboos and farfugiums. There is also often a carpeting of moss, just as would have been found in a traditional tea garden with its shady walks and scattered rocks.

rather than out of any need to hide them – making this style of garden particularly relevant today.

In addition to the entranceway garden, if there was one, most of the original merchants' houses featured a small central garden, which served to separate the trading area from the living quarters, and an even smaller courtyard garden termed a *tsubo-niwa*.

TSUBO-NIWA

The term *tsubo-niwa* derives from a measurement that is equivalent to 2 *tatami* mats. Many Japanese today still measure their houses and rooms in *tatamis*, approximately 1.85 x 0.9m (6 x 3ft), a measurement close to that of the average human being when lying down. So a *tsubo* is roughly 3.3sq m (18sq ft) – an indication of just how small these gardens can be.

THE ELEMENTS OF A COURTYARD GARDEN

In addition to their aesthetic appeal, minuscule courtyard gardens perform the important role of bringing light and air into the home, while the verandas running around their edges join together the *machiya*'s various areas. Though tiny in scale, the quality of the garden's lanterns, rocks and other components were and still are clear indicators of the taste and affluence of the *machiya*'s occupants.

Through the use of sliding screens, fence panels and bamboo blinds, it is possible to view these internal gardens from different angles, with each aspect framed within the rectilinear bounds of doors and window frames. The distinction between indoors and outdoors disappears. Westerners who

Above: *Dry gardens can give surprising life to inner courtyards where few plants would grow. The great waves of sand add a sense of movement in this garden at Ryogen-in.*

Right: *A serene courtyard garden at Kodaiji Temple, a 16th-century Buddhist temple in Kyoto's Higashiyama district. It is spacious enough to include several small trees.*

Another form that a courtyard garden might take is to create a scenic picture with miniature landscapes (*shakkei*) created to be viewed from one of the surrounding rooms.

A MODERN INTERPRETATION

In many ways, the courtyard style – a hybrid between the dry garden and the tea garden – suits the modern world well, and is often highly refined. Some of these gardens have everything from lanterns, water basins, small bridges, gravel and rocks to shady plants and sections of fencing used as a partition or to create privacy. Intricate journeys are hinted at, but it's never more than a hint. Courtyard gardens are often interpreted in a minimalist style today, maybe consisting simply of a single clump of bamboo planted off-centre or a group of rocks with ferns and moss. In fact the courtyard garden is an ideal medium for the contemporary garden designer, as the minimalist style is now so popular.

Roof gardens can also be classified as courtyard gardens, even though they may include views over the outside world. The raw, open, soil-less space on top of a building is perfect for the dry-landscape treatment, particularly where there are worries that excess weight from plants, pots, soil and water might damage the building's structure. The use of sand, lightweight plants and even fibreglass rocks in the Japanese style is often the ideal solution to this.

THE VERSATILITY OF THE COURTYARD GARDEN STYLE

In a sense, the courtyard garden can provide anything you want it to. It can be a dry garden, a tiny tea garden, a miniature landscape, or simply an area that encapsulates nature as a motif, or even a tranquil contemplative space. The courtyard garden can be both a retreat from the busy streets outside and an opportunity for escapist fantasy. It may also function in a mundane pragmatic way, simply by allowing more light to be drawn into the surrounding rooms.

In its design, the courtyard garden absorbs the best of Japanese culture, where one often sees one art form impacting on another. Just as a flower arrangement may influence a tea room, so too does the tea ceremony influence the nature of the garden, and so on. Once we appreciate one art form, we will gain a better understanding of another. This cross-pollination is also at the heart of the courtyard garden style – an art form that is itself in a constant process of evolution.

Above: *The corner of this courtyard garden combines the rocks and gravel from a dry garden style with an oribe lantern, a popular feature of the tea garden.*

Above: *Most Japanese gardens use a grey-white quartzite grit, but this modern garden uses red gravel. Mirei Shigemori designed this garden in the Tofuku-ji temple complex in the 1950s.*

NATURAL MATERIALS

In the Japanese garden, the shapes of nature are celebrated, with great prominence typically given to one beautifully shaped rock or boulder set in subtly coloured gravel. This chapter looks at the natural materials that commonly feature in Japanese gardens. It explains how to source them, how to use them and also offers useful step-by-step features and practical illustrations to demonstrate specific techniques and designs. Paving and stepping stones are used, both decoratively and to create pathways. Gravel, grit and sand are also essential, traditionally designed to imitate the whiteness of a painter's canvas and the flow of water. In combination with rocks, gravel and sand form the vocabulary for the familiar dry-water features of the Japanese garden, such as waterfalls and streams, that are also illustrated here.

Ground cover, in particular moss, and the use of plants both make an important contribution. Moss grows profusely in Japan and is a natural ground cover that allows more freedom with planting than grass. While some gardens eschew the use of plants altogether, especially with dry garden designs, certain garden plants, such as azaleas, are used as substitutes for rocks or are clipped to imitate distant hills using the art of topiary.

Above: *Cobbles feature strongly in dry gardens.*
Left: *The intrigue of a Japanese garden is largely to do with natural forms, used in artful imitation of nature.*

Rocks & boulders

Rocks have formed the foundation of the Japanese garden from the earliest days. No other culture has made rocks so central to its garden art. It is possible to trace the history of the placement of rocks, from their first use in shrines and later as motifs for sacred mountains to their grouping in and around water. Later, in the dry gardens of the Muromachi period (1393–1568), water was replaced by sand, while in the gardens of the Edo period (1603–1867) rocks were replaced by clipped shrubs, which were used to imitate hills and mountains.

Above: *The central rock in this arrangement represents the Buddha, with two subservient attendant stones.*

Below: *The scale and quantity of these rocks at Nijo Castle were intended to express the power of Ieyasu Tokugawa (1543–1616) in the early 1600s.*

SPIRITUAL QUALITIES AND SYMBOLISM
Rocks were originally thought to possess spirits and the ability to draw the gods down to earth. They were later used to represent the mountain homes of the immortals, as well as the Buddha and his attendants. However, Zen monks, who had little time for superstition, rejected much of the esoteric symbolism of rocks and gave them more philosophical and decorative roles.

Although rocks were, and still are, placed in symbolic groups, they now tend to be arranged according to certain aesthetic rules. It takes a well-trained and experienced eye to read the symbolism in a group of stones. Groups of rocks that appear entirely natural may actually possess a number of possible symbolic meanings. Therein lies the genius of the Japanese rock-setters. Do not let this put you off creating symbolic arrangements in your own garden. Historians and Zen practitioners may like to read complex messages in classic rock arrangements, but it is not necessary to have such a deep understanding to compose successful groupings. It was, after all, the study of Chinese and Japanese minimalist ink-and-brush paintings that inspired them. Take a look at some of those paintings. The important thing to remember is that less is more, and not to be too decorative in your approach. What you leave out is almost more important than what you put in, and neither the stones nor the plants need be fancy or remarkable in themselves.

CREATING A ROCK GARDEN

We are fortunate that the Japanese have always rated rocks so highly because excavations of ancient gardens can still give a good idea of what they looked like, and this may help with the placement and grouping of the rocks. One garden in the city of Nara, 48km (30 miles) south of Kyoto, which was excavated in the 1970s (see picure on page 10), was found to be over 1,000 years old. There, the rocks are arranged in a surprisingly naturalistic way around a pond and stream, providing us with a useful example to follow.

Above right: *Gleaming rocks form a dramatic centrepiece in this ryu-ten ("teashop in the garden") in Koraku-en, in Okayama.*

Right: *The setting of rocks, usually within gravel, the latter often representing the sea, is the central creative dynamic in the making of most Japanese gardens.*

Avoid using rocks with fantastic shapes. These have never been popular in Japan, except during a brief Edo/Confucian period. Chinese gardeners, in general, were much keener on using fantastic sculptural rocks, many of which were raised from lake beds, standing them on pedestals as symbols of immortality. The Japanese, on the other hand, are more interested in discovering a rock's natural inner essence.

From a design point of view, there is endless scope when working with larger rocks, but don't get carried away with design ideas and remember the inner essence of the rocks if you wish to achieve a natural effect that does not jar with the rest of the setting you have created in your garden.

MAKING ROCK GROUPINGS

Rocks are generally placed in groups. Seven was an auspicious number to the Chinese, as it is in many cultures, and was the original number of the Mystic Isles. Music was composed in units of 7-5-3 beats, while the prayers recited to Buddha Amida were chanted 7, 5 and 3 times in succession. By the 15th century, all kinds of objects were arranged in groups of 15, including rocks. The Ryoan-ji, for instance, is a 5-2-3-2-3 arrangement.

Most groups will consist of one main stone and up to five accessory stones, with one or more unifying stones to stabilize the group. Others might be used as linking stones to join together the members of one group, as well as different groups. The accessory stones can be placed to the front, rear or side of the main stone, huddled up against it or

Below: *The garden of the Ryoan-ji was first laid out in 1499. The composition of 15 rocks is set in a rectangle of sand, against a backdrop of an oil and clay wall overhung with trees.*

Above: *At the Konchi-in, in Kyoto, the eye is drawn to the rocks as they sit in the centre of a layered composition, with its foreground of raked sand and backdrop of evergreens.*

some distance away, but should never obscure it. Try making the attendant stones respond to or echo the angle or position of the main stone. These stones should respond to the energy of the main stone in one of the following seven ways:

Receptive A rock that is placed to receive the energy from the main stone that is leaning towards it.

Transmitting An attendant rock that transmits energy from the main stone towards others in the group.

Pulling A rock that is angled to counteract a main stone that leans away from it.

Pursuing Set behind a main stone that leans away from it, this rock is angled in the same direction, as if following it

Stopping An upright main stone is stabilized by an accompanying one.

Attacking The accompanying rock leans towards a neutral, upright main stone.

Flowing This rock is a passive conductor rather than a more active transmitter; often flat, it acts as a kind of conduit to others.

These terms are not meant to be rigid, but they help to describe the relationship of the stones to each other and to clarify what might work in a particular grouping. They also highlight the subtle approach that is required to make such a grouping work. If your grouping does not look right, then work through these terms to help give the stones an authentic Japanese touch.

By far the best way of learning how to arrange rocks, however, is by studying good, authentic examples. Because of the static nature of rocks, it is possible to do this from looking at photographs, but note that arrangements must look good from any angle (which a photograph might not show), although they will tend to have one front side that gets the most attention. Also bear in mind that it is better not just to copy an arrangement but to be creative, seeking out and following the "desires" of your own particular rock.

> ### USING ROCKS IN THE JAPANESE GARDEN
>
> The placement and grouping of rocks is crucial to the authenticity of a Japanese garden. The following guidelines should help you:
>
> • study Japanese gardens, in pictures or by visiting good examples;
>
> • go and look at rocks in the wild, by the sides of streams with boulders, or at the seaside. Make sketches of their natural arrangements if you can;
>
> • avoid strange-shaped rocks. It's better to find rocks that would look good grouped together rather than one dominating specimen;
>
> • trust your own instincts and don't be intimidated by the fact that it is such an ancient art and that rocks are supposed to be spiritual and symbolic;
>
> • several rocks with good angles will show up better at a distance than one solitary rock, as they can be placed to complement each other;
>
> • your arrangement should look good from all angles, inspect it from all sides and from the house before you make a final decision on the position of stones;
>
> • imagine the rocks talking to each other, and adjust them to create more harmony between them;
>
> • don't be too rigid, allow room for your own artistic expression.

Left: *Mirei Shigemori's use of rocks at the Matsuo Shrine in Kyoto defies the traditional naturalistic use of rocks, but still uses natural form to create a remarkable sense of drama and mystery.*

Choosing rocks & boulders

Whether you're planning a naturalistic stream garden, a Zen-influenced dry garden (*kare-sansui*) or a small Japanese-style courtyard, the care and attention you spend when selecting the rock elements will have a profound influence on the finished look and feel of the space. Rocks supply the strong yang (positive, bright and masculine) element in Japanese gardens, and larger, more sculptural pieces can be full of character. In dry gardens, they often form the main focus, so the size, shape and texture of individual rocks in a grouping is critical.

Above: *This classic trio of rocks has symbolic meanings in Japanese gardens but also works as a sculptural and harmonious arrangement.*

When selecting rocks for a Japanese garden, choose ones that you find interesting, but are not too eccentric in shape, and which can be partially buried. It is interesting to note that the rocks of the famous Ryoan-ji garden are not individually that remarkable: their hypnotic power lies in their arrangement, inspired by the way rocks and boulders can be seen poking out of the sea or a lake.

The most favoured rocks are often angular, with either pointed or flattish tops. These shapes echo the angular strokes of a paintbrush, but such distinctive shapes also stand out well when viewed from a distance. When you are using rocks as symbols – perhaps to represent Mount Horai, Shimusen or Sanzon, or crane and turtle islands, for example – make sure they are subtly arranged so that they have a quiet, still presence.

WEATHERED STONE

Stone that shows signs of weathering is particularly valued in Japanese gardens of all kinds. In these kinds of stones, a surface colonization of plants – mosses, liverworts and lichens or larger plants rooted into crevices – is of great benefit in the overall effect. This kind of natural weathering is more marked in softer, porous rock types, such as limestone and sandstone, that absorb moisture. However, you can encourage lichen growth on all types of rock by coating them with yogurt or diluted manure, and keeping them moist to get the aged effect.

It is sometimes possible to buy reclaimed stone, for example pieces from a demolished dry stone wall, either from stone merchants or architectural salvage yards. Do not, however, take a beautiful stone from the wild landscape: this is potentially damaging to the environment and individual ecosystems.

ROCKS FOR WATER FEATURES

Harder rocks like granite (a Japanese garden favourite), schist and slate tend to weather slowly, but this can be advantageous in and around water features. Sandstone and limestone are not so successful in water gardens, as porous sandstone quickly darkens with algae when wet, leaving the dry stone surround much paler, while limestone can dissolve into water, raising the pH level and adversely affecting fish.

Large, rounded boulders work very well for natural stream features since they have a water-worn quality and always combine pleasingly with cobbles and pebbles. When building cliffs and banks for a waterfall or other

Left: *Here large rounded boulders with a beautiful patina of age are set well into the ground and are surrounded by plants.*

features, ensure that the rock colours and the direction of strata of sedimentary rocks match up and look as natural as possible.

ROCKS FOR DRY GARDENS
Slate and schist shear in thin layers, producing pieces with dramatic, jagged outlines – ideal for mountainous "islands" in dry gardens. Slate may be very dark when wet with rain and is a particularly good choice for more abstract, contemplative arrangements, including black-and-white schemes. You can purchase plum- and green-toned slates, as well as more colourful kinds with reddish-brown iron deposits. Granite comes in a wide range of shades from almost white through pink and brown to almost black, and is subtly mottled and flecked. Though salts and minerals permeate many different rock types, adding colour and textural interest, it may be safer to go for more restful tones such as greys and browns, especially in a small space.

SOURCES OF NATURAL ROCK
Local garden centres are unlikely to have pieces that are the right size and shape to act as focal points, although they may have smaller rocks to choose from. Stone merchants (listed in your local telephone directory) can usually help, but for very large projects it may be advisable to visit a quarry. There you could discover pieces that have been standing for some time, distinct from the freshly quarried material, and with that all-important aged quality.

When buying by the tonne from a stone merchant or quarry, make sure you specify the rock size and quality to avoid the weight being made up with unusable rock waste. It's very important that you are at home when the stone arrives so that you can supervise the delivery process. Rough handling of rocks may damage the surface patina or cause pieces to shear off, revealing the brighter, unweathered interior, and the stone could take years to recover.

Above: *Decorative stones like these rainbow cobbles can be used sparingly as features.*

Above: *Rockery stones may be too small for Japanese gardens. Always hand select them.*

Above: *Boulders of Welsh green granite offer the perfect way of adding a rugged feel to any garden landscape.*

Do as much preparation as possible before the delivery of your rocks in the way of digging out holes or dry stream courses. You may also need to hire a bulldozer or digger to lift heavy stones into their sockets; alternatively you can use a block-and-tackle pulley system. Ensure that the new rocks are well protected and cushioned to prevent any possible damage caused by cables during lifting.

Above: *The markings on these gneiss boulders are more subtle, making them easier to place.*

Above: *Smooth, sea-worn boulders have a pleasing texture and work well with cobbles.*

Above: *You would be advised to use thicker pieces of slate for stepping stones, as thin pieces tend to crack under any pressure.*

MANMADE ALTERNATIVES
Where access to a garden is restricted or weight is an issue, for example on load-bearing surfaces such as roofs and balconies, use resin or fibreglass rocks and boulders instead. These are hollow and easy to lift but can look very realistic when bedded in and surrounded by plants and perhaps a few cobbles. You can buy them on-line or from landscaping exhibitions.

Moving rocks & boulders

Stones and rocks can vary enormously in weight, size and shape. Your choice of rocks may be determined by your budget, and also by how they can be manoeuvred into place. In a small garden, or behind a house with only a narrow gated entrance, you may have problems in getting the rocks into position. In more open spaces there will be no such limitation, but you should still consider the weight and potential unwieldiness of large pieces and be prepared to hire professionals to move them. If moving smaller rocks, take great care with your back.

Above: *Mount Horai is the tallest of the mythical Mystic Isles, often portrayed by the tallest rock. Moving such large rocks into position requires careful thought and planning, and the right equipment.*

MOVING SMALL ROCKS WITH A BAR

You will need
- two people to carry the rock
- strong straps (from a hire shop)
- a scaffolding pole and shackle

1 If a rock is the right size for strapping, wrap the two loose ends of the strap around a scaffolding pole, securing them with a shackle.

2 Ensure the length of strap is equal to a little less than the height to the carriers' shoulders. This will mean that the rock only need be lifted off the ground a short way, just enough to move it. It will also be safer if the rock is hung as close to the ground as possible, in case it should fall out of the straps.

MOVING SMALL TO MEDIUM ROCKS WITH A SACK TRUCK

You will need
- a sack truck, preferably with pneumatic tyres as this will make it easier to pull over soft ground – hard wheels will easily get bogged down, even in gravel

1 Lift up one end of the rock until it stands on end and slide the sack truck as close up to the rock as you can.

2 Roll the rock over on to the plate of the sack truck. You may be able to slide the plate under the rock without having to roll the rock by lifting one end a little bit off the ground.

3 One person at either end of the pole can lift the pole on to their shoulders, and then the two people can lift and move the rock.

3 Place one foot against the axle of the truck as you pull the handle back. Small rocks are easy to move around like this with the handle at around 45 degrees. It is easier to pull than to push.

NARROW ENTRANCES

If the garden has a narrow entrance, a sack truck is useful to move smaller stones. For larger stones, you may need to hire a crane to lift the rocks over the house. Although expensive, cranes will carry a lot more weight.

MOVING ROCKS WITH A SKID LOADER

You will need
- a hired skid loader
- medium-size rocks

1 You may be able to drive the bucket under the rock without having to move the rock.

2 Otherwise, either prop up one end of the rock using a post or a crow-bar while the bucket slides underneath, or, with help if the rock is too large, roll the rock into the bucket.

SELECTING THE BEST METHOD

The size of rocks you need to move will dictate the method you use:

- to move rocks by hand, they must be small but you can control positioning;
- a sack truck will carry small–medium rocks, and will fit through narrow gaps;
- a skid loader can be used to transport medium rocks, and the weight is taken by the equipment;
- a mini-digger or foreloader can move rocks up to its weight limit.

MOVING MEDIUM TO LARGE ROCKS WITH A MINI-DIGGER OR FORELOADER

You will need
- a mini-digger or foreloader on a tractor, or back-hoe, plus a skilled licensed driver
- hard hats, steel toe-capped boots and gloves
- a block of wood or fencing post
- lifting straps with looped ends – these can be hired, and are classified according to the weight they are designed to carry. Go for heavier straps than you think you will need.
- U-shaped shackles to bind the ends of the straps

1 If the rock is lying flat, prop up the top end in order to slide the straps underneath. Use the digger to lift up one end and slide a block of wood underneath to prop it up.

2 Wind the straps two or three times around the rock at approximately a third of the way from the top. This position should keep the rock secure when the straps tighten around it. Tighten the two ends by pushing one end through the loop at the other end. Make the two ends with equal length to spare and ensure they end up at either side of the rock. This will allow it to hang more vertically when you lift it up.

3 Wind the two loose ends around a secure point on the lifting bucket, and bring the two loops close enough to each other to be secured together. Using a suitable shackle, clamp the two loops together.

4 Lift the machine loader bucket up until the straps are tense and lift the bucket gently and slowly until you can see how the rock will hang from the bucket.

5 It may take two or three attempts until the straps are secure and the rock is hanging so that it can be manipulated into place.

SAFETY NOTE

Before moving the rock, ensure that it is hanging securely and that everyone is at a safe distance.

Paving & stepping stones

Paving is another important element of a Japanese garden. Pathways through the Japanese garden can be made of different kinds of stone, from new or manmade paving stones to reclaimed stone from various sources. Stepping stones are often used in water features or gravel areas. Straight lines and right angles are usually best avoided, as curves and natural forms complement the concept and style of a Japanese garden better. If care is taken at the planning stage, the final result can look completely natural and spontaneous.

Above: *Granite setts are rough hewn and therefore more suitable for Japanese gardens where natural-looking materials are preferred.*

RANDOM PAVING

This kind of paving, using irregularly cut stone pieces, is popular in Japanese gardens. The stone is generally bought by the tonne and needs careful laying to accommodate pieces of varying thickness and to minimize the width of mortar joints. Random stone can be laid as a pathway "filler" in conjunction with straight-edged, rectangular pieces and adjacent to sections of geometric patterning, for example next to pavers set as a line of diamonds. Kerbstones and stone setts are also used to define pathways and to separate areas of differing colour, pattern or function.

RECLAIMED STONES

Paving that is reclaimed, with a rough-hewn look or with worn or weathered surfaces is much sought after. Japanese gardeners will often incorporate pieces once used for other purposes, including original millstones, old gateposts and worn stone door lintels or steps. A good source of reclaimed stones is architectural salvage yards.

STEPPING STONES

A very common feature of Japanese gardens, stepping stones are used in both wet and dry locations. A zigzagging pathway might artfully combine rounded stepping stones with rectangular elements, often also mingled with cobbles or pebbles. Handcrafted granite stepping stones, broadly circular and with softly bevelled edges, are laid following age-old patterns.

Whatever the location – crossing a pool, a mossy woodland floor or in a gravel area – the stones are always set slightly proud of the surrounding surface. Stepping stones should be well bedded into the substrate to give the path stability and also to create a "rooted" quality. This means that individual stones are likely to need a depth of at least 15cm (6in).

TYPES OF NATURAL STONE FOR PAVING

Certain types of sedimentary rock can be split very easily along the overlying layers, making them ideal contenders for paving. These include pale grey or creamy coloured limestone, which often has visible remnants of fossilized organisms and shells. Sandstones, such as buff-coloured York stone paving and millstone grit in Britain, and flagstone and bluestone in the US, are also used for paving. Good-quality reclaimed York stone commands a high price, but nowadays imported Indian sandstone can be more economical and just as effective. It ranges in colour from almost black to buff with pink or yellow tinting. If possible, look at samples of the different colour types laid as paving, both dry and wetted, before making your selection, as the colour may change dramatically when the stone is wet, perhaps making it not the perfect choice after all.

Indian sandstone is widely available in a wide range of sizes, and is hand cut to leave a bevelled, rough-cut edge

Left: *Weathered stone slabs covered with mosses and lichens are used here as stepping stones in a sea of pebbles. Note how they are set proud of their surroundings. Rectangular pieces are often mixed with irregular ones.*

Above: *Indian sandstone comes in a wide range of colours.*

Above: *York stone paving slabs covered with lichen and moss.*

Above: *Limestone is a sedimentary rock that gives an aged patina to paving.*

Above: *Traditional granite stepping stones are usually rounded or irregular in shape.*

Above: *Slate stepping stones look wonderfully glossy and dark after rain.*

Above: *Used sparingly, stepping stones with imprinted symbols or patterns can add interest.*

with a more rustic appearance than diamond- or machine-cut stone. There are, however, some practices to do with the labour and sourcing of Indian sandstone that mean that this material is not guaranteed to be ethically sourced, so you might want to look for alternatives until better standards are established.

When buying any regular-cut stone, buy by the square metre/yard rather than by the tonne, and specify a minimum and maximum thickness.

Granite is traditional in Japanese gardens. As it is one of the most resistant stones to wear and tear, it is much sought after, especially when the surface shows signs of erosion, as this signifies great age. In shady or damp paved areas, granite and other non-porous rock types have an advantage over limestone and sandstone because, with the more porous stone, moisture absorption leads to the growth of slippery algae, which must be removed periodically for safety. This does not apply to granite, which is less absorbent. Choose hand-finished granite paving or tumbled granite setts for a natural effect.

Slate is another excellent paving option, although pieces tend to be cut relatively thinly, so they must be laid on a full mortar bed to give adequate support. Check before buying imported slate to ensure that the pieces are thick enough for external use and that they are of outdoor quality, meaning that they won't shatter or flake on exposure to the elements.

MANMADE ALTERNATIVES

Manufacturers of concrete paving now produce very convincing stone reproductions using old stone pavers as moulds to give a natural-looking effect. But these products can wear and chip, then exposing the concrete interior, and the slabs tend not to be as thick as natural stone. However, driveway setts (small blocks) are a good option for paving close to buildings and in more formal areas.

If used with care, poured concrete can be an effective and inexpensive material for making large stepping stones or areas resembling exposed bedrock. The mix is poured into a mould of sufficient depth to prevent cracking, using curved shuttering. Before it completely hardens, it is textured with a wetted nylon hand brush and various tools. Alternatively, you can add pebbles and shingle to the concrete to create an interestingly textured surface, then use a soft brush and watering can to expose some areas, thus mirroring the processes of natural erosion.

Cobbles, pebbles & paddlestones

Often used for pathways, in open areas or by water features, the smooth, rounded surfaces of cobbles, pebbles and paddlestones make a pleasing contrast to rough-surfaced regular paving slabs or flat stepping stones. They can be a wonderful foil for plants, especially those with linear or strap-like foliage. Different schemes call for different sizes and types of pebbles or cobbles, in keeping with the scale and nature of the garden. Remember that the beauty of the stone may be revealed only when wet, so when you are buying stones ask to see samples in and out of water.

Above: *Graded pebbles camouflage the edge of a butyl-lined pond or stream, creating a beach or natural stream bank effect.*

COBBLES

Acting as a helpful transition from large rounded boulders to smaller pebbles, cobbles tend to be required in relatively small quantities for ordinary domestic garden schemes. In fact, in a compact urban space such as an enclosed courtyard or roof garden, you may need only a handful, which is just as well because they tend to be sold individually and can be quite expensive.

Some cobbles are relatively unmarked but range in colour from white, through brown, red and grey to almost black, reflecting different rock types. Paler greys and browns may also show attractive banding, for which you will pay a premium. When hand-selecting small numbers of stones, look carefully to ensure that they are the colour, shape and texture you want, as cobbles are sometimes split or damaged in transit.

Large cobbles of the sort originally used to surface the roads and stable yards of old are sometimes available from reclamation yards. Bigger garden centres often have a few large cobbles for sale, stored in crates or on palettes. Cobbles may be commercially dredged from the sea bottom or taken from gravel pits. For larger quantities, visit your local stone merchant or a gravel pit if there's one in your area. You can't just go to the beach and help yourself, though – laws normally prohibit the removal of cobbles or pebbles from a beach or the bank of a stream.

Left: *It is important to place larger stones and cobbles by hand to create a naturalistic effect. Here there is the impression of a stream trickling down into a larger, deeper pool. The cobbles are graded by size and infilled with gravel.*

PEBBLES

In nature, pebbles often represent a wide mixture of rock types, fragments of which have been worn smooth and rounded by the action of water or ice. When wet, they glisten and may show an extraordinary range of colours, flecks and stripes. Suppliers normally have samples in buckets for you to examine. Pebbles may also be colour selected so that, as well as the natural mixed shades, you can buy pure white or jet black for special projects.

In small quantities, pebbles are sold in bags or sacks, but they are extremely heavy – the average car could safely transport only three or four bags at a time. You can also buy them bagged or loose by the tonne delivered from stone merchants. Pebbles are graded and sold by size – you'll normally find at least two or three sizes at larger garden centres.

MIXING COBBLES AND PEBBLES

Sometimes cobbles and pebbles are used together in Japanese gardens to create a pleasingly natural look. When you are using these stones as ground cover, mix cobbles and pebbles of different sizes. If you want to create a beach effect at the margin of a butyl-lined pond, or in a dry stream bed, lay cobbles, pebbles and shingle in graded bands and curving sections, reflecting the strata formed by water in nature. Check that the various types you have in mind are compatible in terms of colour and texture. If you intend to use cobbles and pebbles in and around your pond or by a stream, check that they are fish friendly and wash them thoroughly before use to avoid contaminating the water.

PADDLESTONES

These flat or paddle-shaped pieces of stone with gently rounded edges come in sizes from 15cm (6in) across to as much as 60cm (24in). Although they are sometimes used for ground cover and for creating interesting surface textures, these stones are ideal for representing a stream because the pieces can be laid to overlap and "flow" in the direction of the imaginary water. They can also be used to suggest the rippled surface of a pool or, on a much larger and more ambitious scale, a lake or even a sea. Paddlestones have a markedly different look to cobbles and pebbles and are therefore best laid with some visual barrier to separate them from these more rounded, glossy aggregates.

Above: *You can buy pebbles graded by size bagged or loose from builders' merchants.*

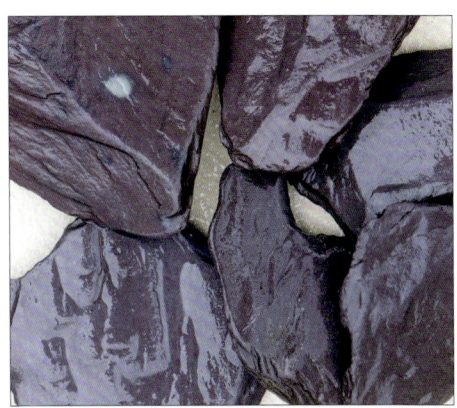

Above: *Slate pebbles eroded by the action of water are softer looking than chippings.*

Above: *These red marble pebbles have been set into cement to create a textured surface.*

PREPARING THE GROUND

Do not lay cobbles, pebbles and paddlestones directly on to soil, because this is likely to contain perennial weed roots and annual weed seeds. Instead use a black horticultural or landscape membrane, which will allow water to pass through but which prevents soil and weeds from coming to the surface.

Above: *Ask to see pebbles wet before you buy as they can look quite different.*

Above: *Paddlestones are characterized by their large, flat, broadly oval shapes.*

Above: *White marble pebbles are sometimes used for more stylized designs.*

Sand, grit, gravel & slate

A feeling of space is very important in Japanese gardens, and open sand or gravel areas help to keep the structure of the garden simple and are easy to maintain if laid carefully. Sand or grit can be raked into patterns, as in a traditional Zen garden, and although gravel cannot be raked into quite such well-defined designs, it makes an interesting and subtly coloured backdrop to a large rock or boulder. Whichever kind of ground cover you choose, make sure that the preparation is meticulous and you will be rewarded with a natural-looking, easy-to-keep area.

Above: *Pieces of natural stone here form an informal pathway. Clay tiles have been used to separate the two types of gravel.*

SAND AND FINE GRIT

A well-known feature of many Japanese gardens is an area of sand or fine grit, raked into swirling patterns to represent forms in nature. (See overleaf for some examples.) This can be a practical option for a newly created Japanese garden if thought is given to the materials, the size of the area and its location within the garden. In dry gardens, the patterns represent the movement of water. More abstractly, in the Zen tradition, these raked sand or gravel patterns can also represent the tranquil mind.

The best location for this effect is in a sheltered garden or courtyard. The fine material traditionally used is not suitable for very open, windy locations as the patterns will be disturbed too quickly. After periods of heavy rainfall or strong winds, you may well find that designs need to be re-raked or brushed quite frequently.

A number of grades and colours of sand and grit can be used to create your design. In bright, sunny locations, and especially for larger areas, avoid pure white sand, as this can create an uncomfortable glare – darker shades are more tranquil. However, paler coloured sands can bring light into a shaded passageway or courtyard area, or an enclosed space that is viewed through a window.

Prepare the area by separating the sand and base material from the underlying soil using landscape membrane. Make sure that you keep the sand or grit well away from areas of lawn as it can damage mower blades.

COARSE GRIT AND GRAVEL

Gravel is a relatively inexpensive ground cover when compared to paving. When laid over landscape membrane, it can also be surprisingly low maintenance. Finer gravels may be used as an alternative surface around rock formations in a dry Zen garden, though they won't allow for intricately raked patterns.

You can buy gravel in a range of grades. The coarser types (up to 2cm/¾in across) are best for walking on, especially if the area is close to the house, because they don't get caught in the treads of shoes and tend to bed down well and stay put. You should try to avoid using fine grit and gravel under trees, as it will be difficult to clear fallen leaves in the autumn. However, you can use a leaf blower on larger diameter gravels and pebbles without disturbing them.

Finer gravel can be kicked about by foot traffic and all too easily makes a seed bed for weeds, so it will need more maintenance than the coarser varieties.

For water gardens, you will find that river gravels and beach shingles give a natural look, being composed of rounded, water-worn pieces that glisten when wet. They normally come in a combination of browns and greys – soft, neutral colours that work well in restful Japanese gardens and also

Above: *Where fine sand is used, be prepared for regular maintenance, even in sheltered areas.*

Above: *Gravel is often used as a representation of water in the Japanese garden.*

combine nicely with pebbles and cobbles (see pages 74–75). Avoid golden-coloured gravels or coloured chippings, which tend not to look very natural.

DIFFERENT SOURCES

To purchase sand or grit for raking, you may need to contact a specialist Japanese garden supplier as it is not easy to find the right grade or colour in ordinary garden centres, stone merchants or builders' merchants. The type of grit used in Japan is made from degraded rock fragments that measure about 3mm (⅛in) in diameter. However, certain types of horticultural grit may make an acceptable alternative if you cannot find it.

Though bagged gravel is readily available from garden centres, you can buy it more economically from builders' merchants. Having bags or truckloads delivered will also avoid unwanted wear and tear to your car. In this case, tell the supplier what area you plan to cover and to what depth and they will calculate exactly how much to deliver.

OTHER GROUND COVER

Stone chippings of hard rocks such as granite are also suitable for ground cover, and they come in a wider range of colours than gravel, including black, shades of grey, plum, green, brownish-red and white. You can purchase a range of grades. Whatever colour you choose, make sure that it blends with or makes a suitable contrast to the type of rock you are using as a central feature. In general, chippings, with their jagged, sharp edges, tend to work better in a dry garden setting than in a water garden. In a water garden you would expect the natural substrate to be smooth and water-worn rather than spiky and frost-shattered.

Slate waste is now widely available in garden centres as an alternative surfacing material to gravel for paths and open areas. The flat shards bed down well and don't tend to get kicked about like fine gravel. This material is also resistant to weed growth, although like the other ground cover materials it benefits from being laid on a horticultural or landscape membrane. Slate is usually sold in bags, and comes in dark grey, or with plum or green tones.

Larger pieces of slate can be laid like paddlestones to create the effect of flowing water in a dry stream feature, and finer grades can be applied as a mulch around plants or to create the illusion of a body of still water in a dry garden. Fine slate works well to make a dry "pool" crossed by an arched bridge or stepping stones, or at the base of a stone waterfall.

Above: *These 5mm (¼in) diameter granite chippings are ideal for traditional-style gardens.*

Above: *Pearly quartz chippings can be used to lighten shady courtyards.*

Above: *Blue slate "waste" is readily available and useful for creating dry pools and streams.*

Above: *Dark-coloured Welsh granite chippings could be used to contrast with pale cobbles.*

Above: *Always lay chippings over permeable landscape membrane to limit weed problems.*

Above: *Use coloured or pale granite chippings sparingly in more naturalistic settings.*

CHOOSING SAND OR GRAVEL

The sand or gravel can be 3–10mm (⅛–⅜in) in diameter. If it is too fine, it will get blown about and will not rake well into patterns, although in the famous garden of Shisendo, in Kyoto, the sand is very fine and is brushed with a twig broom into delicate patterns rather than raked. The ideal size is 4–6mm (³⁄₁₆in) in diameter. A mixture of sizes and a degree of roughness will help the stones in the ridges to bind with one another. If they are too round and smooth, the stones tend to roll and the ridges flatten out too readily.

The sand can be laid over a concrete base, but it is important to ensure that the whole site is well drained. An alternative would be a firm but open base of hardcore overlaid with rough stone and sand mix (known as hoggin or scalpings) in order to allow the surface to drain.

The most sought-after gravel in Kyoto is made of a silvery-grey granite and quartz grit. It is very precious, very expensive and becoming quite difficult to obtain, even in Japan. In other countries it may be difficult to find the ideal kind of gravel or sand, though situations will vary. Avoid white marble chips, as these will be

Above: *With the right type of fine gravel, you can create a range of clearly defined patterns.*

Below: *In the temple garden of Tofuku-ji, "waves" of gravel have been raked into abstractions. The main set of lines runs parallel throughout the garden while those closest to the edge curve to meet it.*

USING GRAVEL: KEY ELEMENTS

Finding the right site Gravel "pools" of water should always be laid on a level site. Don't try to make them on even a gentle slope.

Colour of gravel Don't use gravel that is bright white as this will glare in bright sunshine; try to find a colour that is light enough to feel like water and to show up in moonlight.

Size of gravel Gravel size can be as small as 3mm (⅛in) and up to 10mm (⅜in) in diameter, depending on the kind of pattern you want to make and the area to be covered. The ideal size for raked gravel is 4–6mm (³⁄₁₆in). If the gravel is too small and smooth it will collapse too readily.

Depth of gravel Gravel should be laid to a depth of about 5cm (2in) to give enough material to rake.

RAKING PATTERNS: KEY ELEMENTS

Raking without leaving footprints Simply start in the middle of the "canvas" and work outwards.

Making a satisfying and authentic pattern The bulk of your space should be empty and raked in parallel lines. In the most famous dry garden in the world, the Ryoan-ji, the lines are all parallel except the concentric waves that lap around each of the 15 rocks.

Keeping it simple Avoid making too much of the space busy with too many different and elaborate patterns as this will defeat the calming influence of the water effect. Simple is best.

Imitating the flow of water Around rocks and plants, you can rake as if the waves were lapping against their shores. In other places you can "draw" whirlpools, waving patterns, or patterns that imitate the variable flow in rivers (always remembering that your overall pattern should be simple). Dry streams made of gravel can also be raked to imitate the flow of small brooks.

Stream current

Stylized wave

Ocean wave

Surf pattern

Brook

Stylized ocean wave

Concentric ocean wave

Combination: whirlpool and stream current

Concentric ripples

Whirlpool

Elliptical concentric ripple

far too bright and look a bit funereal. Darker colours can be used but they will tend to look more like muddy water than the reflective purity that is so ideal in these gardens.

If you would prefer not to commit yourself to frequent raking, then any kind of gravel that is not too chunky would do; however, even in this case you will need to rake it from time to time to keep it looking clean and tidy. If you like the raking process, you could make it a regular practice. How frequently you need to rake a dry garden will depend on the degree to which the patterns get disturbed by heavy rains, wind, birds and small animals, or in autumn by how many leaves fall on them. Before you re-do the raking, level out the whole site with a broom, a board or the flat side of a hay rake, so that you are working on a blank canvas.

SAND AND GRAVEL PATTERNS

In Zen temples, dry gardens often have areas of sand or gravel raked into elaborate patterns. These are simple abstract imitations of the movement of waves on water. The simplicity and rhythm are also symbolic of the spiritual life. They create a sense of space and wonder, helping the mind to enter a state of contemplation and quiet – one of the goals of Zen Buddhism. The raking of the sand is part of the spiritual practice of Zen monks, who enter a state of "no-mind" as they walk backwards, drawing their rake and pulling the sand into ridges and troughs.

The traditional patterns made by the monks are a closely guarded secret. If you enjoy the effect of these dry gardens but are less interested in the high goals of Zen meditation, simply imagine that you are "painting" a sea in sand. The sand can be the wide open sea or a river; it also represents the white "canvas" background of a landscape painting. Knowing this can open up numerous possibilities for abstract patterns, but keep the overall pattern simple or you will distract the mind of the viewer, rather than soothing it into a state of calm.

Dry water

The original dry landscape gardens focused on the placement of rocks in moss or grass. In later dry gardens, rocks were set in sand, gravel and among pebbles, with these elements arranged and spread to imitate the qualities of water: either as a stream, when on a flat surface, or as a waterfall, when carefully constructed on a slope (see pages 82–83). The important concept with a dry waterfall is to have high stones at the back of the design to represent the waterfall height. It can then end in a dry stream or pond when it reaches the foot of the slope.

Above: *At Tofukuji, in Kyoto, the 20th-century artist-designer Mirei Shigemori used sand to imitate water, recalling ocean waves lapping at island shores.*

DRY STREAMS: KEY ELEMENTS

Assessing the slope A dry stream can be built down a gentle slope. On a steeper slope you will need to create a series of dry falls, or alternatively make the stream take a wandering course.

Making a meandering dry stream You can use the same principles as for a meandering water stream (see pages 98–101), on a flattish site with a wider expanse of stones.

Paths and bridges Design paths that can cross over the stream or that look as though they can, so that you can build a slab stone bridge across the stream. Bridges will add to the illusion of a real stream.

Adding waterfalls Small "falls" can be built into the stream to make it look more realistic.

Exaggerating the effect Remember that you are suggesting a stream rather than making an exact copy, so the effect should ideally look as artistic as it is naturalistic. If it is too naturalistic, the stream will simply look as though the water has run dry.

Planting Place clumps of plants that have a "wet" look on the sides of the stream, for example sedges, hostas or tricyrtis.

ROCKS AND PEBBLES

The first two great gardens with rocks set in moss or grass were the 14th-century Saiho-ji, or Moss Temple, and Tenryu-ji. At the latter there is a superb dry waterfall, known as the Dragon Gate Waterfall, created with all the power of a real waterfall. At the Saiho-ji, there is a large turtle representation and a hillside with dramatic arrangements of rocks. The

Below: *This dry garden at St Mawgan in Cornwall shows the same kind of enterprising spirit seen in many of Shigemori's designs. The effect is like that of a flooded inland river basin.*

Zen monks who created such dry gardens realized that the imagination is more captivated by a suggestion than by reality. Or, as they might have put it, the power of the imagined shape yields a far greater truth than one locked up in the real. This is what is meant by the poetic term *yugen*, or "the spirit of hidden depth".

Streams, as opposed to still water, are portrayed in their "dry" form by

the use of river-washed pebbles laid out carefully in overlapping patterns to indicate a sense of flow. The image is completed by the use of a few larger boulders or rocks, as well as bridges made of large stone slabs.

MODERN INTERPRETATIONS

There is great design potential for contemporary designers to use a dry rock-and-sand garden to create even more abstract patterns, using quarry-blasted rocks rather than naturally occurring weathered stones. This takes the "suggestive" nature of the dry landscape into the realm of contemporary design. If you are careful with the composition, space and balance of the layout, these gardens can be very successful, as well as fairly easy to manage. Not all modern Japanese garden designers follow Zen precepts; they have become more Western in outlook. However, the overall design of these modern gardens remains essentially Japanese.

Above: *This dry garden at the Brunei Gallery roof garden in London can be interpreted as a river with large natural boulders being crossed by a staggered carved stone bridge that stretches from bank to bank.*

Below: *A dry waterfall in Kew Gardens shows a carp stone placed at the base of the waterfall. This symbolizes the striving of the individual to rise above himself. A carp who reaches the top of the waterfall is transformed into a dragon.*

DRY WATERFALLS: KEY ELEMENTS

Using a flat site In a flat, rectangular courtyard setting, a dry waterfall can be set into one corner.

Using a hilly site In a natural setting, a dry waterfall should be built into the side of a hill or a steep slope to look effective.

Exaggerating the effect Good dry waterfalls should have a "monumental" feel to look impressive, as if a lot of water fell down them at one time. Don't be afraid to exaggerate this effect. Some versions use very large rocks.

Choosing the top stones Find some flat-topped stones for the points at which the water would have flowed over the waterfall. The top stone should always have two larger stones on either side of it. For a simple arrangement, these three stones might be enough.

Imagining the water Always imagine the flow of the waterfall as if it had real water in it. This will help you decide how to lay the stones.

Making pools Some waterfalls have small pools halfway down them. In a dry waterfall these are filled with gravel to imitate the standing water.

Making a dry waterfall & stream

Waterfalls in Japanese gardens can be real sources of water, or they can alternatively be dry cascades (*kare taki*) in which stones simply suggest the movement of a waterfall. *Kare taki* exist in various forms, ranging from a single cascade to a more complex one of multiple stages. Each one is documented in Japan's earliest known manual of gardening, the *Sakuteiki*, which describes ten different forms of waterfall construction, stipulates the proper height and width of a cascade, and advises the reader on the appropriate types of stones to use for such a feature.

This dry cascade is suitable for a garden with a natural slope, and uses a plastic liner and a stepped selection of rocks from the top to the base. Such a dry waterfall is seen as highly symbolic by Japanese garden masters, and the aesthetic positioning of rocks, often in groups of three, is key. The dry waterfall forms part of a dry landscape, which might also include evergreen trees and shrubs, moss and raked sand, which symbolizes streaming water. Here the dry stream at the bottom is represented by gravel and more well-positioned rocks.

Above: *Dry waterfalls are often built on a series of levels, so that the gravel that imitates the water can be held in the "pools" as the dry cascade descends down the slope.*

Opposite: *Sedges and ferns tucked around the rocks recall the plants that you might find alongside a mountain stream.*

You will need
- 2 people to move the stones
- a large backing stone
- 2 side stones
- various other large stones and boulders
- concrete
- plastic sheeting
- gravel
- a long base stone to represent a bridge
- a shovel

1 Prepare the location by digging over the land following the shape of the proposed waterfall and stream. Then dig a hole to fit the backing stone and manoeuvre the stone into position.

2 Set the backing stone and pack the soil around it tightly so that it remains steady. Larger stones and boulders should be set in the hole with concrete to ensure they remain solidly in place.

3 Having achieved the basic stepping-stone shape from backing stone to lower level stone, prepare the ground to accommodate two side stones.

4 Place stones to form a pool structure, as shown here, that is positioned directly below the four key waterfall stones.

5 For the dry stream, prepare the land beneath the pool. The stream should appear on a lower level again to maintain the illusion of falling water.

6 Position further stones to frame the shape of the stream, judging their positions as you go.

7 Having completed your stone structure, cut plastic sheeting to line each of the enclosed areas. This ensures that plants will not grow into the gravel.

8 Shovel gravel on top of the plastic sheeting to cover it fully. Ensure that the gravel layer representing the stream is at least 2.5cm (1in) thick.

9 As a finishing touch, position another long, flat stone across the two base stones around the stream to represent a bridge.

MAKING A DRY WATERFALL & STREAM 83

Plants & planting

The "hard" elements of a garden – gravel, rocks and architectural features – are important in Japanese garden design. However, "soft" elements – plants, trees and shrubs – are also vital. Many people regard Japanese gardens as making little use of plants, and while it is true that they are often less central than in, for example, a traditional English cottage garden, many Japanese gardens use a great range of plants. The crucial point is that the plants are always subservient to the overall design, and will be carefully placed and managed to this end.

Above: *On the west coast of Europe, near the sea, there is enough moisture in the air for moss to grow on the ground and over the trees.*

GROUND COVER

An important ingredient in most Japanese gardens for ground cover, moss requires the right balance of sun and shade to grow well. In Kyoto, for example, it will grow virtually anywhere because of the high rainfall during the summer. The variety of different species of moss gives the surface of the garden a beautiful velvety texture in all shades of green, often highlighted by the dappled sun if the moss is growing beneath trees. By contrast, the popular Western ground cover of grass is not widely used in Japanese gardens. The advantage of growing moss rather than grass is that it gives the Japanese designer much more freedom in terms of positioning plants, as it does not need to be mown in the same way as grass. It does, however, need to be cared for and weeded to keep it in shape. Rocks can also be positioned without the constraints placed on gardens in which grass is the main foundation. If you are not blessed with a climate in which moss grows freely, you can easily improvise by using a ground cover of mondo grass (*Ophiopogon*) or perhaps instead some shorn bamboos.

Below: *It is important to have the right amount of light and shade to maintain the moss cover. Too much sun and it burns out; too little and it dies out. Many species of moss have combined to knit this carpet at Sanzen-in.*

Below: *This uneven chequerboard of stone squares sunk into a sea of moss and edged with roof tiles is at the garden of Tofuku-ji; this garden harmonizes the natural, the architectural and the contemporary.*

84 NATURAL MATERIALS

Right: *Although most Japanese gardens exhibit restraint in their colours, some late Edo-period gardens grew a number of brightly coloured azaleas, such as these at the Karlsruhe Japanese garden in Germany.*

Grass is rarely used as ground cover in the Japanese garden except in very large gardens, where drought-resistant zoyza grass can be planted. This deep-rooting grass is not mown tight to the ground, and should be left at a height of approximately 8cm (3in), which gives a dense, cushiony turf. However, this grass does turn brown in the winter. Grass on banks and between rocks in Japanese gardens should be trimmed and clipped as neatly as in a Western garden.

SYMBOLIC PLANTS

While plants are not used as much as in Western gardens, when they are used they are not simply a design element but often hold symbolic significance too. So most Japanese gardens will contain one or more of the most symbolic plants, such as plum, cherry, bamboo, pine or maple. The Japanese plum (*Prunus mume*) is a symbol of purity and hope; the cherry (*Prunus serrulata*) with its short-lived blossom reminds us of our mortality, while the Japanese maple (*Acer palmatum*) is a symbol of longevity.

JAPAN'S NATURAL FLORA

Although Japan's mountains, streams and coastlines are brimming with superb flora, the disciplined restraint of Japanese gardens focuses on certain types of plants. The native plant area in Kyoto's botanical garden is full of plants that Western gardeners would relish, but most of them would not find a home in a Japanese garden.

The problem with many Western imitations of Japanese gardens is that designers cannot resist using attractive Japanese plants that would not normally be chosen by a Japanese designer – for example, those that are considered too colourful or are the wrong shape. However, this restraint does not mean that the Japanese do not appreciate plants. On the contrary, the Japanese celebrate flowers perhaps more than any other nation, especially flowers that signify seasonal change or are associated with certain festivals.

SEASONAL VARIETY

As the last snows melt in spring, the plum trees (or Japanese apricots) start wafting out their scent and are appreciated with a quiet reverence. The cherry blossom season then attracts thousands to gardens with the best displays, with parties gathering under their boughs. Although there are a number of native shrubs that flower in late spring – some deutzias, spiraeas and kerrias – they are considered as secondary to the cherries, wisterias, peonies, azaleas and camellias.

The summer begins with a show of irises that grow in swampy ground at the heads of ponds, and in pots as prized and cosseted specimens. Hollyhocks (*Alcea rosea*), hydrangeas, the lotus (*Nelumbo*) and the morning glory (*Ipomoea*) are all cultivated to keep the season going as long as possible. Many plants originating in different climates do not grow well in the hot, wet Japanese summers, but will revive in the spring and autumn.

Right: *Garden with azaleas in bloom in the Rikugien Garden in Tokyo, Japan.*

In Autumn Japanese maples are just as important as the spring cherries in the Japanese calendar. Their fiery reds contrast with the deep greens of the evergreen pines and the fleeting blossom of the autumn-flowering camellia (*Camellia sasanqua*). Bush clover, balloon flower, toad lilies and *Farfugium* all add extra interest.

The most favoured plants for winter interest are bamboos and pines, and these can withstand the cold impressively. Snow-covered pines make a beautiful sight. Japan is also blessed with an exceptional number of evergreen shrubs that thrive in its acidic soil and temperate climate.

PLANTING STYLES

Most shrubs in the Japanese garden are set out in random, natural-looking groups or as individual specimens. Formal, symmetrical styles are rarely used, and shrubs and flowers are not planted for their textures or colours.

Below: *A pathway through the bamboo garden at the Hakone Gardens in Saratoga, California. This part of the garden contains many highly prized types of bamboo, including a black-stemmed variety.*

In tea gardens, you will find plants such as ferns that lend a wild quality to the design. In stark contrast, other gardens are planted with clipped evergreens, a look at its most artistic in the 17th-century art of *o-karikomi*, in which groups of shrubs, usually azaleas and camellias, are clipped into abstract topiary shapes (see pages 88–91). Hedges are another important feature for which a great miscellany of shrubs can be used. While some hedges look fairly uniform from a distance, they may actually contain as many as 20 or more genera from a list including *Elaeagnus, Pieris, Camellia, Rhododendron, Ficus, Aucuba, Osmanthus* and *Nandina*.

The Japanese garden is by no means devoid of colour and scent. Town gardens might include hydrangeas, hollyhocks, sweet peas (*Lathyrus odoratus*), morning glories and clematis or azaleas growing in pots outside the door. This planting effect is something that would be simple to recreate in any small city garden. The pots themselves can be in all shapes and sizes but in Japan are often quite small. The compost (soil mix) would be annually renewed to ensure a good supply of nutrients.

Above: *A dwarf Japanese red pine creates a much softer look than the harsher and more rugged black pine.*

PLANTS THROUGH THE SEASONS

Spring
Plum blossom (*Prunus mume*)
Cherry blossom (*Sakura*)
Deutzia
Spiraea
Japanese rose (*Kerria*)
Wisteria
Peony (*Paeonia*)
Azalea
Camellia

Summer
Iris
Hollyhock (*Alcea rosea*)
Hydrangea
Lotus blossom (*Nelumbo*)
Morning glory (*Ipomoea*)

Autumn
Japanese maple (*Acer*)
Evergreen pines
Autumn-flowering camellia (*Camellia sasanqua*)
Bush clover (*Lespedeza*)
Balloon flower (*Platycodon*)
Toad lily (*Tricyrtis*)
Farfugium

Winter
Bamboos
Evergreen pines and other shrubs

PLANTING TECHNIQUE

Although you can plant pot-grown plants at almost any time of year, you may need to water them more frequently if you plant in late spring or summer. The ideal time of year for planting is autumn but if your chosen plant is tender, especially when young and small, it would be better to wait until the late winter or early spring. It is not a good idea to attempt to plant anything when the ground is very hard and dry, very wet and boggy, or when it is frozen solid.

The standard planting technique shown below should be adapted around the different types and sizes of plant available as well as around the type of roots the plant has. Before you start the process of planting, you will need to be prepared with a garden spade and fork, some well-rotted manure, a rake and a watering can.

Right: *Take care when planting some species of bamboo as they can be invasive. Root barriers can be placed in a circle around the plant to prevent it from invading the garden.*

1 Place the plant, still in its pot, where you want to plant it and mark around the spot with your spade or place a cane. Then put the plant to one side, digging a hole 50% wider than the pot and 5–7.5cm (2–3in) deeper. Break up the soil in the bottom of the hole and replace it.

2 While holding the pot, turn it over. Squeeze the sides gently with the hand holding the base of the pot and ease it off with the same hand. If it doesn't come off readily, give the rim a firm tap on something hard and check that no roots have emerged through the holes in the pot and are holding the plant in.

3 Before planting, check that the hole is the correct depth – normally, the same as it was in the pot. In very heavy soil, planting slightly higher would help to avoid waterlogging, and in light soil you could plant deeper to increase the water supply. Add one or two forkfuls of well-rotted manure to the soil that you removed from the hole and mix the two.

4 If the plant has been well grown then you will not need to tease the roots out, but if the plant is at all pot-bound, spread some of them out. Now, still holding the plant with one hand on the top and one underneath, turn the plant over and carefully lower it into the hole.

5 Backfill around the plant with the manure/soil mixture. There is no need to put any of this mix under the plant as most "feeder" roots grow out laterally.

6 Firm the soil with your foot. If it is very wet, wait before you do this, as the firming may cause compaction and bad drainage. Water the plant generously to help the soil settle in around the plant and remove air pockets. Water at least once a week until established.

PLANTS & PLANTING

Topiary

The Japanese love clipping plants. Often this is simply to manage the growth of a tree or a shrub so that it doesn't become too overgrown, or it may be to allow more light into a garden or on to the mossy woodland floor. In many gardens in Japan, almost every shrub is clipped into rounded mounds, in layers or in squares. This clipping, known as *o-karikomi*, is something very familiar to Westerners when they think of Japanese gardens. But don't make the mistake of attributing very elaborate topiary to the Japanese, when that particular style is, in fact, more Chinese.

Above: *These massive blocks of clipped azaleas in Raikyu-ji resemble huge waves, cloud formations or even mountain ranges.*

AUTHENTIC STYLES

Topiary has been part of the way the Japanese have represented the abstraction of nature in their gardens since the earliest gardens of the Nara and Heian periods. It is worth taking a closer look at how the Japanese approach topiary. In the most famous traditional Japanese gardens, you will find very few examples of the kind of "cloud pruning" that you often find in copies of Japanese gardens, especially in the USA, where all kinds of plants from juniper to boxwood are clipped into a series of rounded "cloud" forms. These sculptured plants can be spectacular but can also, in the wrong setting, look rather comical. Topiary needs a skilled eye; without it, these plants can look more like clipped poodles than part of an elegant design. This brings us back to the recurring theme of the Japanese garden: that the overall composition should not be overwhelmed by excessive forms or colours that may be too distracting.

Although "cloud" pruning is an oriental practice, it was originally (and still is) highly developed in China and Korea. The practice of these countries influenced the art in Japan, but the Japanese way is different. The art of clipping shrubs, like so much of their art, is modest and meaningful when carried out by good designers. In the same way that the Japanese enjoy the simple and natural form of rocks while the Chinese enjoy eccentric and convoluted forms, Japanese garden designers also use their form of topiary with sensitivity and restraint. In the 16th and 17th centuries this practice of *o-karikomi* reached its peak of artistry. With consideration, it can be utilized in a Japanese garden in any of the main styles, using all kinds of plants.

Pines are often trained rather than clipped into remarkable shapes, but this is not strictly *o-karikomi*. These trees are restructured to imitate the weathered, windswept look of wild seaside and mountain-top pines – a favoured feature of many gardens.

Left: O-karikomi *reached its peak during the 17th century. Although the clipping in this garden imitates natural forms, the artistic hand is very apparent. The plants are made up of a mixture of azalea, camellia, pieris and photinia.*

Above: *This natural hill form of clipping has become popular in Western-style gardens. Sometimes all you have to do is follow the "desire" of the plant. Here, the result is a gentle flowing outline of a range of small hills.*

Below: *Planting azaleas or boxwood so that they can be clipped into rounded shapes of differing sizes will create a dynamic design, especially when placed to contrast with the natural outline of rocks.*

Above: *Cloud pruning is used to give plants an eccentric individual character. Although intriguing, these forms are not always easy to fit into an overall design, and are generally best placed as individual specimens.*

KOBORI ENSHU

The man acknowledged as the master of *o-karikomi* was Kobori Enshu (1579–1647). A soldier, town planner, tea-master and garden designer, Enshu introduced the clipping of great masses of evergreens, most often blocks of azaleas but using mixed plantings too, into abstract forms that suggested the movement of waves, the folding of hill ranges, and even, in the garden of Daichi-ji near Kyoto, a treasure-ship on an ocean. In the temple garden of Raikyu-ji, in Takahashi, Enshu combined the art of *o-karikomi* with the art of *shakkei*, clipping blocks of azaleas into forms that, in one part of the garden, imitate ocean waves around the Mystic Isles of the immortals, while in another the forms echo and draw in the outline of the surrounding hills. The overall effect makes for a brilliant composition.

AZALEAS IN TOPIARY

Clipping into such ambitious schemes is not the commonest form of topiary. It can also be the simple trimming of evergreen azaleas into rounded shapes on the banks of a small hill, by the side of a path or pond, or virtually anywhere in the garden. These shapes should complement each other. In the dry garden of Shoden-ji, the clipped azaleas are used in place of rocks and are arranged in artistic groups in a 3-5-7 arrangement, as in the Ryoan-ji. Rounded mounds of azaleas are often seen with square clipped hedges or camellias trimmed with a stem and a round head. This can be seen at Sanzen-in, in Ohara.

There are two varieties of azalea that are clipped differently. 'Hi-ra-do' is a large-leafed evergreen azalea, usually with pink or white flowers, that is clipped into large mounds, while 'Satsuki', with its tighter growth and deeper pink flowers, can be shorn very low, sometimes only 15cm (6in) from the ground. This technique can be used to make the azalea flow down hills, or hug the bases of rocks. Clipping, often carried out in spring and autumn, can result in many plump flower buds being removed.

Above: *This white-flowered form of* Camellia sasanqua *has been clipped into three layers. The autumn flowering should not be affected.*

Enough flower buds remain to give a display, but the number is moderate compared to the profuse flowering that azaleas might otherwise produce, often smothering the plant with so much colour that no leaf can be seen.

WHEN TO CLIP

To maintain a neatly trimmed look, follow these guidelines:

• azaleas, box, hollies and most other evergreens can be clipped from autumn to spring, preferably straight after flowering, followed later in the year by a gentle autumn tidy-up;

• hard prune in spring, to give the plant time to recover its vigour by the end of the growing season;

• avoid serious pruning from mid- to late summer, as this might stimulate a late flush of growth that is likely to be damaged by early autumn frosts.

Left: *This juniper,* Juniperus chinensis, *has been clipped into an elaborate Chinese-style "cloud" formation.*

SQUARE FORMS

Some gardens use linear hedge clipping to draw the eye into the garden or as a device across the line of vision to separate the foreground and background – a feature that actually unifies the composition more than it divides it. Rectangular topiary or clipping into square forms is more familiar in Western gardens. In Japan this kind of topiary and square shaping is used as an interplay between the architecture of the buildings and the informal landscapes beyond them. This may have been influenced by the culture of Western design, since this art developed in the 17th century when the Japanese were first exposed to Western culture after centuries of isolation.

By the 19th century (the late Edo period), much of the clipping of shrubs lost the genius of Enshu's art and became rather over-elaborate. This clichéd style has often been imitated by Western gardeners.

MIREI SHIGEMORI

In the 20th century, Mirei Shigemori (1896–1975), who was a landscape architect and scholar, transformed the design of the Japanese garden, incorporating old motifs and new together in a dramatically abstract manner. His work was also known for using the Western formality of squares, particularly in the gardens around the Hojo of Tofukuji. Here he used the device of repeated low squares of azaleas positioned in a chequerboard pattern.

PLANTS SUITABLE FOR *O-KARIKOMI*

Although deciduous shrubs could be used, the following plants are exclusively evergreen and are the most common ones used for *o-karikomi*:

Genus	Species	Common name
Rhododendron	vaious hybrid azaleas	azalea
Camellia	sasanqua	camellia
Camellia	japonica and others	camellia
Ilex	crenata	holly (Japanese holly)
Taxus	baccata	yew
Taxus	cuspidata and others	yew
Buxus	sempervirens	box
Buxus	microphylla	box

For large blocks and hedges of mixed evergreens, you could include:

Pieris	japonica and others	pieris
Photinia	glabra and others	photinia
Aucuba	japonica and others	spotted laurel
Prunus	lusitanica	Portugal laurel
Prunus	laurocerasus	cherry laurel
Nandina	domestica	heavenly bamboo
Osmanthus	heterophyllus	osmanthus
Osmanthus	delavayi	osmanthus
Osmanthus	burkwoodii	osmanthus
Taxus	cuspidata	yew
Taxus	baccata	yew
Thuja	plicata	western red cedar
Chamaecyparis	obtusa	hinoki cypress
Cryptomeria	japonica	Japanese cedar
Juniperus	chinensis	juniper

For clipping as individuals into cloud formations and other dramatic forms, choose:

Camellia	sasanqua	camellia
Osmanthus	burkwoodii	osmanthus
Prunus	lusitanica	Portugal laurel
Taxus	baccata	yew
Chamaecyparis	obtusa	hinoki cypress
Cryptomeria	japonica	Japanese cedar
Juniperus	chinensis	juniper

Far left: O-karikomi *can be used to enhance, or play with, existing architectural forms; this idea is similar in many ways to Western-style topiary.*

Left: *At Tofuku-ji, a Buddhist temple in Kyoto, Mirei Shigemori took some of the Western influence of topiary to create a chequerboard of clipped azaleas to evoke an old system of land use in China. The bold squares contrast with the white wall and its blackened vertical wooden posts.*

WATER FEATURES

The original Japanese word for landscape was *shan-shui*, meaning "mountain-water". Most Japanese gardeners find their inspiration in the mountain landscapes of their country, with their pools, tumbling streams and waterfalls. For this reason water and rocks have become central to Japanese garden design.

While sometimes it is the spirit of water that is encapsulated in dry water features such as waterfalls made with rocks, and streams and still areas of water constructed with sand or gravel, actual water features give lifeblood to any garden they are used in. This is true whether they are pond or stroll gardens with large ponds, meandering streams and natural waterfalls, or tea and courtyard gardens with smaller-scale examples of ponds and streams and self-contained features, such as *tsukubai* (water basins), *shishi-odoshi* (deer scarers) and *sui-kinkutsu* (echo chambers). At whatever level they are used, the Japanese are always meticulous about integrating water features sensitively within the garden landscape.

Above: *A waterfall in the gardens next to Himeji Castle, Japan.*
Left: *This pond view illustrates the technique of* shakkei, *a way of incorporating a distant view into a garden.*

Streams, waterfalls & ponds

Water has a naturally mesmerizing quality and it is easy to understand the spiritual significance of its various incarnations in the Japanese garden. The choice of Kyoto as the new capital in the 10th century was partly due to the way the hills frame the area, but also to the southward and westward flow of its rivers. In geomantic terms, the southward course towards the sun (fire) was said to bring life, growth and good fortune. While mountains were said to have a meditative quality, and were seen as symbols of the gods and the Buddha, water was a source of joy and detachment.

Above: *A naturalized stream in the Japanese garden at Newstead Abbey, England.*

WATER IN THE JAPANESE GARDEN

In the past, streams would have been used on ceremonial occasions in Japan as settings for poetry readings and for drinking tea and saki. They would typically lead in and out of shallow ponds, often home to koi and the common carp. Ponds were also combined with small islands, and a pine on an island is one of the classic images of Japan. The bridges that cross from the mainland to the island give a good viewing point for the fish and flowers in the shallow water.

Waterfalls are the third water element, believed by Japanese gardeners to be best placed where they can reflect the moon. This stunning effect can be recreated in your garden so long as you take care to place the waterfall so that it looks as natural as possible.

STREAMS

The first Japanese gardens of the Nara and early Heian periods had winding streams that bordered the courtyard before feeding the main pond. These were often edged with rocks, the two forming an important relationship. An august stone might be used to mark the headwater of the stream as it entered the garden. Other rocks would "follow the desire" of this stone, responding to its position and shape, forcing the water this way and that, changing its mood as it approached the pond. Mountainside, torrent-style streams required the scattering of many more random stones, which caused the stream to divide and flow rapidly through narrowing channels.

A *yarimizu* is a meandering stream of the type that might be found flowing through a meadow, and it can be used in gardens to create a wetland area including an estuary planted with reeds and irises – popular in the Japanese garden. The stream's point of entry into this wetland should be indiscernible, and the water level should be kept fairly high, like a flooded estuary. These estuaries are often crossed by zigzag, eight-plank bridges (*yatsuhashi*) that weave over iris beds or baskets of irises secured to the stream or pond bed. (See pages 134–135, *Making a yatsuhashi bridge*.)

Left: *This is a quintessential and perfectly enchanting Japanese garden at Hosen-in, Ohara. The pond reaches almost up to the veranda.*

Above: *With its naturally crushed quartzite beaches and well-formed boulders, the stream that tumbles down the mountains above Nagoya is shaded by groves of wild Japanese maples.*

Below: *Shigemori's double winding stream is highly abstract. The rocks, set in a naturalistic manner, contrast with the smooth-set cobbling and gravel beaches. The idea owes some of its inspiration to the streams of the Heian period.*

STREAMS: KEY ELEMENTS

Assessing the flow A meandering stream will need a large pump to keep a good flow of water. The smaller the flow, the narrower the channel should be. Narrow channels will produce a more rapid flow.

Using intermittent flow If the flow is intermittent, make your stream into a series of small pools that have the look of a stream. This way, when there is no flow from a pump or a natural source, the stream bed will not empty out.

The sound of water Streams make a pleasant sound if allowed to trickle over stones and pebbles.

Planting Be careful not to let plants draw too much water from the sides of a stream. Thirsty plants can lower water levels considerably, so make sure the supply is always topped up.

WATERFALLS

These are another essential feature of pond and stream gardens and stroll gardens. They are often built to represent the Buddhist Trinity, with one large stone at the centre, over which the water tumbles, supported on either side by two attendant stones that stand slightly further forward. Large and important waterfalls were often known as dragon-gate waterfalls after the Chinese symbol for waterfall, which included a dragon and water.

A stone might be placed at the waterfall's base to represent a carp, as if it were about to leap. This "carp stone" symbolized spiritual and mental effort in Buddhist and Confucian terms. The carp, symbolically, would change into a dragon on reaching the top of the waterfall. The carp stone points to the strivings of an individual to better themselves. It is also, on a more practical level, the part of the waterfall that receives the full force of the flow as it hits the bottom.

Above: *A thin stream of water falls on to a flat stone, creating a louder sound and making a more decorative pattern than if it had simply fallen into a pool of water.*

Left: *The eccentric rock forms in the Huntington Botanical Gardens are more Chinese in spirit, but the overall design follows the natural ethos of the Japanese.*

WATERFALLS: KEY ELEMENTS

Position Waterfalls will look too artificial if mounded up in the middle of a garden. Try to use a natural hill or slope near the edge of the garden.

Siting the inlet Try to disguise the inlet of the water as much as possible. To do this, choose a dark, mysterious corner of the garden for the emergence of your stream.

Installing a pump It will usually be necessary to use a circulating pump for artificial waterfalls.

Losing water It is easy to lose water down the sides of a waterfall through splashing, so be thorough and generous in laying out a liner beneath any nearby rocks and make sure the water is channelled back into the system.

PONDS

Whether it moves through a stream or waterfall, the water needs eventually to flow into a pond. In Japanese gardens, ponds tend to be no deeper than 45cm (18in), so that they are easily kept clean and clear, and the fish can be seen. Try to include a stream flowing out of the pond for authenticity, they are believed to carry away evil spirits. When planting the pond with lotuses (*Nelumbo*) or water lilies (*Nymphaea*), make sure that they do not become too choked or the pond may silt up after a few years.

The proposed design of the pond edges will determine what happens to the water. For example, the water might appear to lap against a rocky shoreline, with a few solitary stones jutting out into the water, or it could become a wide inlet bordered by a sand bar. One sand-bar scene – the Aminoshidate peninsula in western Honshu – is so famous that it is cited as one of the three most important landscapes in Japan. It is often symbolically reproduced in Japanese gardens, often shown with a lantern on a promontory to represent a lighthouse. The shapes of ponds should, wherever possible, recall a natural scene, perhaps even the seaside.

The edges of ponds can be supported by rocks or timber posts. If you are using a pond liner, ensure that the liner is hidden by edging stones, timbers or plants. Japanese ponds are often designed using the shape of an ideogram, maybe symbolizing the word for "heart", "water" or "gourd", or they can be loosely outlined in the shape of a turtle or crane, however, it is more usual to find islands in these shapes representing the Mystic Isles.

ISLANDS

The islands in Japanese gardens might reproduce special scenes, such as the hundreds of extraordinary rocky islets in Matsushima Bay, near Sendai, in northern Honshu. Some of these islands are very small, but most have some kind of plant life, particularly pines, growing in their rocky crevices. The pine is a resilient tree that can take on fantastic forms as it is buffeted by salty winds. The Japanese take great care in pruning the pines in their gardens to give this characteristically wizened and windswept look.

Apart from the pine-covered island, there are other island styles, including the Rocky Islet and Cove Beach Island, all described in the *Sakuteiki*. The Meadow Isle is made up of low rocks, moss and autumn grasses. Forest Isles have random trees and grass, while Cloud and Mist Islands have sandy beaches planted in a spare, wispy way. These styles can all be recreated in your Japanese garden by growing suitable plants to set an atmospheric scene.

Islands were originally placed towards the middle of the pond, but slightly off-centre, to create a sense of mystery so that, whether you were boating or walking, you might find an inlet, waterfall, grotto, or even another island behind them. Use this element of surprise if you are designing a pond with islands.

Below: In the gardens of Nijo Castle, the shogun used unusually large rocks as a means of exhibiting his own power.

> **PONDS: KEY ELEMENTS**
>
> **Shape** Mimic the outline of natural ponds or choose a Japanese ideogram.
>
> **Using streams** Most ponds have a wider inlet for the stream. This could be a good place to plant water irises.
>
> **Stepping stones** When placing stepping stones across ponds with a butyl liner, make sure the liner is well protected from their weight.
>
> **Edging the pond** Beware of how much the edges of a liner might show if there is a big drop in water level. Exposed liners are unattractive and can be damaged by animals and too much sunlight.
>
> **Position** Choose a site where water might naturally lie in your garden.
>
> **Drainage** Beware of any potential problems with drainage, and make provisions for overflow water.
>
> **Pumps** Before buying a circulation pump for your pond, be aware of the running costs – it may have to run throughout the day to keep a pond healthy and clean.
>
> **Stocking a pond** A pond with a good balance of plants and fish will stay naturally healthy.

Preparing the watercourse

Running water in the Japanese garden gives pleasure in terms of both sight and sound, but careful thought and planning is needed to make a water feature such as a stream or a series of cascades look natural. It may be easy to decide on the kind of feature you like, but its setting and the way it blends with other parts of the garden should be considered. As always, the preparation of the ground is vital, and you will need to use a variety of ground cover materials in the surrounding areas to hide tanks and pumps.

Above: *A carp stone at the base of a waterfall in the gardens of the Golden Pavilion. This tall upright stone is traditionally used in waterfalls.*

PREPARATION

Whether you are designing a broad, shallow stream to meander gently through the landscape (ideal for a flat site), or a rocky cascade feature (for a sloping garden), the watercourse first needs to be dug out as accurately as possible. Next you should remove any sharp stones. You will need a rubber liner, but before you lay this on the bed of the watercourse you should cover the channel with soft sand and/or a cushioning underlay to prevent the rubber liner being punctured. Specialist mail order companies and larger aquatic garden outlets will make a stream course liner for you, saving you the difficult task of manhandling, cutting and sealing a large, heavy piece of butyl rubber.

If you wish to make a waterfall on flat ground, the garden would have to be artificially contoured with the addition of several tonnes of soil, hardcore or subsoil covered with topsoil to achieve a suitable height. At the same time the rear of the waterfall feature should be camouflaged so that the water appears to be coming in from beyond the garden boundary. If this all sounds like a major upheaval, why not make a stream with a broader course on a gentle manmade slope instead? These can look and sound just as delightful in a Japanese garden.

ARRANGING THE ELEMENTS

Whether you are making your water feature on a natural or manmade gradient, carefully arrange the wall of rocks to create your cascade or waterfall, especially in the steeper sections. The strata and rock seams should line up to look as natural as possible. Use spare pieces of liner folded over several times to cushion the impact of large rocks sitting on the pool or stream liner and be careful not to tear the liner when arranging the stone.

Whatever liner you use, ensure that the overlapping pieces make a good seal and do not allow water to seep back through into the ground. For the same reason bring the edges of the liner well up on either side of the stream course, tucking them under the soil to hold them firmly in place to preserve the water.

Left: *This broad, meandering stream with gravel banks and large rocks in the Augsburg Japanese garden in Germany creates a restful scene. Artificial stream beds such as this are lined with butyl rubber.*

Right: *In the Augsburg Japanese garden, the water curtain provides movement within a static composition of clipped evergreens. To create the impression of a stream-fed pool, position a rock barrier with a hidden reservoir behind and pump water over the edge.*

Camouflaging the water inlet and outlet of your stream requires a certain amount of ingenuity. For a re-circulating system where the stream appears to run through the garden, the water flows into an underground reservoir made by burying a plastic dustbin (trashcan), hidden by plants and perhaps a large slab of stone or a galvanized metal grill covered with pebbles and cobbles. Alternatively, the water can flow into a base pool or pond. A submersible pump sends water back from there to the top of the stream via a length of corrugated plastic delivery pipe buried underground and protected with a row of tiles.

Ask an aquatic or pond specialist to calculate the size of pump needed for your scheme and the diameter of delivery pipe required. You can do a rough estimation of the required flow rate by pouring measured buckets of water down the watercourse over a set time to achieve the look you want. Multiply up to calculate a litres-per-hour or gallons-per-hour figure.

A header pool, which could be made using a small, preformed fibreglass pond, at the top of a rock cascade ensures a steady flow of water with no sudden surges when the pump is switched on. The stream could also appear to rise directly from a spring, if you camouflage the end of the delivery pipe with rocks and plants.

Take time to select the piece of rock needed at the top of a large waterfall as it will be quite a feature even when the water is switched off. A flat spillstone on top ensures that the water curtain cascades evenly over the stone. Different shapes, sizes and arrangements of stones will affect the fall of water over cascades and, with careful positioning, a relatively small water output can be made to look like a much bigger flow. After cementing in the main rocks, experiment with loose stones, seeing how they can further deflect and direct the cascading water in a pleasing manner.

READY-MADE ALTERNATIVES

Stream courses and cascade features can be purchased ready made as rigid fibreglass sections, and are obtainable from aquatic specialist outlets as well as mail order or internet companies. These are fashioned to resemble rocky watercourses, but will need to be carefully camouflaged. This will be achieved by bedding them well into the earth and rock surroundings, giving them a more natural appearance. Adding gravel, pebbles and cobbles along the length of a fibreglass-lined or butyl rubber-lined stream softens the look, especially with the addition of overhanging plants and the occasional large rock or boulder.

Above: *Choose a preformed stream unit to blend in with the surrounding rocks and gravel.*

Above: *A preformed stream unit and water basin with a sandstone rock finish.*

Above: *Simple, dark stream liners may blend more easily. Use gravel to camouflage them.*

Building a meandering stream

Japanese gardens often have a meandering stream on a site where there is little natural gradient, and this is made using a flexible liner. The stream does not have to be dominated by rocks but can have softer, more rounded stones and boulders along its course, looking as if they have been deposited naturally along an old river bed. If you don't want to have a pump running continuously, the stream can be built as a very long narrow pool or series of pools with small falls along its length that are designed to overflow as soon as the pump introduces more water.

The header pool for a meandering stream does not have to be conspicuous – it simply provides the illusion of natural water entering the garden. The essential factor in creating a natural-looking scheme is to devise a wandering route that widens in parts and follows as closely as possible the direction that water would take naturally when flowing over a flat site.

The first thing to do is to check the garden levels. This is because even a relatively flat site will have a slope, no matter how slight. If you can identify the highest point, plan a scheme that has this as the source of the stream. This will not only avoid the difficulty of building the stream against a slope but also do away with the need to make slight changes in the levels.

Above: *This stream wanders through a moss-covered landscape. The shadowy enclosed garden and the shafts of sunlight breaking through give a feeling of solitude.*

Below: *The winding stream that runs into the large ponds at Motsu-ji has been restored to show how they were used during the 11th and 12th centuries. The placing of rocks and plants is understated, in the style of a slow stream weaving through a meadow.*

You will need

- string, canes or garden hose
- wooden pegs, about 2.5cm (1in) in diameter and 15cm (6in) long
- a hammer
- a straight-edged piece of wood
- a spirit level
- a spade
- a plastic sheet
- a rake
- underlay and flexible liner
- a thin, flat stone
- ready-mixed mortar
- a mortaring trowel
- cobbles or river gravel
- corrugated plastic pipe, measuring 1–2.5cm (½–1in) in diameter
- roof tiles
- rounded boulders
- a submersible pump
- a flow-adjusting valve

1 Having chosen the source, mark out the route of the stream with string, canes or a hose, working back from any existing pool.

2 Knock in the pegs about a metre (yard) apart along the route of the stream. Place a length of straight-edged wood and a spirit level on the pegs to identify any slight depressions or rises in the ground so that the surrounding soil can be adjusted if necessary. If the outlet point from the stream into the base pool is lower than the pool sides, there will be a flow when the pump is turned on. If this point is established first, then you can ensure that all the other edges are higher.

3 If the route of the stream is through a lawn, remove the turf and lay it elsewhere, if needed, or stack it upside down to rot down. Leave the pegs identifying the level in place.

4 Dig out the soil from the stream to a depth of 38cm (15in) in the centre. If the stream is wider than 60cm (24in), create shallow marginal shelves, 23cm (9in) deep, along the sides. Stack the soil on a *plastic* sheet to be used after the liner is inserted. Rake the stream bottom and the shelves to make them level, removing any sharp stones.

5 Place underlay along the stream length and drape the single length of liner into the stream contours. Use rocks to hold down the sides of the liner to stop them blowing about.

6 Create a spill point and prevent soil erosion by securing a thin, flat stone on the liner with a dab of mortar where the stream enters the pool.

7 Take some soil from the heap of topsoil and put it on the liner to form a shallow saucer shape inside the excavation. This will help to protect a cheap liner from ultra-violet light and provide a medium in which plants can grow. Top-dress the soil with rounded cobbles or river gravel to stop it from being washed away.

8 Bury a corrugated plastic delivery pipe along the side of the stream so that it runs from the base pool to the source. Cover the pipe with roof tiles before replacing the soil.

Above: *Winding streams are usually quite shallow, so care must be taken to disguise the liner at the edges, and cover the stream bed with varying sizes of gravels and cobbles.*

9 Position a few rounded boulders on the liner at the source to simulate a small spring.

10 Install a pump in the base pool and connect the outlet to the plastic delivery pipe. As the water will only trickle through this stream, a flow adjuster should be fitted to the delivery pipe to regulate the flow. Fill the pool with water and turn on the pump to check that the stream is running satisfactorily.

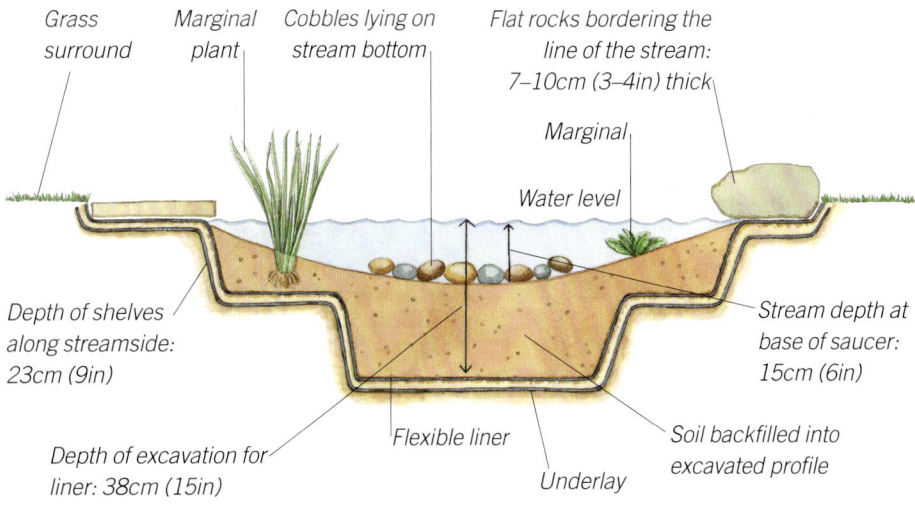

Pond liners, pumps & filters

Pond liners and pumps are the invisible workers that enable you to create your Japanese water feature. They should never be seen, but are vital elements in the construction of a beautiful *tsukubai*, waterfall or stream. The pump ensures a constant supply of fresh, oxygenated water for fish, and special filtration systems help to keep water clear and process fish waste. The flow rate of a pump decreases over time so ensure you have spare capacity. Buy the best you can afford and you will be rewarded with a natural-looking water feature that lasts for years.

POND LINERS

Today's standard pond liner is made of black butyl rubber. It resists degradation by UV light and, being flexible, it is easy to fit and tolerant of stretching. It also resists puncturing and tearing. Undisturbed, good-quality butyl lining could last for thirty years. For naturalistic pools and ponds in Japanese gardens butyl is practical, versatile (fitting any irregular shape) and relatively easy to install compared to, say, a rigid fibreglass pond.

Butyl rubber comes in different grades, so discuss with your local aquatic garden specialist which will be suitable. For large ponds, liner made from one of the thicker grades could be very heavy and difficult to manoeuvre into position without several pairs of hands. The thickest grades are also less flexible and therefore trickier to lay or fold in tight bends and corners. Laying out the fabric on a sunny day allows it to warm up and become more flexible.

Above: *Wait a little while until the pond filters are mature before buying koi carp. Japanese koi are normally exported in November and December, but the best time to buy is in the spring when the water has warmed up.*

Below left: *The pool in this garden has been made with a flexible liner and is now being filled with water. The liner should not be exposed above the water line.*

Below: *This pool uses polythene (polyethylene) sheet as a flexible liner. Only trim the liner when you are certain the water level and edging are satisfactory.*

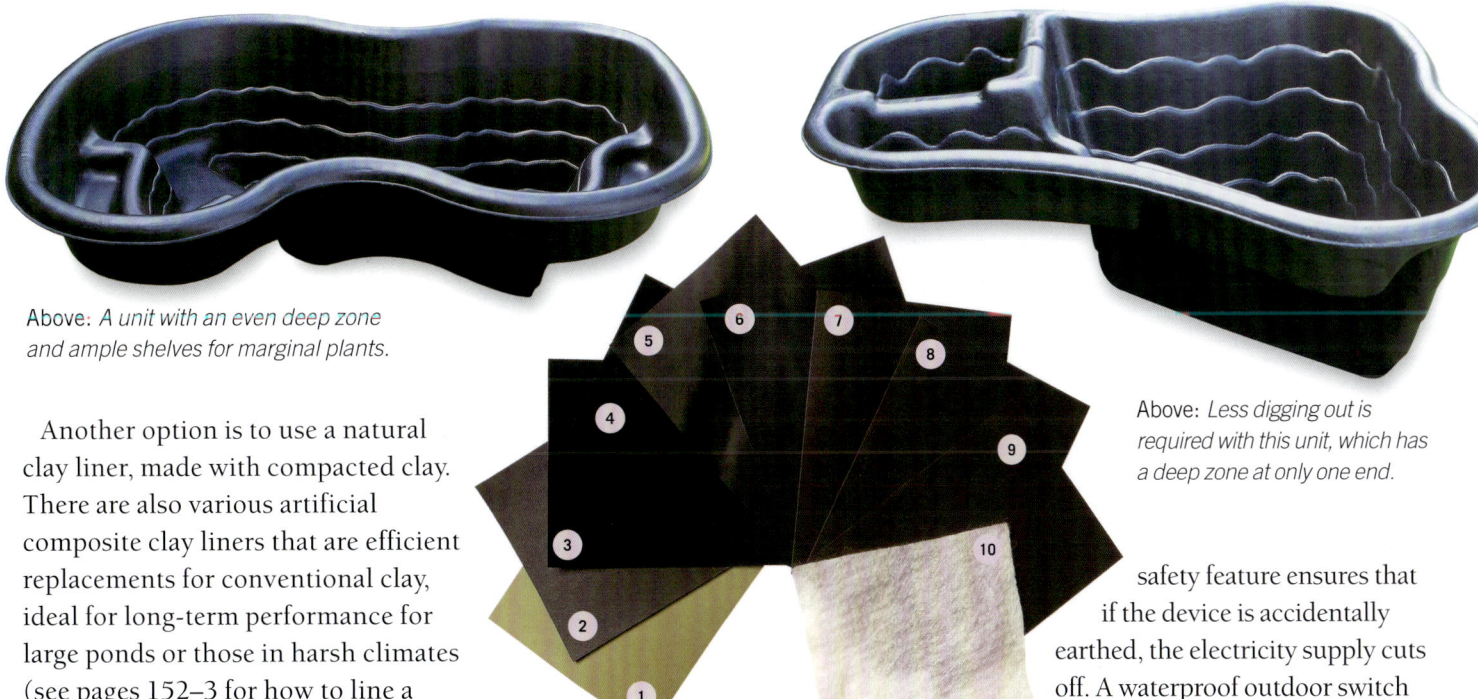

Above: *A unit with an even deep zone and ample shelves for marginal plants.*

Above: *Less digging out is required with this unit, which has a deep zone at only one end.*

Above: *Flexible liners are available in a variety of materials, thicknesses and colours. From left to right: 1 Butyl liner; 2 Butyl liner; 3 Low-density polythene (polyethylene); 5–9 PVC in different grades; 10 Underlay.*

Another option is to use a natural clay liner, made with compacted clay. There are also various artificial composite clay liners that are efficient replacements for conventional clay, ideal for long-term performance for large ponds or those in harsh climates (see pages 152–3 for how to line a pond with a soil liner). Mail-order companies specializing in pond liners or larger aquatic centres may offer a made-to-measure service.

Before you lay a flexible liner, you should use a geotextile membrane underlay to protect the butyl from being punctured by sharp stones and roots. You can use soft sand as an alternative, but the underlay is easier to keep in place over sharp corners and steep slopes. Use extra underlay and folded offcuts of butyl liner to provide a cushion beneath individual rocks and boulders laid on top of the liner (see pages 188–9 for how to line a pond with a flexible liner).

PUMPS

For moving water features, such as streams or waterfalls, you will need a pump. Designs vary depending on the task they have to perform and they have different power outputs, so ask a water garden specialist to advise you. The data needed includes:
- the distance over which the water is travelling around the circuit
- the gradient
- the height of the starting point
- the diameter of the pipe
- the flow rate, which affects the appearance of a waterfall and speed of filtration.

Large schemes will require a submersible pump running off the mains (utility) voltage and so, unlike pumps operating via a transformer, the electrical cabling must be run through protective ducting buried to a depth of 60cm (24in). Make sure that you fit residual current devices (RCDs) or circuit breakers for all pieces of electrical equipment, including lighting. This safety feature ensures that if the device is accidentally earthed, the electricity supply cuts off. A waterproof outdoor switch can also be fitted.

FILTERS

For ponds containing fish, you will need a filtration system. This will either be a system submerged in the pond or, most efficiently, biological filters held in a header tank above the water. Fitting an ultra-violet clarifier causes green algae cells to clump together, making it easier for a biological filter to extract them. Fish and water lilies need a minimum pond depth of 45cm (18in) to overwinter, especially in colder regions. Consider installing a water heater for fish ponds, which keeps part of the surface ice-free.

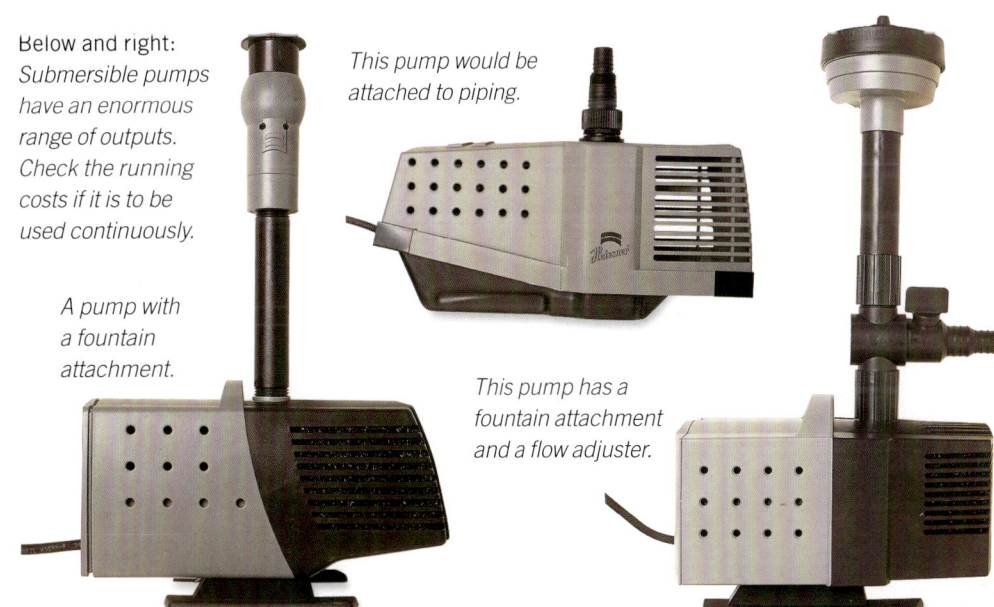

Below and right: *Submersible pumps have an enormous range of outputs. Check the running costs if it is to be used continuously.*

A pump with a fountain attachment.

This pump would be attached to piping.

This pump has a fountain attachment and a flow adjuster.

POND LINERS, PUMPS & FILTERS

Creating edges for a pond

The edges of most small ponds, especially those in small gardens, are best lined with rocks. Larger ponds in stroll gardens, however, often include stretches of cobbled beaches or grass rolling up to the very edge of the pond. The edges of ponds always need careful attention, as the water may run out or evaporate and this leaves an ugly view of the liner. Whichever kind of edging you choose, make sure that it covers the edge of the pond well and that it is a practical solution for the kind of pond you have made.

Above: *Cobbled beaches are popular around ponds, at times set loosely and at others set in mortar to create an even surface.*

CONCEALING A POND LINER
If you are using a butyl liner, make sure that you conceal 10cm/4in of the liner below the water line with rocks or gravel, and any part of the liner that might show above water level. Bear in mind that in summer, with increased evaporation, the pond level may drop and expose the liner. It is also worth noting that butyl liners deteriorate more quickly when exposed to sunlight and frost.

ROCK EDGING
The rocks around a pool should be partially submerged to achieve a natural effect. The rocks will also need to be supported on a foundation slab or concrete footing.
- If you are using a liner, pass it over the slab or footing and under the rock, embedding the liner into a layer of stiff mortar or concrete.
- You can use a sandwich of underlay above and below the liner to help protect it.
- Ensure that the liner finishes above the level of the water under the rock at the side of the pool.

COBBLE EDGING
The essential thing in introducing naturalness to a cobble edge is to arrange the sizes so that the main body of cobbles increases in diameter from below the waterline into the drier margins.
- Sort your cobbles into size before you lay them.
- To prevent the cobbles from rolling to the pool bottom, a concrete support should be constructed at the edge.

GRASS EDGING
An edging of grass is very easy on the eye and is suitable for larger pools and stroll gardens.
- The edge of the pool can become worn fairly quickly, which can cause the sides to crumble.
- Avoid this by underpinning the turf with a small foundation of stones or timber edging (see below right).

TIMBER EDGING
An alternative method of taking grass up to the water's edge is to construct a vertical timber wall, which will extend from below the waterline to just below the level of the grass. The timber wall looks most attractive if it is made with timber rounds, at a measurement of 5–7.5cm (2–3in) in diameter. These are placed tightly side by side to form a palisade-like barrier. Proprietary lengths of "log roll" could also be used

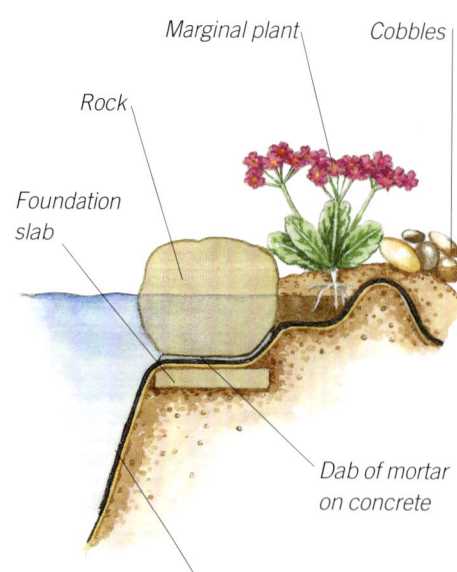

Rock edging *A rock that is being used at the edge of a pool is best when it is partially submerged, and supported with a foundation slab under the liner.*

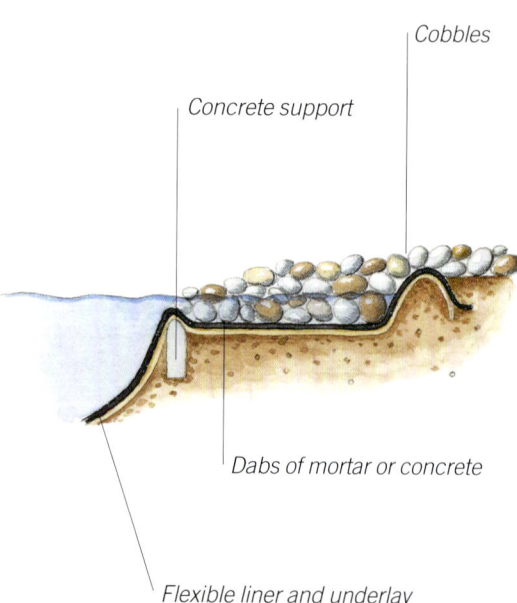

Cobble edging *To prevent cobbles from rolling into the deeper zone of the pond, make a shallow shelf with a raised edge under the flexible liner in order to give extra stability.*

Right: *Paving with a slight overhang around a pond edge can hide flexible butyl liners.*

instead of complete rounds, and these log rolls are already joined together by galvanized wire strands.
- To make either of these systems of timber edging stable enough not to crumble into the pool, a small trench, approximately 15cm (6in) deep and 10–15cm (4–6in) wide, must be dug out at the pool edge.
- A concrete support should be added in front of this trench.
- The pool liner is then run over the concrete support and into the trench, finishing above the waterline.
- A mix of stiff mortar is placed on the liner and the timbers bedded into the stiff mortar before it hardens. Make sure that the timber rounds are straight and tight together because they cannot be moved once the mortar sets.
- After a day or two, when the mortar has set hard, soil can be backfilled behind the timber edge and the liner can be wedged upright so it is held above the waterline.
- Turf can then be laid right up to the timber edge on the fresh soil, which is now supported by the concrete at the water's edge.

PAVED EDGING

A more formal and solid design can be made with paving stones arranged around the edge of the pond.
- Prepare the area by scraping away some topsoil. If the subsoil is not firm, replace it with 7.5–10cm (3–4in) of hardcore. Top this with about 5cm (2in) of damp sand, rake and level, then cover with the underlay and liner.
- Place the perimeter paving stones along the water's edge, checking that they fit well and that they overlap the water by 2.5–5cm (1–2in). Use the largest piece to give stability, with the straight edge overlapping the water.
- Mix some mortar on a board, then lay the first stones on to dabs of mortar trowelled on to the liner.
- Press the slab down on to the mortar dabs and bed it down firmly before laying the adjacent slabs.
- Check the slabs are level with a spirit level. To adjust the height, tap with a club hammer over a block of wood.
- The gaps between the slabs must be filled with a fairly wet mortar mix in order to hold each slab in place. Lay on a slight slope to reduce run-off from any adjacent paving or grass.

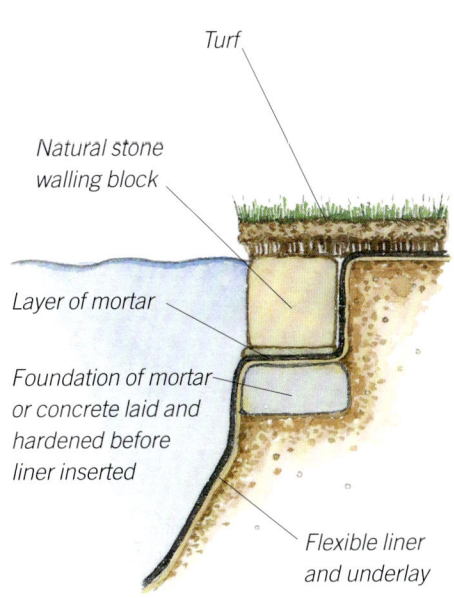

Grass edging *A grass edge is subject to heavy wear and tear. It should be supported by a natural stone walling block, which is placed on a deep foundation of stiff mortar or concrete.*

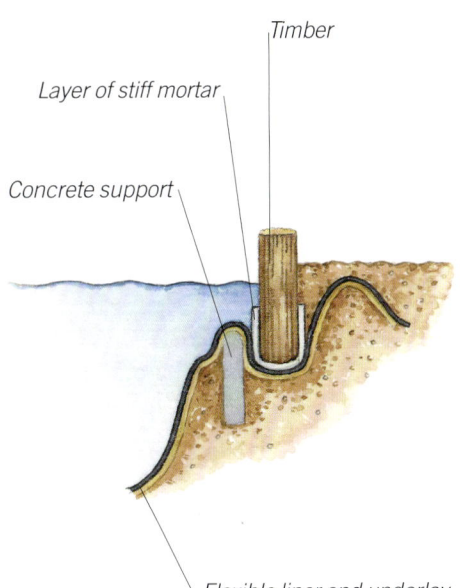

Timber edging *Log roll or timber rounds placed side by side make a good edge when mortared into a thin trench under the level of the water. Turf edging can then run up to the timber edging.*

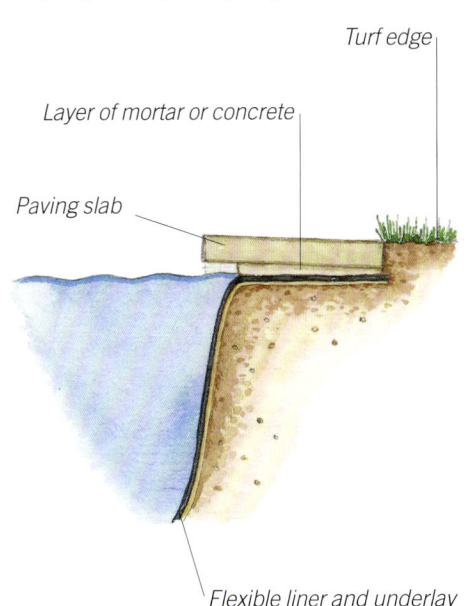

Paved edging *When using a paving slab to provide an edge, ensure that there is a small overlap above the water, and mortar the slab on to the liner above a foundation of hardcore.*

Tsukubai & shishi-odoshi

Some Japanese gardens contain very distinctive water features called *tsukubai,* or water basins. These water basins were often found in traditional tea gardens and were used for providing drinking water. They were usually fed by a natural spring. Taller basins, *chozubachi*, are sited nearer the house. Another traditional Japanese water feature, the *shishi-odoshi*, was designed as a deer scarer and uses running water to make a knocking noise with a bamboo pole against a stone basin, a sound loud enough to deter marauding animals from eating tender plants in the garden.

Above: *Water basins were traditionally made from stone and were fed with water from a bamboo spout called* kakei.

WATER BASINS

The principle of spiritual and physical cleanliness has been adapted for use in Japanese garden design from the earliest days. You will often find a water basin or other standing water feature in a Japanese garden, and sometimes even two or three such features.

Water basins are not always kept full, except those that are fed from a concealed bamboo pipe that is allowed to drip into the basin to keep the water fresh, rippling and constantly overflowing. Water basins that are not automatically filled will need cleaning out and topping up with fresh water. In addition, just as the path can be cleaned and damped down before the guests arrive, the sides of stone water basins may also be wetted to darken and intensify the natural colours and markings of the stone.

The water basin itself may be a simple rounded bowl carved from a single piece of granite, but traditional designs (copied from various historic shrines and temples in Japan) vary, and some are surprisingly geometric, cube-shaped or cylindrical, with carved patterns and designs around the outside. These intricate designs tend to stand out more than the rustic bowls, making a pleasing contrast to the surrounding rock forms and

Above: *A 17th-century crouching basin in the temple garden of the Ryoan-ji. This has been one of the most copied of all water basins.*

Above: *A cube-shaped water basin with regular square indentations in a private garden in Ohara. This design, made from granite which has* tarnished and discoloured over time, is copied from an original basin in the gardens of the Silver Pavilion, or the Ginkaku-ji Temple in Kyoto, Japan.

plantings. Nowadays, materials other than granite are often used, and the more porous they are, the more quickly they will develop a pleasing patina of age due to the moist environment.

There should be good drainage around a basin, as the fact that the basin is frequently topped up, and so overflows, could make the area swampy. If the basin is being refilled constantly from a pipe, a drain will also be needed to take the water away. The area around the water basin is often surrounded by cobbles or large-sized gravel to keep it dry. This combination of gravel and water basin is another opportunity to express artistry. You can place a special stone that does not get wet in the surrounding gravel area for people to stand on.

TALL WATER BASINS

Although tall water basins come in all shapes, sizes and materials, such as cut and natural stone, ceramic and wood, there are essentially two types: *chozubachi* and *furisode*.

Chozubachi basins are usually up to 1m (3ft) high and are placed on verandas where they can easily be reached from the house. These basins may have a slatted bamboo cover to keep the water fresh, to stop birds from drinking there and to prevent leaves and debris from falling in.

Furisode basins come in the form of a narrow, naturally rippled rock that is shaped like the long sleeve of a kimono. A bowl is carved into the stone, sometimes in the shape of a gourd. (The gourd is a symbol of good hospitality, being the traditional holder for the Japanese rice wine sake.)

A more elaborate tall basin can be found in some Japanese gardens, one example being the *ginkakuji*, which is named after the famous garden of the Silver Pavilion, near Kyoto, with tiled patterning on the sides.

LOW, OR CROUCHING, WATER BASINS

The *tsukubai chozubachi* is a low, or crouching, basin placed on or just off the *roji* (the path to the tea house). The act of crouching to reach the basin, like the bending needed for the middle crawl-through gate and the tea house's small hatch-like entrance, compels guests to humble themselves.

Above: *A simple* tsukubai *will work in naturalistic settings as well as in Zen gardens.*

One famous anecdote recalls how the great tea master Rikyu had hidden the view of the beautiful inland sea in his tea garden with dense plantings. His guests and visitors could see the view only at the moment when they bowed down to cleanse themselves at the *tsukubai*. This is a perfect expression of Zen – that true beauty is available to us only once we have lowered our heads (and therefore our minds) lower than our hearts.

CHOOSING A WATER BASIN

Water basins were originally made of granite, which makes them very heavy and therefore expensive to transport. However, fake stone (fibreglass), glazed ceramic and concrete versions are easy to come by nowadays and may be found in garden centres, especially those that specialize in Japanese garden ornaments.

Above: *Still quite simple, this flower-like* tsukubai *looks best in plain surroundings.*

Above: *This* tsukubai *is hewn out of a rock, a dramatic feature with a strong presence.*

Above: *This reproduction, like many others, is based on original Japanese designs.*

Above: *This cube-shaped* tsukubai *would make a good courtyard feature.*

Left: *Purification is ritualized by the Japanese. Outside all Buddhist and Shinto shrines there are water basins for cleaning the hands and mouth.*

Below left: *Two tall water basins (*chozubachi*) that can be reached from the veranda of Sanzen-in, in Ohara. These are square basins set on stone pillars.*

As well as this, pottery or stone urns can be used, and these make excellent alternatives.

Recycled materials are another option – maybe some hollow, second-hand architectural pillars, or old *stupas* (a feature in many Buddhist temples). So use anything that might take on a new life as a water basin, including old stone water troughs or a stone with a natural deep depression.

PLACING A WATER BASIN

A *tsukubai* should always be placed by a path and a *chozubachi* by a house, but apart from that there is no need to get too caught up in the idea that everything should be set exactly according to a pre-ordained plan. Japanese gardeners do not consider this to be in the true spirit of Zen. In fact, Rikyu, the master of the Japanese tea ceremony, would have disapproved of an approach that meant everything was too rigidly correct. For instance, it is traditional to place the *tsukubai* on the sunny side of the path, so that guests do not have the sun on their backs and necks when they kneel down to take water from it. This kind of tradition is just respectful, intended to be attentive to the comfort of the guest, and it is therefore not necessary to copy it precisely. The key consideration here is that the exact placement depends on the conditions within the garden – if it is shady enough, your guests will not need to shelter from the sun.

There are often special stone arrangements around the basin, featuring worn, rounded cobbles and pebbles, with accompanying stones, a lantern, ferns and evergreen shrubs. Often a special flat-topped stone is placed to the side of the basin for guests to stand on or to rest their fan or bag.

In wooded wilderness settings, the arrangement can be quite lush and atmospheric, but as with so much that is connected with the tea ceremony, the *tsukubai* is full of symbolism. This gives the garden designer plenty of opportunities to take the concept of the *tsukubai* and the lantern that often accompanies it, to abstract it and give it a modern interpretation, as befits a contemporary garden.

The fact that water basins symbolize cleanliness and hospitality means that they are not only found in tea gardens or off the verandas of houses: they will also be found in courtyard gardens and along passageways to the house.

Above *Visitors to the Meiji Shrine in Tokyo, Japan, use the traditional bamboo ladles provided for washing and purification.*

Below *A stone basin, or* tsukubai, *covered with moss in the gardens at Ten Juan Temple, Kyoto.*

Below: *Water basins are often filled constantly by fresh water, the excess draining away among rocks and pebbles. A sump could be built under the stones to collect the water, which can then be recycled using a submersible pump.*

Below *This basin in the Seiryu tea garden at Nijo Castle is carved from natural rock.*

TSUKUBAI & SHISHI-ODOSHI

Above: *The water in a* shishi-odoshi *is circulated with a small pond pump, placed below water level in a bowl, and hidden with a metal grill and stones. One outlet makes the water surface ripple and the other trickles into the swinging arm.*

DEER SCARERS (*SHISHI-ODOSHI*)

Another traditional Japanese garden water feature, the *shishi-odoshi*, or deer scarer, is sometimes found in kit form in garden centres, but you are likely to find more authentic-looking *shishi-odoshi*, or the individual elements and raw materials for making your own, from specialist Japanese garden suppliers. This can be an enjoyable do-it-yourself project, and means you can choose the elements to fit with your garden.

The *shishi-odoshi* consists of a piece of bamboo 60–90cm (24–36in) long, drilled through to accommodate a pin on which it pivots. One end rests on a piece of stone called a sounding rock and the other end fills with water fed from a bamboo spout. When it contains enough water, the pivoting bamboo tips, releasing the water, and then flips back up, striking the stone and making a noise. This is very similar in basic construction to the *tsukubai*, with an underground, camouflaged reservoir containing a submersible pump and a length of plastic tubing that links the pump to the bamboo feed pipe.

Above: *This deer scarer was featured in Horoshi Namori's show garden at the Chelsea Flower Show, London, in 1996.*

Below: *A traditional Japanese fountain, the* shishi-odoshi *was originally used to deter deer from feeding on shoots in rice paddies.*

Making a *sui-kinkutsu*

A *sui-kinkutsu* is a water echo-chamber, or more literally a "water harp chamber". It is constructed so that you can listen to the dripping of water falling into an underground chamber by means of a hollow bamboo pipe held to the ear at one end and to a hole in the ground above the chamber at the other. The sound is like that of the traditional stringed Japanese musical instrument called the *koto*. This might also make you think of a stream in a mountain cave. In very quiet surroundings you should be able to hear the sound without the aid of a bamboo pipe.

Purists believe that a *sui-kinkutsu* should be constructed only in conjunction with a *tsukubai* arrangement (see pages 106–110), as it collects water dripping and draining away from the water basin, which is itself fed by a dripping bamboo pipe. However, a *sui-kinkutsu* may also be constructed as a separate feature, independently from a *tsukubai*, perhaps simply collecting water from a dripping hose that is switched on especially for visitors or at your personal discretion.

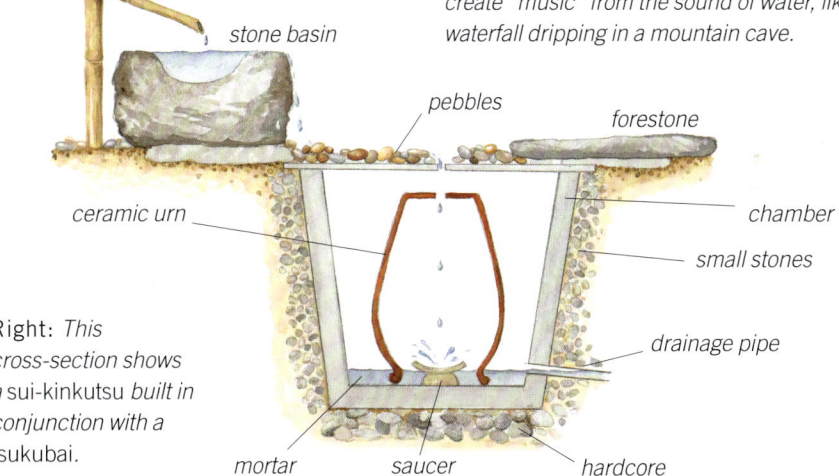

Above: *The idea behind the* sui-kinkutsu *is to create "music" from the sound of water, like a waterfall dripping in a mountain cave.*

Right: *This cross-section shows a* sui-kinkutsu *built in conjunction with a tsukubai.*

You will need
- a piece of cylindrical shuttering or an old plastic barrel
- concrete mix, 1 part sand to 4 parts cement
- an Ali-Baba-style urn about 80–100cm (32–40in) high and 40cm (16in) in diameter with a single drainage hole in thits base
- a small ceramic plant saucer
- rope to lower the pot
- a paving slab, 1m (40in) square, with a hole 4cm (1½in) wide drilled in the centre

1 Dig out a pit around 1.2m (4ft) deep and 1m (40in) wide. Create a circular shuttering around 70cm (28in) in diameter using an old plastic drum or some other mould that can be removed easily after surrounding it in concrete. Line the base of the hole and the outside of the mould with 8–10cm (3–4in) of concrete. Make sure the bottom of the hole is level. Make a drainage outlet 10cm (4in) above the bottom of the chamber to take the excess water away to a soakaway or an approved watercourse.

2 Leave the concrete to set for two days before removing the mould and proceeding with the next stage.

3 Place the ceramic saucer at the bottom of the hole. The saucer should be smaller than the rim of the vase.

4 Tie a rope around the rim of the Ali Baba vase and (with assistance to balance the weight) lower the upturned vase carefully into the chamber so that it completely covers the saucer, with the drainage hole directly above it.

5 Lay the paving slab over the chamber. Then direct your chosen water source to the hole in the paving slab.

6 You will need to disguise the paving slab and the water source (for example a hose). You can do this using small stones and cobbles. An alternative camouflage idea is to place a water basin over the slab, but position it off-centre so that the water spilling out of the basin finds its way into the hole above the chamber.

Constructing a reservoir

Water basins and deer scarers both need a reservoir and pump to make a circulating water system, unless they have a natural source of water. The reservoir for the water will sit immediately under the water basin (which is usually made from a hollowed-out rock, but any basin that is dignified enough, including a stone trough, could be used) or at the spilling end of the deer scarer, and it gives the illusion that the water feature is stream fed. If the site is in a windy location, check that all the water flows back into the reservoir, otherwise it can empty, causing the pump to burn out.

Above: *Ladles are laid over or by the side of the basin supported by a rack of bamboo. Guests use them to cleanse their hands, mouths and faces before entering the tea house.*

The amount of water that circulates around a water basin is much the same as that for a deer scarer (*shishi-odoshi*), where both require a mere trickle for best effect. Thus the reservoir need be no more than 100 litres (22 gallons). The reservoir can be set almost directly below the feature, but in a place where you can access it for cleaning, and where, if it were to overflow, there is some suitable drainage around it.

The small amount of water spillage likely from the basin will not need an extensive drainage system, but it is a good idea to cover the immediate area around the reservoir with loose stones and gravel to aid drainage. This will also give a more authentic appearance.

Below: *The* shishi-odoshi *reservoir differs little from that of a water basin. Always ensure that the spillage goes back into the reservoir.*

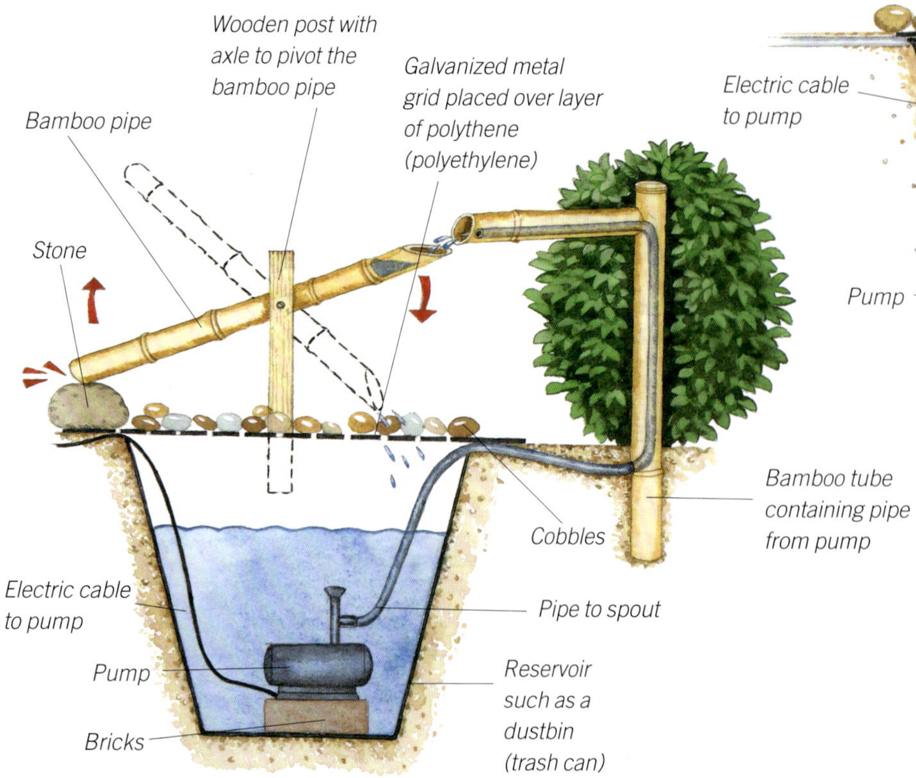

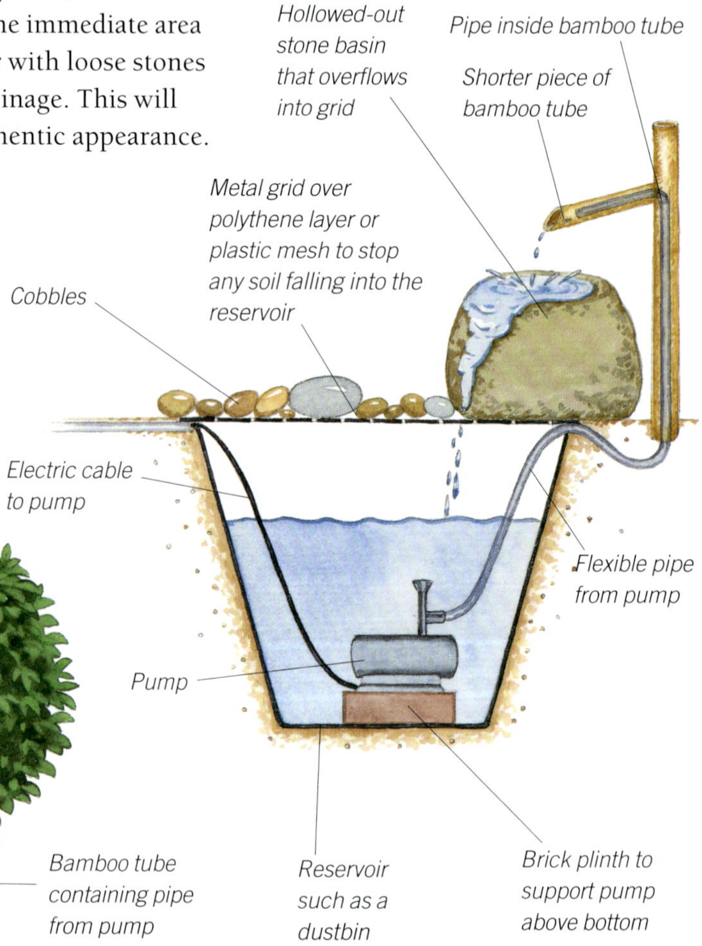

Above: *Be sure when you build a reservoir of this kind that you leave a place to check the level of water. Pumps should be equipped with float switches or they will burn out if the reservoir is allowed to dry out.*

112 WATER FEATURES

You will need

- a reservoir kit from a specialist supplier (see pages 248–9), which should include a reservoir, a metal grid, a sheet of plastic mesh, a polythene layer, a small pump with a cable, and a length of ribbed hose to join the pump to the delivery pipe of the deer scarer or water basin

Or you can make your own kit using

- a strong plastic bin at least 60cm (24in) deep and 45cm (18in) wide, such as a cold-water storage tank sold for central heating systems
- a small pump kit from your local aquatic centre – the pump should have a variable pressure valve so that you can modulate the flow
- a polythene layer to cover the bin
- a sheet of plastic mesh
- a metal grid, which can be made of a piece of concrete reinforcing mesh from a builder's merchant

For both options, you will also need

- lengths of pre-drilled bamboo tubes to deliver water to the feature
- some cobbles or large gravel
- a spade to dig a hole
- some sharp sand
- a spirit level
- a waterproofed electrical source or socket for the pump

1 Choose a small, level site. The cobbles can extend as far as you wish, but the area need be no bigger than a circle of the diameter of the reservoir. Mark out the diameter and dig out a hole wider and deeper. Line the base and sides with sharp sand to protect the reservoir from stones and to make it level.

3 Backfill the gap between the reservoir and the hole sides with soil and ram it until firm with a piece of timber, such as a cut-down broom handle. Rake the surrounding soil and remove any stones.

5 Before lowering the submersible pump on to the plinth, attach a flexible delivery pipe to the pump outlet. Take the pipe over the side of the reservoir (or through a hole in the top edge) and push it through a tube of bamboo, 60–90cm (2–3ft) tall, next to the reservoir.

2 After placing a 4–6cm (1½–2½in) deep layer of sand at the bottom of the hole, lower the reservoir into the hole and check that the rim is just below the edge. Then check that the sides are level with a spirit level. If necessary, you will need to adjust the base of the hole until it is completely flat.

4 Remove any soil from inside the reservoir as, if it is left, this may silt up the pump and stop it functioning. Make a plinth in the reservoir with two bricks or a piece of broken paving.

6 Push the pipe through to a further bamboo spout positioned to spill into the basin. These can be made by cutting away the end of the pipe. Lay the polythene layer over the depression and the reservoir and cut out a hole 5cm (2in) smaller than the bin diameter.

7 Lay the galvanized metal grid on top of the reservoir. This should be larger than the diameter of the top of the reservoir. Fill the reservoir with water.

8 Lay a sheet of plastic mesh over the grid to stop any soil falling into the reservoir. Position the spill basin at the side of the grid, but make sure that it slightly overhangs the reservoir so that it will overflow on to the cobbles.

9 Test the flow of water, adjusting the regulator on the pump or moving the position of the spout so that the water falls into the saucer part of the spill basin. Arrange the cobbles over and around the metal grid. Test the system to make sure there is minimal water loss through spillage or splashing, and adjust accordingly.

CREATIVE CONSTRUCTS

This chapter looks at the elements that are designed and created to fit within the Japanese garden. Manmade constructs such as paths, fences, bridges, lanterns and water basins add form, character and scale to a garden. When used well, these can contribute to its beauty. Such artefacts are not placed to be admired as sculpture as in Western gardens, but blended into their surroundings to form an intrinsic part of the whole composition.

The Japanese garden designer is deeply interested in the quality of these objects, choosing them very carefully so that they form part of the design of the garden. Most fences and garden buildings are built of raw timber, bamboo, sisal and reeds, exhibiting the pure natural qualities of those materials, while lanterns and water basins are often carved out of the finest stone and encouraged to weather. Paths and bridges should be designed with great care and creativity, using a combination of natural materials and balancing the gardener's deliberate artistry with nature's own perfection.

Above: *A path in a bamboo grove near the Tenryu-ji Temple.*
Left: *A Japanese garden, featuring a curved bridge, ablaze with the colours of autumn.*

Paths

Japanese garden paths have evolved from the simple surfaces of gravel and fine sand that were originally used for paths that circled around ponds, to the stepping-stone paths of the tea garden where each step carries a special significance for the traveller. Some of the path styles used today are simple and naturalistic whereas others use a highly sophisticated mix of materials and designs. The only requirement is that whichever kind of path you choose blends well with the natural style of your garden.

Above: *Ginkgo leaves fall on to a path. Paths are often edged in imaginative ways.*

THE PURPOSE OF PATHS

The main purpose of paths is to control the visual experience of the stroller, with each change of direction introducing a new view. From the earliest times, paths have suddenly stopped or turned abruptly – a device that encourages the stroller to hesitate and scan a view that was deliberately composed to be seen from a particular spot. Zigzag paths and bridges take this idea to a greater extreme.

Paths found their true significance in the tea garden and were originally known as dewy paths (*roji*). The tea path recalls the pilgrimages that philosophers, painters and Zen monks made on their visits to China in search of renowned Chinese artists and sages, who lived, often alone, in huts and hermitages in the hills and mountains. As the tea guest is drawn along the *roji*, they are made more conscious of each step they take through the use of stepping stones. These had previously been used only for practical purposes: to cross water and swampy, muddy ground. Their addition to the tea garden was initiated by Rikyu, who was one of the great Japanese tea masters of the 16th century.

The strategic placement of some larger stepping stones on a path gives the visitor the freedom to be less conscious of where their feet are falling. This means that they would be able to look up to take in a special view of the garden or cleanse themselves at a water basin. Stepping stones were always kept scrupulously

Left: *The formality of this path cutting through the dry garden of Tenju-an is softened by an enveloping carpet of moss. The path takes a sudden right-angled turn at the end, a black pine (*Pinus thunbergii*) grows alongside it.*

Above: *In some climates, moss will readily creep over gravel paths, and may create a desirable effect.*

Above right: *In the gardens of Rheinaue in Bonn, Germany, a naturalistic path of stepping stones set in gravel crosses a cobbled path, which gives way to more formalized paving set in grass.*

clean, brushed and even damped down to give the impression of mountain dew. Damping down paths is considered to be a very hospitable way to welcome guests into a tea garden or the tea house itself. However, great care must be taken to keep stepping stones free of slimy algae, which can become extremely slippery when wet.

In some Japanese gardens, especially dry ones – which were mostly designed to be viewed from one particular place, such as the veranda of a building – the paths of stepping stones might be set to weave right across the garden. In the past, these paths were rarely walked on, but were used by the garden designers of the day to suggest movement and to draw the viewer's eye across a particular scene. If a path was not

EDGING GRAVEL PATHS

Gravel is a loose material, so it is always best to contain it carefully within solid edges. If you don't edge these paths, the gravel will tend to get pressed into the surrounding soil or kicked around and will eventually disappear.

Edging materials	Where and when to use
Paving and cobbles	Paving stones or cobbles should be chosen for the appropriateness of their setting. Make sure the size and shape of paving stones complements the surrounding garden.
Granite setts	Near the house, more formal granite setts might be used.
Random stones and other materials	In more naturalistic areas you could choose to use random stones. In Japanese gardens it is common to find imaginative use of all kinds of "found" materials such as old roofing tiles, long strips of chiselled granite or even charred post tops. Such elements need to be placed with great sensitivity.
Wood and steel	The use of easy-to-install wooden boards and steel edging would be possible in any area, as these materials are subtle and will blend in with the surrounding shrubs or mossy areas, especially once they have weathered. Steel is best used sparingly for a more authentic design.
Bent bamboo	Paths in Japanese parks and some private gardens are edged in hoops of bent bamboo, which adds style and rhythm to the path, as well as discouraging visitors from stepping on the garden.

Right: *Changes in path angles encourage the stroller to take in new views. The random paving stones in this path at Koto-in are bordered by long rectangular strips of granite.*

supposed to be taken, for reasons of privacy or in order to delay the tea guests from entering the inner tea garden, a small, round boulder bound with a knotted string, rather like a small parcel, would be left in the middle of a paving stone. This would indicate to any visitors to the garden that the path was not yet meant to be used for crossing the space.

SAND AND GRAVEL

By the Kamakura period (1185–1392), when the first stroll gardens were constructed, garden paths were likely to have been laid with a mixture of compacted fine sand and a light grit surface, similar to the one used for ceremonies in the courtyards of Heian residences. Both materials are readily available today. Although gravel paths need maintenance, they are one of the easiest and cheapest means of providing an all-weather surface in gardens, particularly in rainy climates such as that of Japan. The paths need to be topped up occasionally with fresh gravel, weeded and then raked or brushed with bamboo brooms.

PAVING AND COBBLING

Whole paths are frequently made with randomly or formally arranged paving or cobbling. There are numerous designs to choose from, as shown on pages 120–121. The joints between the paving or cobbling are usually filled with compacted sharp sand, which is a good medium for the colonization of moss. If the moss is left uncontrolled in damp climates, it may grow until it almost envelops the surface; this is not always discouraged, because moss is both natural and beautiful.

In many Japanese gardens, the paths do become soft and mossy and this is a perfect surface to wander on. You can fill the joints of paved areas with a soft cement mix (1 part cement to 12 parts sand) to give a firm binding but also grow less vigorous mosses and other plants. To exclude all vegetation between the joints, use a stronger mix (1 part cement to 6 parts sand).

DRAINAGE

Even on loose gravel paths, make allowance for the run-off of surface water. This is best done by creating a slight camber to the path, by sloping one side or raising the middle so that excess water can run off to one or both sides. This will be important on sloping paths, where heavy rain can cause erosion. On solid paved areas, provision may need to be made with land drains and soakaways, especially on poorly drained ground.

WIDTH OF PATHS

You can make gravel paths as little as 1m (1yd) in width, but bear in mind that only one person will be able to walk down the path at one time. If paths are too narrow, rain-soaked shrubs will wet you as you pass. If you want to be able to walk two abreast, the minimum path width should be 1.5m (5ft), though a more comfortable width for two people would be 2m (7ft), which will allow for plants that have grown over the sides of the paths.

Tea paths that are made of stepping stones are designed for one person to pass along them at a time. The width of such a path will depend on the design effect and how comfortable you want the path to feel. Some tea paths in Japan can be quite tricky to negotiate. This is a deliberate device, used to make the guest much more aware of each step they take. If you want to achieve a more relaxed stroll, then place the stones about 70–80cm (28–32in) apart. You can experiment with this spacing by marking out where each foot falls at your own natural pace.

It is difficult to make any stepping-stone path without the walker having to be aware of where their feet land, but if you make the joints between them quite tight, no more than 10cm (4in), and level with the height of the stone, the transition between each stone will be easier. Most stepping-stone paths are placed higher than the surrounding soil, but this will depend on how thick your stepping stones are. You may find it difficult to obtain random stones of the quality and thickness that you could find in Japan. The use of substitutes such as logs, or concrete logs with strips of bamboo, is fine as long as you keep them clean of slimy algae. All stepping stones, especially those that are sawn rather than riven, can become slippery, especially in shady gardens, so be prepared to clean them occasionally to reduce their slipperiness.

KEY CONSIDERATIONS

Materials	Sand and gravel are commonly used but need careful solid edging. Alternatively use paving stones or cobbles and encourage moss to grow between the stones.
Drainage	All paths will need to be drained by shaping the path with a slight camber or slope.
Width	Bear in mind how many people will want to walk along the path together, and the direction and shape of the path.
Purpose and meaning	Some paths lead to a destination; some require the visitor to wander and pause to look at the view; others are for show, not for walking on. Make sure you have thought about the purpose and meaning of your path before you lay it out.

Below: Small stepping stones sunk in a carpet of moss wander through this private garden in Ohara. The small symbolic "lantern" by the tree is made of stones piled up on top of each other.

Path styles

To the Japanese, a path is not simply a way of moving around the garden without getting your shoes muddy – it is a precisely designed element of the garden that directs you to certain points, where the view is carefully constructed to be seen from that point. A path can be of great spiritual significance, as in the stepping-stone paths of the tea garden, symbolizing the progress of the spiritual seeker. There are three specific styles of path used by the Japanese: informal (*so*) paths, semi-formal (*gyo*) paths and formal (*shin*) paths.

Above: *This* shin *path uses formal paving blocks that are combined with a formal pattern. Moss is used to link the two elements.*

INFORMAL AND FORMAL STYLES

Around the turn of the 17th century there was a movement away from pure naturalism in the use of stone paths, and towards a greater emphasis on the design element. A greater freedom of expression allowed designers to use a variety of materials and patterns and to exhibit more formalism. While the original tea paths were laid out with a series of informal stepping stones, natural slabs of stone or buried boulders, later paths tended to blend in more formal shapes.

The Japanese expressions for the varying styles of path are *so* (informal), *gyo* (semi-formal) and *shin* (formal). This was linked to a social means of determining the level of formality for greeting people of varying status.

Stepping-stone paths were designed to unite separate parts of a garden, areas often with different atmospheres. The path may start near to the house, being set with formal paving or cobbling, and then launch off across a sea of sand before entering a more earthy and mossy "forest" area planted with maples and shrubs. In each case a different style of paving can be used.

Informal (*so*) paths

These are paths that may be made of rough, uncut stepping stones set in a weaving motion. It also applies to straight paths made up of random stones, without well-defined edges.

Semi-formal (*gyo*) paths

This mixing of the rough with the smooth, the informal with the formal, can be expressed in different ways. Square stepping stones can be set in the

Left: *An interrupted line of formal rectangular granite slabs helps to contain a* gyo *path of mixed natural cobbles and stones.*

CREATIVE CONSTRUCTS

Above: *These formal paving stones combine with an informal surround of other stones.*

Above: *This* gyo *path through a rock garden uses formal materials in an informal pattern.*

Above: *A* so *path through a bamboo grove uses informal materials and an informal pattern.*

same weaving motion as rough uncut stepping stones, but being of a formal shape they will give a different impression. Rectangular or square paving set out in this manner could flow through planted areas or across areas of moss or a sea of sand. Another mixture might use informal random stones bordered by straight-edged granite setts or long strips of paving. Other semi-formal paths might have square forms with sections of informal cobbles, roofing tiles set on edge and natural paving. The use of old roof tiles, mill stones and reclaimed relics is seen as a sign of good taste.

Formal (*shin*) paths

These paths may be made of square paving, bordered by long, rectangular granite setts, or paved in random but rectilinear patterns. This kind of path will look quite familiar to the Western gardener as it is commonly used in terraces, patios and driveways.

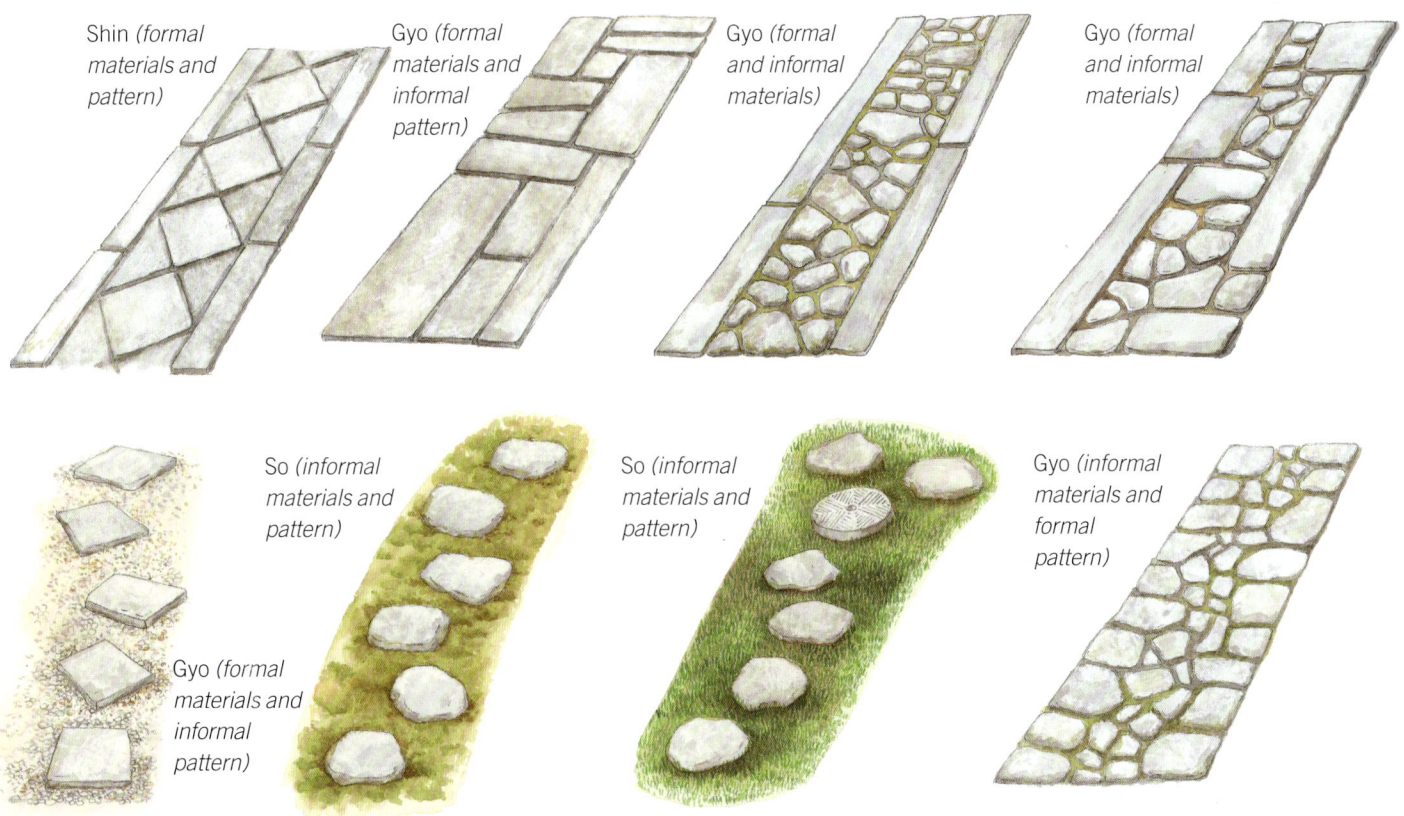

Shin *(formal materials and pattern)*

Gyo *(formal materials and informal pattern)*

Gyo *(formal and informal materials)*

Gyo *(formal and informal materials)*

Gyo *(formal materials and informal pattern)*

So *(informal materials and pattern)*

So *(informal materials and pattern)*

Gyo *(informal materials and formal pattern)*

Tea houses & other buildings

Early Japanese gardens had Chinese-style viewing pavilions, designed to give a view of the pond and garden, often built at the end of a long covered corridor that was open to the sides. The introduction in the 16th century of the unique Japanese tea house would come to influence the style and character of Japanese garden buildings to the present day. Apart from the traditional tea house, other buildings can also be a feature of the Japanese garden, such as small pavilions and arbours surrounded by plants with a place to sit and look at the view.

Above: *Wisteria-covered arbours are popular in Japanese gardens. They are simple constructions of robust timbers to carry the weighty stems of wisteria, with very little, if any, ornamentation.*

THE JAPANESE TEA HOUSE

The tea house was originally conceived by the Japanese as "a mountain place in the city", and it was often built as a rustic hut that was thatched with grass, but later became increasingly sophisticated in design. Originally, the tea house was the place to which the tea garden path led, and it was a place of reverence and social intercourse; it was not a place from which to view the garden. However, by the 17th century, especially in the exquisite gardens of the Katsura Palace in Kyoto, the tea house had opened up its sides and front so that its visitors could look out over the new pond and stroll gardens.

If you want to build a tea house in your garden, then you can easily create a structure that can be used as an outdoor room, but still retains the key elements of the ancient style. Paying close attention to the design of the building and the materials will give your tea house an undeniable air of authenticity.

TEA HOUSE COMPONENTS

All the materials you might need to build a tea house are readily available. The main elements are:

• a mixture of natural raw materials blended with finely planed, high-quality timber;

• a floor consisting of a layer of straw mats (tatami) bordered by fabric;

• the supports for the buildings might be made using the whole trunks of small trees with the bark left on;

• the walls are often finished with plaster, lined with bamboo strips, or painted in weathered gold and pale blue.

Left: *This unusual tea house was shipped from Japan to the English garden of Heale House in the early 1900s, where it stands on stone pillars so that it can straddle a stream.*

TEA HOUSE INTERIORS

The essential elements of tea house interiors typically include the entrance hatch, which in 16th-century tea houses was a small 76cm (2½ft) square sliding-door hatch, so that guests were forced to enter on their knees and demonstrate a suitable level of respect for the ceremony to come. Other window-like openings are often round, like the moon, or rectilinear with sliding rice-paper panels. There is often a sunken hearth for heating the tea water, which is placed off-centre. Calligraphic scrolls might hang in a special alcove (*tokonoma*) in the back wall. There might also be a vase containing a simple, seasonal, "country-style" flower arrangement.

You may not wish to go to the trouble of building a sunken hearth in your tea house, but even if you are simply using the tea house as an outdoor shelter or gazebo, you might still include some classic Japanese design features to give the structure an air of authenticity. There is nothing ostentatious whatsoever about these tea houses, and they blend beautifully into the landscape.

OTHER BUILDINGS

Different types of building might include a small open-fronted waiting room, similar to a rustic shelter with benches, where guests can relax before being invited by the host to proceed to the tea house. There might also be outside toilets for a tea garden built in a similar style to that of the tea house. Raised boarded walkways are also common in stroll gardens, used for viewing the cherry blossom, and these could lead to a thatched pavilion. You might find umbrella-shaped arbours, with a single pillar supporting a circular or square thatched roof, for viewing the garden, or Chinese-style hexagonal shelters, similar to modern Western gazebos. In and around such a shelter were often portable benches and tables, some in the style of Chinese porcelain tubs. These arbours and pavilions are often placed in more prominent places than tea houses, such as on a hill crest or other vantage point.

In some ancient gardens, the contrast of bright red paper umbrellas over tables draped in red cloth, set against dark green evergreen trees and shrubs, can be quite startling, an approach that would even suit a contemporary Japanese garden.

Above right: The waiting room alongside the tea path is often of the simplest design, such as this one at Newstead Abbey, England.

Right: A Japanese tea house gets an English touch in the form of a wicker chair. The Japanese usually sit directly on tatami *mats.*

Far right: The interior of a tea house at Toji-in. The materials are natural and simple, but the craftsmanship is detailed and refined.

Boundaries

Ever since Heian times (794–1185), when the city of Kyoto was laid out on a strict grid system, Japanese gardens have invariably had distinctive boundaries. This approach did not really change until the Edo period (1603–1867), when gardens became large enough for their perimeters to be of secondary importance to the overall design. Now that the average garden is fairly small, the walls, fences and hedges have once again become an important element in the design, and are made to be admired.

Above: *There are hundreds of fence designs to choose from, and the attention to detail typically extends to every tie and binding.*

WALLS

The outer boundary walls of large houses and temple gardens that were constructed before the Edo period were designed as a reflection of the architecture of the buildings. They also became an important backdrop and could be seen from within the garden. These boundary walls were often built of clay and tiles, and were usually neatly plastered. With a stout wooden framework and bracket as a cornice, they were usually crowned with ornamental tiling, although they were sometimes thatched on the top with a ridge of protective tiles.

These walls were rather grand structures, suited to palaces and temples, but smaller residences used many of the same techniques and materials. Modern brick and stone were used more rarely in traditional Japanese gardens, although many garden boundaries on slopes were supported by stone retaining walls, sometimes with azaleas growing in their crevices. Incidentally, internal walls around courtyards were often kept lower than perimeter walls, giving views of trees or distant hills.

Walls in Japanese gardens tend not to be used for growing exotic plants or fruits, as they are in Western gardens. When climbing plants are grown, in large and small gardens, they are allowed to twine through light bamboo trellising.

If you would like to give a Japanese look to conventional brick or concrete block walls, including walls around a courtyard or Zen-style dry garden, the careful use of plaster, paint and some timber uprights at intervals can be effective. Top with large reclaimed or new terracotta pantiles for an authentic finish.

FENCES

Beyond the practicalities of privacy and security, fences were, and still are, considered an important garden feature. In the use of bamboo, in particular, the Japanese have excelled in their inventiveness. An ornate bamboo fence may be woven into wonderful patterns,

Left: *The wall surrounding the garden amid the sweeping roofs of the temple of Tofuku-ji is an intrinsic part of the overall design, with its vertical blackened timber supports and heavily tiled coping.*

Above: *The use of vertical boarding is generally seen as aesthetically the most pleasing and is very practical when changes of ground level require adjustments in the levels of a wall or fence.*

Left: *Vertical bands of reeds seem to mimic the trunks of the trees in this elegant bamboo fence found in the Nanzen-in temple, in Kyoto. The use of raw natural materials such as unpainted wood or bamboo allows a boundary fence to merge with the trees beyond.*

Below: *Horizontal bands of split bamboo, tied to the main fence with black jute, add strength and beauty to this fence. The Japanese use these bands to create many different designs.*

bundled together, tied with jute, or combined with branches, twigs, thatch or bundles of reeds, to flow alongside a path or to help direct the way.

Generally, timber fences are left raw and unpainted. At their most rustic, planks might be old and weathered or sometimes deliberately chiselled and charred to give an instantly distressed and aged effect.

A hybrid between a fence and a wall is the wattle-and-daub fence. The upright support timbers are often left exposed and stained black. Posts with horizontal, vertical or even angled boarding are also used, sometimes with the boards staggered to allow air and light through and occasionally with gaps that are wide enough to allow visitors to peep out.

Japanese bamboo fences can be expensive to buy or build but you can make suitable and more affordable fences using simple methods. Try rolls of bamboo tied to posts, and add superficial framing with other materials such as timber or pine. If you are unable to find authentic fencing for a traditional Japanese tea garden or pond garden, you can use willow or hazel hurdles, chestnut paling or rustic pole fencing. These alternative fencing materials are usually available from larger garden centres and fencing specialists, the latter often providing an on-site construction service if you require it.

SLEEVE FENCES (*SODE-GAKI*)

These are screens of bamboo and reeds that were, and still are, used for two reasons: firstly to deflect the view to another part of the garden, and secondly to create privacy. This is often the case in Japanese restaurants, where guests do not want to be aware of other diners, yet still wish to have a view of the garden, usually a courtyard (*tsuboniwa*). Sleeve fences are usually about 2m (6½ft) high by 1m (1yd) wide, often curved at shoulder level and pierced by an aperture. They come in different designs, from rustic to more formal, and work well in modern gardens.

Above: *A granite water basin and an artificial bamboo fence constructed in a fan shape with jute ties. There is also a Donald Duck figure, a popular feature in contemporary Japan.*

Below: *This main entrance gate to the Huntington Botanical Gardens needs to be secure so is built of more substantial materials such as timber and roofing tiles.*

Above: *Sleeve fences are a classic feature used to frame a view.*

Above right: *A bamboo panel tied with jute is framed between two branches. At the step, guests remove their shoes before entering the tea house.*

Above far right: *Brushwood, reeds and bamboo are combined in this sleeve fence.*

Below right: *These bamboo fence posts tied with jute give a dense, yet informal, barrier to this entrance gateway.*

SCREENS

Western-style brick walls, fence panels, wooden sheds and outbuildings can be camouflaged or blended into your Japanese garden by fixing on bamboo roll or other screening materials such as the darker, more rustic-looking heather screening. Rigid panels, made of framed sections of split bamboo, heather or willow, are also available to conceal pre-existing buildings.

Traditional Japanese screens, including curved sleeve or wing panels, come in a wide variety of designs made from bamboo or brushwood and feature many different knotting patterns and styles of construction. For more contemporary settings, plain square trellis panels, either bought off the peg or constructed from pressure-treated roofing laths, can also be used for creating screens and divides. By making trellis you can customize the panels to be more Japanese looking than the standard models that are available from garden centres and fencing specialists. Paint or stain them black and, for privacy, attach bamboo, heather or brushwood roll to the back using an industrial staple gun.

TREATING NATURAL MATERIALS

The Japanese tend to leave fences unpainted to retain their natural look:

• achieve a blackened effect with several coats of dark wood stain;

• treat the base of posts that go into the ground with wood preservative;

• bamboo fences last longer painted with a layer of matt varnish diluted with white spirit;

• wooden fences can be preserved using linseed oil or oil-based stains.

BOUNDARIES 127

Left: *Zigzagging down the hill, this bamboo post and rail fence helps to emphasize the garden's contours.*

WATER AND PATH EDGINGS

Although on a smaller scale, these boundaries are also important in the Japanese garden, both practically and aesthetically. Water features and pathways will always benefit from neat but natural-looking edging. This approach is practical too, as a firm edge will help to retain and strengthen pond banks and define areas of gravel and other loose material. If you are making pond edgings, or outlining paths and raised beds, use lines of tanalized or pressure-treated logs or rounded posts set in a bed of concrete to hold them rigid. The advantage of this approach is that this edging is 100 per cent flexible, creating curves and following the rise and fall of the land as required.

GATES

Often at the main entrance to the garden, the gate is the threshold between the busy outside world and the calm and tranquil mood of the garden beyond.

The entry gate to a Japanese garden is often a low wooden structure with a roof. This has a humbling effect reminding visitors of their stature in comparison with the space they are about to enter. It may be simply an opening in the wall or fence or a hinged structure often made from latticed bamboo. Particular attention is given to the floor of the entry gate. Stones are carefully selected for this area and positioned with much care.

A classic *Torii* gate, consisting of two vertical posts joined with a double crossbar and often painted red, may be used to indicate that you are entering a sacred space.

Except perhaps in the case of contemporary Japanese gardens, one desirable feature is that any constructions look attractively weathered even when relatively new. Though bamboo tends to take a couple of years to fade and lose its sheen, after washing and rubbing down it can be treated with stains, oils, waxes or varnish as required. Bamboo can also be effectively "aged" and blackened using a gas blowtorch.

HEDGES

Japanese box hedges (*Buxus microphylla*), evergreen oak (*Quercus ilex*), Japanese cedar (*Cryptomeria*), photinia and podocarpus are common. Where they thin near their base, they may be backed by bamboo fencing.

Japanese hedges are almost always evergreen, so plant a mixture for a varied texture. Camellias and other flowering plants can be used, especially the autumn-flowering *Camellia sasanqua*.

Left: *This entrance is flanked by sections of traditional Japanese bamboo fencing, which is lashed together with black twine. This see-through fencing style blends in well with the natural surroundings.*

Left: *A residential road in Kyoto, Japan with a succession of identical bamboo gates and brush and bamboo fencing.*

Gates were very popular in tea gardens, developing their most elaborate and ritualistic style by the early 17th century. The traditional tea garden is often divided into two or even three parts: an inner, middle and outer garden, linked by a *roji* (dewy path), featuring specially designed gates opening into each area.

The main entrance gate (*roji-mon*) may be a large tile-covered gatehouse or a simple thatch-covered bamboo gate. The second gate into the middle or inner *roji* might be a small crawl-through opening or stooping gate (*naka-kuguri*). One type has a door that is hinged at the top so that the guest has to push it forward and up to get through, being forced to bow in the process. This can be propped open.

You can simulate this effect with a series of sections, each with their own entrance, to enhance the feeling of deference as you approach the tea house, and give the garden authenticity.

You can buy ready-made Japanese gates, or make your own from natural materials, using a simple shape hinged at the side or top.

Right: *This gateway, with its thatched roof, is a symbolic statement as well as a physical entrance to the tea garden at Nijo castle. Such roofs can also be finished with wooden shingles.*

READY-MADE STRUCTURES

A wide range of traditional Japanese structures are available direct from Japan or through specialist importers. These include garden screens, fence panels and roofed gateways. Details can be found on the internet, through mail order firms advertising in specialist directories and in the classified sections of home and garden magazines.

In addition, a number of companies outside Japan manufacture structures either to catalogue specifications or as bespoke items. The best of these use traditional materials and methods such as split bamboo and black hemp for tying and knotting.

DO IT YOURSELF

If you like the idea of having your own construction project, build or adapt screens, fences and walls using a variety of raw materials. There are mail order and internet supply companies selling the basic materials, from bamboo poles to lengths of split bamboo and wooden roof shingles.

BOUNDARIES 129

Making a tea-path gate

Small lattice bamboo gates are very lightweight and are easy to install. Gates are very common features throughout Japanese gardens, from the main entrance to key points within the garden or along the tea path. The gates that are sited on the tea path itself are often not meant to keep people or animals out of the garden, but are more of a symbolic feature, for example the middle crawl-through gate (see also page 172). In the case of the tea-path gate, it is quite usual for the gate to be found standing alone with no fence on either side of it.

The simple design of this gate gives the garden an airy feel, especially when associated with live bamboo plants, maples and glossy evergreens, the kind of plants that you would find in a tea garden.

This system for hanging a gate is only suitable for very lightweight gates that are made of bamboo or light wood, as we have used light posts and heavy twine for the top hinge. For heavier gates, you will need to use stronger posts and a hinge at both top and bottom, but the methods of measuring and levelling will be the same. This bamboo gate is also hinged in such a way that gravity will ensure that the gate naturally swings to a close behind you.

Above: *The semi-transparent nature of this jute-tied bamboo trellis gate gives a light and airy feel to a garden.*

As the gate is merely symbolic and not designed to be child or animal safe there is no latch, but a loop of twine could easily be attached to the top of the gate to keep it firmly shut.

You will need
- a lightweight lattice bamboo gate
- 2 x 7.5cm (3in) round softwood gateposts, ideally pressure treated or with wood preservative on the base
- an L-shaped gate hinge with a pin that will fit inside the bamboo frame
- a short length of black jute or nylon rope
- a hammer
- a crowbar
- a small sledgehammer
- a spirit level
- a hand saw
- dark ash black wood stain and a paintbrush (optional)
- an electric drill or hand wood drill

1 Having chosen the site, you must decide which way the gate will open and on which side the hinge should be. Now make the first hole for the post that the gate will hang on. This needs to be deeper than the "receiving" post. Prepare the hole with a crowbar, to a depth of at least 30cm (12in).

2 Prepare both posts for the gate by staining them, if you like, and making sure that the part below the ground is protected with wood preservative. Place the hinge post in the hole and check by eye that it is more or less vertical. If you have an assistant, ask them to hold the hinge post while you knock it into the ground with a sledgehammer. It is a good idea to protect the top of the post with a block of wood to prevent the top of the post from being damaged by the sledgehammer.

3 Using a spirit level, check that the post is upright. Check the distance to the other post by laying the gate in place. The receiving post can be at a slighter narrower width than the gate so that the gate will lean against it when closed. Prepare the second post hole with the crowbar and knock in the receiving post.

4 It is better that your posts are set a little too high, so that you can cut them off to the right height. The tops of the posts should line up with the top of the gate or can be slightly higher. Using a spirit level, check that the two posts are level with each other. If they need to be cut, mark the cutting line.

5 Cut off the tops of the posts with a wood saw if necessary to ensure they are level. If you have stained the post to give it the blackened and charred look that the Japanese love to create, you will need to paint some more wood stain on to the cut surface at the top.

6 Check the height of the gate against the post, positioning it so that the bottom of the gate will hang just off the ground, clearing any stones or paving slabs. Mark on the hinge post where the bottom hinge needs to be.

7 Select a drill-bit slightly smaller than the diameter of the hinge. Drill to the depth needed. Alternatively you can buy a hinge with a flat plate that can be drilled directly on to the side of the post.

8 Knock the hinge in firmly with a hammer. Drop the gate on to the hinge and tie a piece of black jute in a figure of eight around the post near the top. You may need to adjust this until the gate hangs and swings comfortably.

9 The gate can now swing until it just touches the side of the receiving post. If the gate hangs well, you may not need to secure it, but another loop of jute could be used to secure the gate to the receiving post.

Right: *The gate acts as a transition into the inner* roji *of a tea garden with its* tsukubai *arrangement of lantern and water basin.*

Bridges

Always a dominant feature, bridges tend to be particularly associated with Japanese gardens. One of the most well known is the Chinese-style bridge (*sori-hashi*), lavishly ornamented, high-arched and lacquered red or orange. While the islands in a pond represented the abodes of the immortals, bridges symbolized the crossing over to that world. These red-painted bridges are often closely associated with Japanese gardens in the Western mind, but they are in fact rarer in authentic designs than those made of more natural materials and unpainted wood.

Above: *A moss-covered log bridge in the gardens of Saiho-ji, the Moss Temple in Kyoto, where over 60 species of moss are said to grow.*

STYLES OF BRIDGE

In the garden of the Tenryu-ji, built in the 14th century, a Chinese-style, curved red wooden bridge was replaced by a series of flat, natural stone slabs, propped up on rock pillars. Later gardens used single pieces of wrought granite, supported by granite piles. Some of these granite slabs were carved with a gentle curve. This was the dominant style of Japanese bridges until Chinese high-arched bridges returned to favour in the Edo period (1603–1867). These semicircular bridges, known as full-moon bridges because their reflections in the water make up a complete circle, are so steep that the only way to cross over them is by means of steps going up one side and down the other.

YATSUHASHI BRIDGES

Especially designed for viewing iris beds, the *yatsuhashi* style of bridge, which is still popular today, is constructed from a series of single horizontal planks, which are supported by short wooden piles that are driven into the mud at the head of the pond, where the Japanese love to grow beds of irises. The planks cross the swampy beds in a zigzag fashion, forcing the visitor to loiter, watch the fish and admire the flowers. This simple style of bridge can easily be incorporated into today's Japanese garden, perhaps designed to sit in a boggy area in which moisture-loving plants such as irises and sedges can be grown. See overleaf for instructions for making a *yatsuhashi* bridge.

WATTLE AND LOG BRIDGES

Bridges were also often made from wattle (woven branches) then covered in earth, or from batches of logs bundled and laid across a timber frame and then covered with earth and gravel. These were designed more for effect because they were fairly fragile, and did not usually feature a hand-rail. Those that link up the islands at the famous Moss Temple, in Kyoto, for example, are quite rotten, but they blend in with the deep shady mystery of the garden. If you want to construct this type of bridge, consider how long you want it to last and whether the logs should be treated in order to improve their longevity. Nowadays, wattle is not easily available, so it is best to use bundles of logs that have been coated in a wood preservative, or use a good hardwood, such as oak, which needs no treatment.

WISTERIA BRIDGES

Sturdy wooden bridges with a trellised canopy to carry twining wisterias are popular in Japan. This style of bridge was immortalized by Monet in his

Left: *This style of red-painted bridge, seen here in the gardens at Heale House in England, is Chinese in origin, and became popular in Japan in the Edo period.*

BRIDGES: KEY ELEMENTS

Making a decorative effect Bridges can be placed simply to be part of a scene that will be viewed from a distance and not necessarily used for practical purposes. A small wooden curved bridge, for instance, can add to an illusion of scale in a miniaturized landscape.

Making a solid construction Always make sure that bridges to be walked on are given deep footings, and that any wooden supporting posts (piles) are made of a durable hardwood such as oak or treated timber. Alternatively, use concrete pillars and bolt the wooden bridge to the concrete.

Protecting a pond liner Bridges across ponds lined with butyl rubber will need special footings to protect the liner from being punctured by the bridge's weight. Further instructions can be found over the page.

Keeping it authentic Consider whether a natural stone or timber bridge might look more authentic and blend better with your garden design than a Chinese-style red-painted bridge. Choose the bridge to suit your location – they all have their place.

paintings of his garden at Giverny, in France. The effect of the long racemes of the Japanese wisteria (*Wisteria floribunda*) is doubled when they are reflected in the water, and cascades of wisteria flowers create a shady, scented walkway to stroll on.

STEPPING-STONE BRIDGES

These bridges can be made of recycled pillars or natural rocks. Like the *yatsuhashi*, the stones zigzag across the water instead of taking a straight line, offering a variety of views as you cross streams, inlets and ponds, and possibly echoing the wandering nature of the path it joins at either end. If you are lucky enough to have a large garden with an expanse of water, a stepping-stone bridge would make a delightful feature.

Top: *This massive curving slab of schist in the grounds of Nijo castle is a symbol of strength. The original garden was thought to have been designed as a dry garden with no water at all.*

Above: *Another style of bridge, borrowed from China. The high arch allows the passage of boats underneath but the sides are so steep they require steps to cross over them.*

Right: *This stepping-stone bridge in the garden of Tenju-an is made of unusually shaped piers – possibly recycled temple-pillar bases.*

Making a *yatsuhashi* bridge

The *yatsuhashi* bridge is a popular form in Japanese gardens. The origin of the name *yatsuhashi* is a poetic reference to a timber bridge made of eight planks that zigzag across a river. The idea is to delight the eye of visitors to the garden with unexpected sights as they make their way over the bridge and across a pond or swampy area filled with flowers. It should also encourage them to linger and admire an unexpected aspect of the garden. A *yatsuhashi* bridge is relatively simple to construct, as it requires only a few posts and planks.

Above: *Although appearing to be complex in design, the actual construction of a* yatsuhashi *bridge is relatively simple.*

This unique kind of bridge is mostly found in gardens where the inlet of a stream flows into a pond, or any other area that is similarly ideal for the growing of the Japanese water iris (*Iris ensata*). *Yatsuhashi* bridges do not have to have eight planks – they can be made up of as few as two planks, and whatever their size, they are an excellent addition to any small or large pond or stroll gardens. In some cases the device can simply be a design that is viewed but not actually used to walk on.

When constructing the bridge, make sure that your measurements are accurate, so the planks will be level. If possible, drain the pond water first.

If you cannot drain the pond or other water feature, it is still possible to construct a bridge but you may need to get professional help as setting the posts into water can present problems.

1 Measure the exact span for the bridge and make a sketch of how many planks will be needed to cross your inlet, iris bed or pond, and the length of the planks. The directional changes do not have to be at 90 degrees – they can be at even sharper angles.

2 Measure how deep the water is at different points to calculate how many posts you need and how long they should be.

You will need
- planks or boards at least 5cm (2in) thick – the number and length of planks and posts will be determined by the span and depth of water you are working with, and the width of the planks can also be variable
- supporting posts, 7.5cm (3in) square or round
- cross beams, 7.5cm (3in) deep x 5cm (2in) thick – the length of these will be determined by the width of the planks
- bolts, minimum 1cm (½in) wide by 15cm (6in) long
- an electric drill with wood bits
- cement and concreting sand/aggregate
- metal post holders (for a butyl-lined pond)
- a shovel
- a spade
- a crowbar
- a coarse-toothed wood-saw
- a sledgehammer if you are driving posts into the ground or a clay-lined pond

POSITIONING YOUR BRIDGE

When considering the design of your *yatsuhashi* bridge, use the angles to encourage the garden visitor to take in varying views. You may even place a bench at a strategic position on the bridge.

3 Start on dry land by setting two posts in the ground exactly the width of one plank apart, or two plank widths if you are laying two planks side by side. The posts need to be dug into the ground to a depth of 45–60cm (18–24in) and their bases set in two or three shovelfuls of concrete (1 part cement to 6 parts concreting sand or aggregate). If the first set of posts will be in the water, follow step 7 opposite.

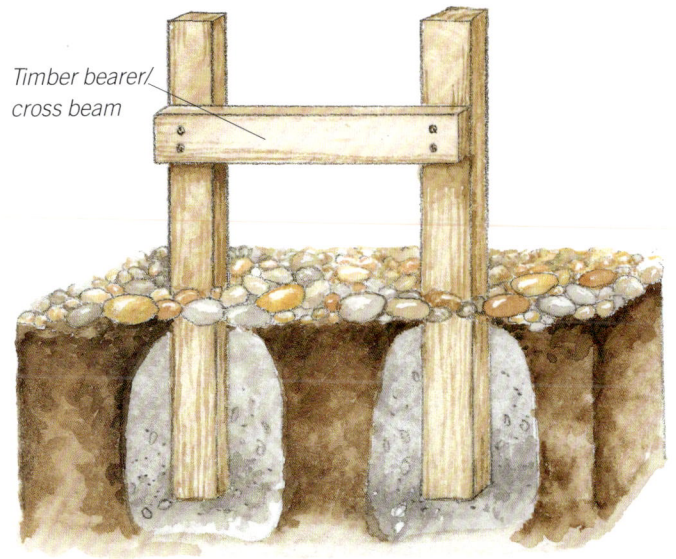

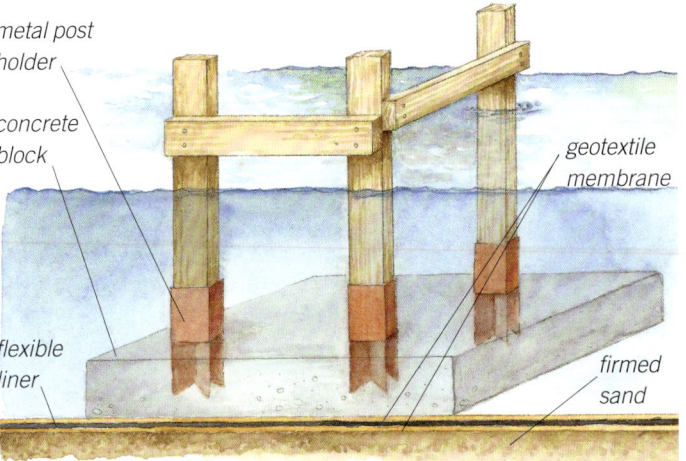

4 Measure how high you want the bridge to be off the ground and make a mark on one of the posts. With a spirit level, mark across to the other post. Attach the cross beam on to the posts using bolts. Stout screws may suffice but bolts will be stronger and last longer. The first set of planks may overlap these first posts by up to 30cm (12in).

5 Drain off the water if possible, as this makes it much easier to construct the bridge. Driving posts into the clay base or mixing cement directly into water is very tricky and unreliable.

6 Measure across to where the next set of posts will stand. The first set of planks will overlap the second set of posts by the width of a plank, as the next set of planks will lie over the top of the first.

7 The second set of posts may be dug or driven directly into the base of a clay-lined pool, but in a pool with a butyl liner, they will need to sit in post holders and be set in a concrete base (1 part cement to 5 parts concreting sand). You can use fast-setting concrete that is specially designed for posts and will set in less than 15 minutes.

8 Leave the concrete to set for at least a day before laying the planks and two days before you walk on them. You only need three posts at each junction, but four will make the bridge more stable. If you prefer the look of three posts, include a fourth one for strength and trim it off flush to the top of the cross beam. Attach cross beams as in step 4 and continue one set of posts at a time, testing them for measurements as you go. On the far side you may need another pair of posts on dry land.

Below: *A* yatsuhashi *bridge of planks, resting on wooden piles, staggers past baskets of irises towards an impressive stand of cycads.*

MAKING A *YATSUHASHI* BRIDGE 135

Decorative artefacts

The addition of objects without any useful function is generally avoided in Japanese gardens. The garden is regarded as a completely integrated composition, and the introduction of unnecessary features can destroy the unity of the design. Many Japanese garden designs are either inspired by nature or reproduce famous views; they avoid distractions that might divert the eye from reading the composition as a whole. However, the useful objects such as water basins and lanterns that are found in gardens can be beautiful in their own right.

Above: *A pagoda stands in the middle of an island in the gardens of the Golden Pavilion (Kinkaku-ji), in Kyoto.*

In the Japanese garden, specimen plants, focal points, sculptures and statues are usually shunned, as are overt colour schemes, textural combinations, surprise effects and most of the elements that are the bedrock of many Western gardens.

This general emphasis still accommodates the more focused effect of sculptural forms with a religious connotation. These include garden stupas, pagodas, water basins, lanterns, or images of the Buddha. Although these artefacts are still integral to modern Japanese gardens, their religious significance can be more diluted.

PAGODAS AND STUPAS

These are structures of the Buddhist treasure houses where relics and scriptures were stored to commemorate a saint. Like lanterns, they were found close to temples, but when used in the garden they do not dominate because they are such familiar images that they readily blend into the scene. Indeed, both pagodas and stupas represent very recognizable features, from a Western viewpoint, of the Japanese garden and what it should contain.

WATER DEVICES

There are one or two playful devices found in Japanese gardens that recall a distant rural past. Deer scarers (*shishi-odoshi*) are the best known of these. They use water to make a noise intended to startle any deer feeding on plants in the garden (see page 110). A more unusual device is the *sui-kinkutsu* (see page 111). It literally

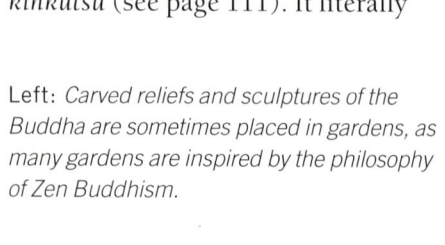

Left: *Carved reliefs and sculptures of the Buddha are sometimes placed in gardens, as many gardens are inspired by the philosophy of Zen Buddhism.*

136 CREATIVE CONSTRUCTS

means "water harp chamber" and distills the sound of water dripping in an underground chamber.

Wells may also be found in Japanese gardens, constructed of timber or natural stone, and often with a bamboo rack as a cover to prevent leaves from falling in. The use of wells, whether real or decorative, is common in conjunction with tea gardens to indicate a pure source of water for making tea.

Left: *A stone pagoda stands in a grove of the rare Chinese fir (*Cunninghamia lanceolata*) in the stroll garden of Syoko-ho-en, Kyoto.*

Above: *This water mill, sited in the gardens of the Nijo castle in Kyoto, has been decorated to become a feature.*

Below left: *Kasuga, temple-style lanterns are very impressive and can be very large, often standing over 2m (7ft) high.*

Below: *Wells are often found in tea gardens, with a stone at the side for the water bucket. Many, such as this one, are purely ornamental.*

Lighting

There is a large selection of garden lights available, from tiny concealed uplighters made to highlight individual plants or rocks, to Japanese-style lanterns, which are among the most distinctive sculptural artefacts in the Japanese garden. Originally these lanterns stood outside Shinto shrines and Buddhist temples, sometimes in their hundreds, lining up in avenues of flickering lights. On a more practical level, lighting allows you to view the garden at night from the house rather like a painting. It also makes the garden usable at night and can create different moods.

Above: *Cast-iron lanterns are hung from trees and verandas and are used less as part of the overall garden design than stone lanterns.*

LANTERNS IN THE TEA GARDEN

Like other artefacts such as the water basin and the stepping-stone path, lanterns found their way into the Japanese garden, by way of the tea garden. They were originally placed to illuminate tea paths and water basins, as many tea gatherings were arranged in the evening. They were also placed near pond edges to represent lighthouses, or at the base of slopes or near wells. Despite their popularity, stone lanterns (with oil and wick lamps or candles placed inside) did not give much light and were, to a large extent, ornamental.

Below: *Lanterns in Japanese tea gardens have taken on numerous forms, from the large temple-like "Kasuga" lantern to small lanterns designed to look best when covered in snow.*

THE WEATHERING PROCESS

Sculpted ornaments are rare in Japanese gardens, so stone lanterns, especially granite ones, give an opportunity to create something interesting and distinctive. Brand new granite lanterns are often bright silvery grey and the colour can be too startling. It can take many years before granite weathers naturally to give that patina or aged effect that is evoked in the term *wabi-sabi*. The term, with no literal translation, roughly means "withered loneliness" and became an essential part of the tea ceremony philosophy. When applied to ornaments, it implies the patina of age. So encourage your lanterns to discolour and grow algae, lichen and moss. The more porous sandstone lanterns weather more quickly.

There are ways to speed up this process. One effective method is to smear a lantern with yogurt or manure (soak some manure in a bucket of water and just paint it on), promoting the growth of algae. Repeat this monthly for three months, especially in the autumn when it is damp. In summer, in hot exposed positions, algae and lichen will not take a hold so readily as in the cooler, wetter months. Some gardeners even used the slime of crushed snails to achieve dampness. Another method is to drape them in pine boughs for a month or two. Stone ages more quickly when placed in the shade.

Kasuga

Snow scene

Mile post

Valley

Rikyu

Above left: Many temple-style lanterns still carry Buddhist motifs, such as this one crowned with a lotus bud.

Above centre: Organic rock forms can be layered on each other to create a lantern shape. These naturalistic forms can add an unusually animistic quality to a garden.

Above right: The valley lantern has been specially designed to place by the water's edge where the light from the lamp, usually an oil wick, can be seen to reflect in the water.

Left: The introduction of the stone lantern into Japanese gardens came through the development of the tea garden, where they were used to light the path (roji) and water basins.

Below: Short and stocky lanterns are often placed near water or at the end of gravel spits to evoke lighthouses.

LIGHTING 139

Above left: *In some Japanese gardens, lanterns are the only architectural artefacts to be found. Most are never lit, but this one is. Rice-paper panels diffuse the light from the lit oiled paper.*

Above: *Lanterns were often designed to look dramatic within the larger landscape – this one is majestically placed within a pond.*

STYLES OF LANTERN

Lanterns play such a large part in Japanese gardens that long ago they were classified into different types. Some were named after famous tea masters or gardens; the most well known and popular of these is the Oribe lantern. Oribe was an eccentric samurai tea master active at the end of the 17th century. The Oribe lantern often has a Buddha carved on the front of the pillar base. In some gardens this image was disguised and purported to be of the Virgin Mary, an image that was banned after the Christian Westerners were evicted from Japan in the 17th century. The Oribe lantern is easy to install (see pages 178–9). Taller and statuesque lanterns such as the Kasuga sit on a round plinth, some of them with elaborate carvings of lotus petals. More squat stone lanterns and low lanterns that rest on a tripod or four feet are often placed by the sides of ponds.

In gardens with ponds designed to include a symbolic reproduction of the Amanohashidate Peninsula, a famous scenic spot on the northern coast of Honshu, a lantern is usually placed at the gravelled promontory. This is a classic example of *shakkei*, a small-scale version of real scenes or objects. Some of these poolside lanterns are designed to look especially beautiful when covered in snow, a regular feature of the Japanese winter.

Although most lanterns are made of stone, some are also made of wood and thatched with reed. Hanging lanterns made of bronze are also popular and can easily be moved around, hung from a tree or simply placed on a rock.

TSUKUBAI ARRANGEMENTS

The most popular way to use lanterns is as part of a *tsukubai* water feature in tea gardens (see pages 176–7), a classic arrangement that consists of a lantern placed near a water basin, with one or two paving stones in a sea of gravel at the base, and surrounded by ferns, camellias and sedges. Versions of *tsukubai* arrangements can also be found in courtyard gardens or along passages that lead to the front doors of houses and restaurant entrances. These often include a backing piece of bamboo fence, a water basin, and a pine or maple tree to provide shade and promote the growth of moss.

CONTEMPORARY USE OF LIGHTING

In the Muromachi and Momoyama periods, special platforms and gardens were made for "viewing the moon". Moonlight was especially revered and was considered to be at its most moving when seen across a dry garden. These days in Kyoto, many of the most popular gardens are open during the autumn months at night, when artificial lighting is

Above: *There are many styles of Japanese stone lantern. This is a* kodal rokkaku.

Right: *Subtle feature lighting can highlight chosen parts or elements of the garden, in this case to create drama.*

laid out to highlight the main buildings, the reflections of water and the autumn colours of the maples. Modern dry gardens can also be lit in a surprisingly adventurous manner.

As traditional lanterns give off very little light, in a contemporary Japanese garden electric lighting could be used effectively. Low-voltage and wattage systems that are cheap to install and run are ideal. Many of the traditional stone lanterns and other Japanese-style garden lights that you can buy today can be fitted with low-voltage electric light. Another way to supplement the meagre light is to hang bronze lanterns or hurricane lamps from trees or posts.

In naturalistic Japanese gardens, small black uplighters are used to light rocks, plants and ornamental features. Other kinds of low-level lighting can be installed to illuminate a pathway or steps, and in decked areas, small LED or halogen lights can be recessed into the wood to great effect. Low-voltage garden lighting sets running off a transformer are relatively easy to install. Not connected directly to the mains supply, the cabling can lie close to the surface and does not have to be buried in armoured ducting, though great care must be taken to hide the fittings and wires so that they are not visible during the day, as this would spoil the romantic effect. It is advisable to use an electrical contractor to install lighting projects, however, and you must fit residual current devices, or circuit breakers, as a safety measure.

Right: *A low-level wall light is discreet and effective. Such lights can be fitted to help light the way to a door or gate.*

Far right: *LED uplighters can be set into wooden decking or into pathways that are paved with setts.*

CREATING A GARDEN

Japanese gardens will always include a selection of the classic components that we have so far encountered. When it comes to planning your own garden, start on an achievable scale. Choose either to plan a small garden, or focus on a specific area in a more spacious garden, the rest of which can be developed over time.

After an outline of how to plan a garden design, this chapter looks at the five main garden types – pond gardens, dry gardens, tea gardens, stroll gardens and courtyard gardens. Each section explains the style and presents a colour plan showing the typical elements. This is followed by a design proposal for a garden in this style. Three practical sequences showing the three stages for each one then show how to bring the design to fruition. Some of the features, such as constructing a pine island, involve detailed planning and logistics; others, such as setting a lantern or laying a paving stone path, are relatively simple. They can all be adapted to the requirements of individual schemes, and many can be used within other garden styles.

Above: *A "hillside" of clipped azaleas at Sanzen-in, Ohara.*
Left: *A turtle island in Huntington Botanical Gardens, Los Angeles.*

Making a plan

Once you have decided on the style of garden you want to make, taking into consideration all the criteria of space, type of site and natural features, you will need to make a rough plan of the layout. This need not be too sophisticated, but it should be accurate enough for you to position any pool or any new trees, for instance, in relation to existing items such as buildings, walls, trees and slopes. It is worth measuring the site as accurately as you can and making a sketch of your plan from various viewpoints, especially if the site is not flat.

Above: *Measurements need to be taken with some precision, especially when calculating pond levels and drainage requirements.*

WHAT TO INCLUDE IN YOUR PLAN

If you are planning to make new water features on different levels, and are considering the fall of water for waterfalls and streams and any drainage that may be required, you will need to take some fairly accurate levels. This can be done using a spirit level placed on a long straight board, which will be accurate enough for most of your requirements. Knowing the levels at different points in the garden is especially important with water features but will also help with your overall design. When you are preparing your plan, make sure that you include all of the features mentioned below before you even begin to consider anything exciting like future planting. It might seem laborious, but it will definitely be worth it in the end. Japanese garden designers pay special attention to detail, scale, viewing angles and ways of framing those views from different vantage points.

CHECKLIST FOR YOUR PLAN

Marking the features identified in the plan shown here will allow you to see the areas that might be problematic for planting (those in shade, those with underground service supplies and those in windy areas, for example) while identifying where you definitely do want plants (such as places in sun and those that can be appreciated from the windows of the house). Only when you have identified all the existing characteristics of your garden will you be in a position to get down to the creative planning.

Orientation

It is important that you do not forget to mark the position of the sun in relation to your garden, as this may affect the placing of plants.

Utilities

Identify and mark the position of all underground services, such as water pipes, gas pipes, electric cables, drains, sewer pipes and manhole covers. If you

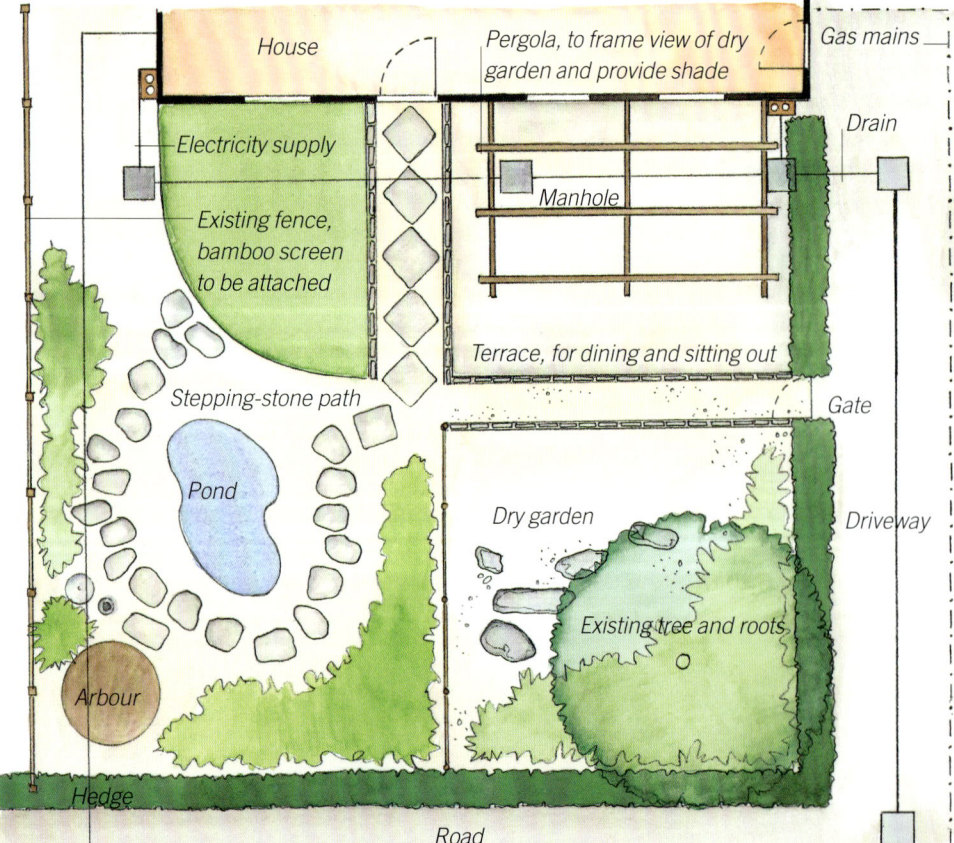

Left: *Before you plan your garden you must familiarize yourself with the location of all the utilities. Your garden design should keep them accessible and prevent them from being damaged by excavations.*

are planning to excavate a pond, you should avoid these rather than have them diverted. Most of them are deeper than the average depth of an ornamental pond, but do not assume that this is the case. If you have no idea where they are, contact the utility company involved, which will have the equipment to trace the route of its pipes if no plan exists.

Trees
The position of existing trees will affect the siting of a pond or any new plantings owing to the shade they cast, the extent of their roots and their falling leaves. The leaves of some trees, such as yew, release toxins if they accumulate in water, so avoid placing a pond near such trees. Some trees, such as birch, rowan and pine, produce only light shade, but many, including beech, sycamore and horse chestnut cast dense shade, and any area under them that is in shade constantly, rather than for just a small part of the day, should be marked on the plan.

Boundaries, outbuildings and viewing points
Walls and fences, as well as outbuildings such as sheds and garages, should be marked on the plan because they, too, will cast shade. They also cause eddies of wind, which gust around the walls on an exposed site. The main ground-floor viewing windows are most important to include on your plan because they will help to identify view lines. Doors inevitably mean paths to various points, and in a new garden it is important to establish the route of paths early on in the planning process.

Wind tunnels
Suburban gardens are notorious for having wind tunnels between buildings and fences. Even if you cannot entirely avoid a wind tunnel, you can plant windbreaks or erect trellises in order to filter the wind.

Filtered wind, such as that which occurs in the area behind a hedge or trellis, causes much less damage than eddying wind on the leeward side of a solid barrier. In fact, wind strength will still be greatly reduced some distance away from a trellis – so it is actually a better, and usually cheaper, shelter option than building a wall or fence.

Top: You can use spray marker paint or a trail of powdered lime to mark out the principal design outlines in your garden. Be sure that you plan a logical sequence of tasks, so that any heavy or disruptive work will not disturb plantings.

Above: Turfing should be left until last, as new turf should not be walked on for several weeks after it has been laid. Any loose stones and building rubble should be raked off the surface of the ground prior to turf laying.

The pond garden style

Starting with the very earliest gardens influenced by the Chinese and developing over the centuries to the most up-to-date designs, pond gardens have always been enormously popular in Japan. The pond will, naturally, be the central feature, and should ideally be big enough for you to incorporate an island or two, and, for greater authenticity, to make a ride in a small rowing boat possible. For this you will need space – it is obviously not suitable for a small town garden – as well as the time and energy to plan on a large scale.

Above: *At the Heian shrine, in Kyoto, the staggered stepping stones are made of recycled bridge piers and temple column bases. Borrowing old architectural fragments is known as mitate ("to see anew").*

Below: *Chinese-style red-painted bridges, such as this one at the Tully Japanese Garden in Ireland, were popular in the early days of Japanese gardens of the Heian period. They were also used extensively in later Edo gardens and copied in Western versions.*

ELEMENTS OF A POND GARDEN

The pond gardens of Japan were originally found only in city complexes. Despite being surrounded by buildings, these gardens were very naturalistic and much less stylized than the later stroll gardens. Ponds (with pine islands) and streams are the main features, along with naturalistic planting and a strolling path.

Pond

The edges of the pond should have a varied and natural outline resembling a coastline, with coves, grotto-like caves and beaches. Rocks can be placed at the edges of ponds and by waterfalls so long as their shape is considered carefully, and also in the water, where they can be used as stepping stones or supports for naturalistic bridges.

Island

There are many styles of island to choose from, but the most popular is the pine island, planted with one very picturesque pine, or a group of pines set in a tight group. In pond gardens the island is often reached by a bridge, especially an old-style Chinese wooden bridge that is painted red or orange. You may of course prefer a different style of bridge, perhaps aiming for a more minimal, neutral effect.

Stream

Another main feature of a pond garden is a winding stream that either feeds into or empties the main pond (or both). This would originally have been used for ceremonial purposes, but even without the ceremonies it makes an attractive addition. Again it should follow a naturalistic course, and be planted at its edges with hostas and other waterside plants.

Plants

Planting in pond gardens should be in naturalistic groups of trees and shrubs that celebrate the seasons. Groves of cherries, maples and pines can be underplanted with azaleas, kerria and spiraea for contrast.

Path

A strolling path is the final essential feature that should be added, in order to encourage the visitor to experience every part of the garden by wandering around the pond, over the stream and through the groves of trees.

Above left: A valley-style lantern, typical of the type used to arc over the edges of ponds at Pureland Zen garden, England.

Above right: Stepping stone paths that continue across ponds help to create a unity of design within a garden.

Below: The use of large rocks and clipped evergreens gives this pond garden a sense of scale that is much larger than in reality. The waterfall design carefully observes the natural flow of mountain streams.

Garden plan: a pond garden

The design of this pond garden would suit people with a large garden. The main feature is the pond fed by a winding stream or by a spring spilling over a waterfall. Pine islands and rocky islets are artfully placed, some of them reached by Chinese-style bridges and viewed from a pavilion that might double as a boathouse. The overall feel of the planting and rock placement is naturalistic.

MAKING A TURTLE ISLAND

Turtle and crane islands were built to lure the immortals to earth and learn their secrets, especially the recipe for the elixir of eternal youth. These islands can be made anywhere in a pond, just from a few well-placed rocks.

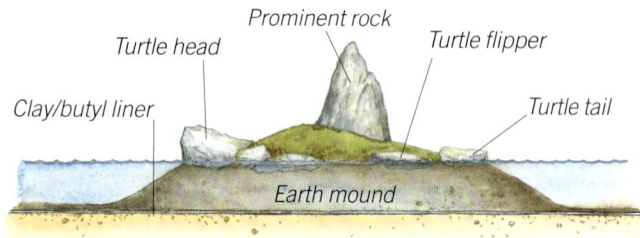

Turtle head · *Prominent rock* · *Turtle flipper* · *Clay/butyl liner* · *Turtle tail* · *Earth mound*

1 Make a rough sketch, then select rocks to represent the turtle parts. The island is the body of the turtle, made up of earth and a collection of supporting rocks. You also need rocks to represent the turtle's head and the four flippers. Just suggest the shape of the head and use wider rocks that reach out into the water at the four corners of the island for the flippers.

2 Construct the island before the pond is filled with water. You can build the island on a butyl liner, or add the liner after the island is complete, but if you are planning an elaborate arrangement then lay the liner first. If using machinery to transport the rocks and soil, you can roll back the butyl liner to avoid puncturing it. You can also lay out some extra layers of liner and underlay for protection.

3 Build the soil up in layers, making the base twice as wide as the island itself, so that the sides slope gently into the water. This will ensure that the rocks are sitting on stable ground. Place a ring of rocks just below water level around the soil to add stability.

4 Now place the rocks to signify the different parts of the turtle. Upright rocks will need to be buried by up to a third of their height to be stable and safe.

5 The island can then be planted with grasses and a pine tree. According to the myth, the turtle carries on its back one of the Isles of the Immortals. This could be represented by placing one particularly prominent rock on the "back" of the turtle.

Small hill with waterfall

Gravel path

Rocky s[tream]

Small bridge over winding stream

Left: *Winding streams emulate a natural type of stream, with the rocks used to modulate the flow.*

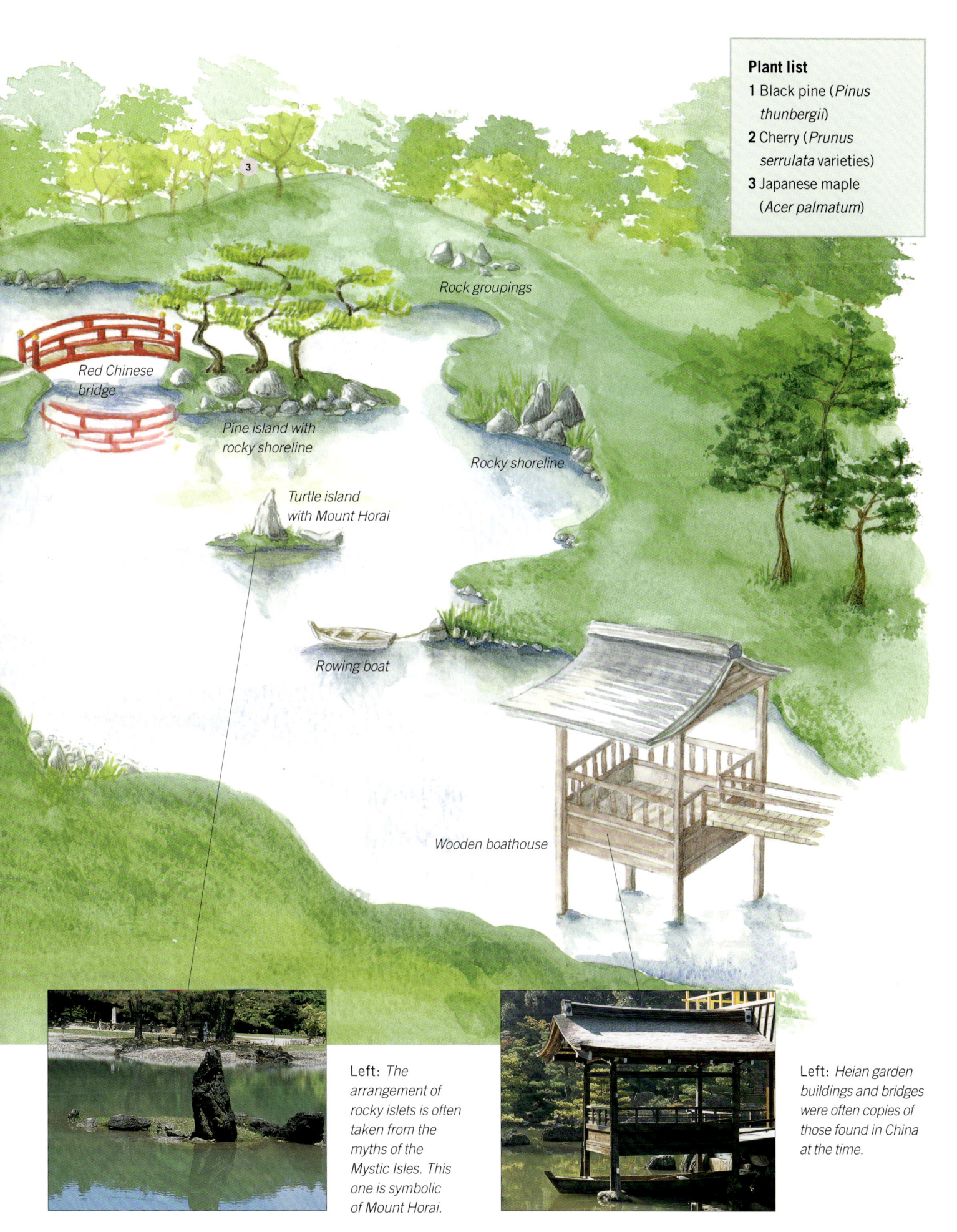

Left: The arrangement of rocky islets is often taken from the myths of the Mystic Isles. This one is symbolic of Mount Horai.

Left: Heian garden buildings and bridges were often copies of those found in China at the time.

GARDEN PLAN: A POND GARDEN 149

How to make a pond garden

Pond gardens do not necessarily require a spectacular country setting. They were originally made in Japanese cities in large walled spaces, which means that the pond garden is a style that can easily be reproduced in Western gardens. However, a minimum of a quarter of a hectare (over half an acre) is required to make the style effective. Here is a suggestion for a pond garden created with a clay-lined pond, a pine island and a waterfall, all of which are key elements of the style. On the next few pages follow practical sequences on each of these three elements, with instructions on how to prepare and install them. This will give a good foundation plan for creating a pond garden and you can then vary these elements and introduce others in order to suit the needs of your own garden or your individual preferences.

Above: *The autumn colours of maple leaves are reflected in the pond at Tenju-an. Much of this garden dates back to the 13th century, with its simple design of two ponds, two islands and rocks arranged around a waterfall.*

Above: *The most stable way to support the edges of a pond is to use rocks, even if you want grass to grow close to those edges.*

TYPICAL FEATURES

The following elements are the most important to include in a pond garden:

- ponds with rocks around the edges and cobble and sandy beaches shelving into the water;

- one or two islands, typically planted with pines and grasses among rocks;

- red-painted Chinese-style bridge;

- meandering stream or waterfall feeding the pond;

- boathouse with small boat;

- undulating hills around the pond;

- winding gravel paths;

- plants such as cherry trees, Japanese maples, kerria, azalea, spiraea.

PLANNING AND VISUALIZATION

First think about the site you are planning to use and how it might need to be adapted for a pond garden. A series of features such as these would have a minimum area requirement of 45 x 45m (147 x 147ft). The size, position and style of a pond will need to fit the location, and you may also want to imitate ponds you have seen in other gardens.

When you are choosing a site for a waterfall, find the most natural place in your garden for a fall, ideally a raised hill from which the waterfall flow can be created. If you want to build islands in the pond, these must be planned before you build the pond. Sketch your ideas for how the garden will look and what will be included (see also Making a plan on page 144). The coloured design opposite shows how an initial concept and visualization of this scene might work and how the elements will link together when everything is in place.

WATER PRACTICALITIES

Water sources It is obviously essential to have a source of water. If you own a natural source, such as a spring or a stream, make sure that it is sufficient to keep the pond clear and healthy in the dry summer months. If not, or if you have no natural source, consult a water garden specialist on what type and size of pump you will need for your pond. Remember that the power of the pump you need has a cost implication for running the electricity to drive the pump.

Loss of water You should also get advice on how to top up the pond from losses due to evaporation, and from inevitable leakages and splashing.

Draining excess water You will need to make provision for too much water from excessive rain, and also allow for drainage.

Making a pond with a soil liner

For creating a small pond the flexible liner method shown on pages 188–9 is the best option; this liner is easy to install and readily available at garden centres. Alternatively, a large-scale pond may be required, one to include in a pond or stroll garden with more generous dimensions. In this case you can use either a natural clay liner, or more conveniently an enhanced soil liner or geosynthetic clay liner, shown in the method below. Manmade liners such as these are now more commonly used than clay.

A natural clay liner needs to be created from naturally occurring clay within the garden site. It is also advisable to get professional advice for this type of pond because it has to integrate within the natural landscape of the site. Because of these requirements, if you want a substantial pond, especially one that won't be damaged by aquatic animals or other wildlife, an enhanced soil liner such as the one shown here is usually a safer choice, while having many of the advantages of a natural clay liner.

In the following method, a synthetic clay liner is combined with sodium bentonite crystals to produce a strong seal. For effective installation, the pond should be empty.

Sodium bentonite can be used either in the construction of a new pond, or to repair an existing pond. It is absorbed into the soil at the base of the pond and then swells to create a block so the moisture cannot escape. Treating a pond in this way will create a watertight seal

Above: *Synthetic clay liners are the best method of sealing large ponds in areas where there is no natural clay subsoil to use for the job.*

that will last for many years. What is more, it is environmentally friendly and safe to use. Make sure you use a high quality sodium bentonite, apply it following the manufacturer's instructions and use the recommended amount depending on your soil type and the area that is being treated.

You will need
- string, sand or canes for marking the outline of the pond
- 5 x 5cm (2 x 2in) stakes (for a pond more than 2m (6½ft) across)
- a laser level
- a spade
- rolls of synthetic clay liner that are sufficient to cover the sides and floor of the pond, allowing for a 15cm (6in) overlap between each sheet
- a sufficient quantity of sodium bentonite crystals to cover each of the overlapped joints of the liner to expand and seal it
- garden hose
- topsoil to overlap the liner by 30cm (12in)
- a tile or stone slab

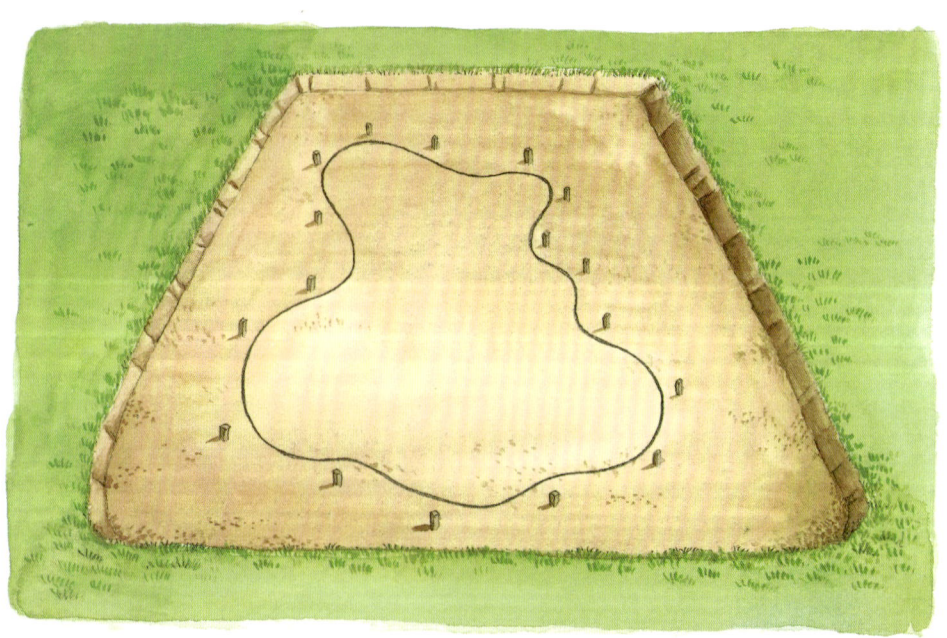

1 Remove at least 30cm (12in) of soil to a generous distance from the main working area and stockpile it for later use. If this excavation goes into the subsoil, keep the topsoil and subsoil in separate piles. Mark out the outline of the pond on the ground with string or sand or with a series of canes. With a large pond, drive in the stakes to indicate the level of water, as shown here.

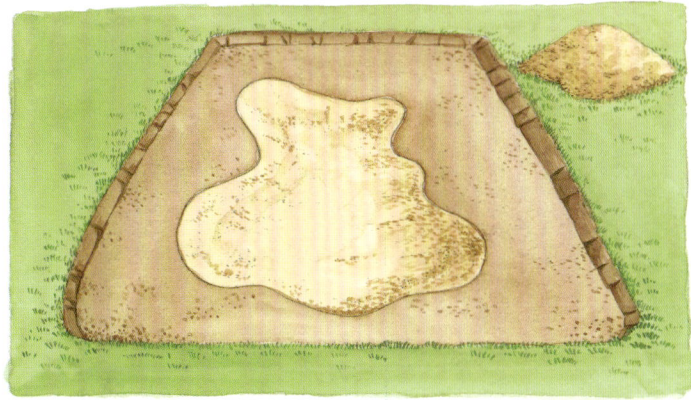 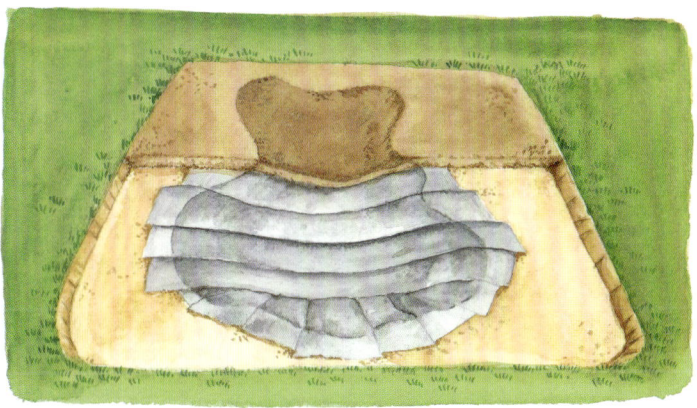

2 Excavate a saucer-shaped depression to a minimum of 60cm (2ft) and a maximum of 1.25m (4ft) at the deepest point. The sides should slope at no more than 30 degrees. Save the soil for replacing on the pond liner later and for grading around the sides.

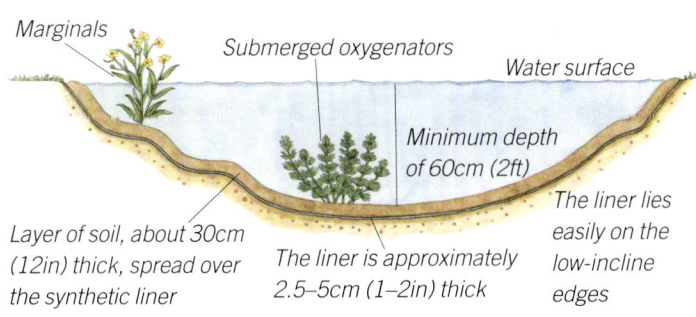

Above: *A cross-section of a synthetic clay-lined pond.*

Below: *A large and complex pond like that at Syoki-ho-en could be lined using clay or a geosynthetic clay liner.*

3 Roll sheets of the liner over the excavation and over the edges of the pond, overlapping them by about 15cm (6in). Sprinkle sodium bentonite crystals between and over the joints: once they absorb water, they will swell to fill any cracks, so completing the seal.

4 Cover the liner with a 30cm (12in) layer of soil, avoiding soil with heavy levels of fertilizer. The liner expands when in contact with water to several times its original thickness. This process will reverse and the mat may crack if it is allowed to dry out, so once the mat is in contact with moisture, either from rain or from the soil layer, keep it wet by laying a plastic sheet over the completed areas or by sprinkling it until you are ready to fill the pond.

5 Add water by resting the end of a garden hose on a tile or stone slab and letting the water in slowly. This prevents the freshly added soil from being dislodged.

6 Fine particles of debris, silt and clay suspended in the water may take several days or weeks to settle on the bottom, but the water will then begin to clear.

Making a pine island

A pine island can be one of the finest features of a traditional Japanese pond garden. This small rocky island would be planted with a twisted, weatherbeaten pine tree, and is reminiscent of the Matsushima islands off northern Japan (*matsu* means "pine" in Japanese). A pond of virtually any size could accommodate a small pine island, though obviously the pond and island will need to be in suitable proportions to achieve the desired effect. These islands are best surrounded by stones, which give a more natural look to the feature and can also be used to support the soil.

Above: *This pine island is located in the tranquil lake setting of the 19th-century Heian shrine, in Kyoto.*

Although it is possible to build an island after the pond has been made, it is always advisable to plan for an island during the pond-building process, rather than as an afterthought. Driving machinery or wheelbarrows across butyl-lined or clay-lined pools could damage the lining. If, however, the pond has been made, make a layer at least 30cm (12in) deep of protective soil, free of sharp stones, over a clay liner, or simply roll back a butyl liner.

Japanese black pines (*Pinus thunbergii*) are the best variety for pine islands as they can be easily shaped to give a picturesque windswept habit and they are also tolerant of wet roots. They do not like waterlogged soils, so build up the island to at least 60cm (2ft) higher than the water level to ensure that the pine roots have plenty of soil, not only to grow in but also to ensure they are sturdy enough to withstand winds.

PINE ISLAND PRACTICALITIES

Size The size of the island should be in proportion to the size of pond.

Shape Small islands should be simple in shape. Larger islands can have a more interesting outline.

Bridges If the island is close enough to the edge of the pond, you can link it to the mainland with a bridge.

Foundations Make sure that the foundations are at least twice the area of the exposed island.

Plants Pines do not like waterlogged roots, so make sure they have access to dry soil. Dwarf miscanthus looks good with pines and rocks.

Wild areas Leave some long grass to encourage wildfowl to nest.

Rocks Rocks blend well with pine trees. You can make a turtle or crane island by suggesting the shape with rocks.

You will need
- underlay and flexible liner
- scissors to cut underlay
- a number of rocks to support the soil
- interestingly shaped rocks to place on the pine island
- topsoil
- a spade
- a crowbar
- a wheelbarrow or small dumper truck
- a Japanese black pine tree (more than one in different sizes will also look good)
- grass seed or any ornamental grasses to decorate the island, including *Miscanthus yakushimenis* and *Molinia caerulea*

CONSTRUCTING A PINE ISLAND OVER A BUTYL LINER

1 Drain the pond, if necessary, then roll back the butyl liner and underlay. Make a large mound of soil where you want your island to be.

2 Lay the underlay and flexible liner over the top of the soil mound. Cut a hole in the underlay and liner so that an area of soil is exposed, but ensure that the liner is taken well above the waterline.

3 Add a further mound of soil on top of the foundation to create a gently curving island. Stack rocks on top of each other all around the edge of the island in order to hold the dry soil in place.

4 Plant the pine(s) and sow the grass seed, or plant grass plants. Keep well watered until established.

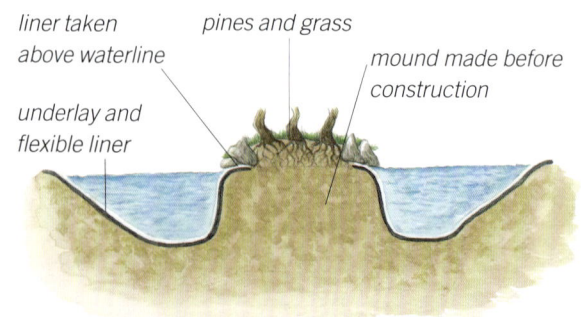

Above: *This method ensures that the pine roots do not become waterlogged.*

CONSTRUCTING A PINE ISLAND OVER A CLAY OR SYNTHETIC CLAY LINER

1 Drain the pond, if necessary, then protect the clay liner with an extra 30cm (12in) of soil. If draining is not possible, use a tracked vehicle to build the island. Alternatively, you could use a large digger with a long reach, if the island is made close enough to the edge of the pond.

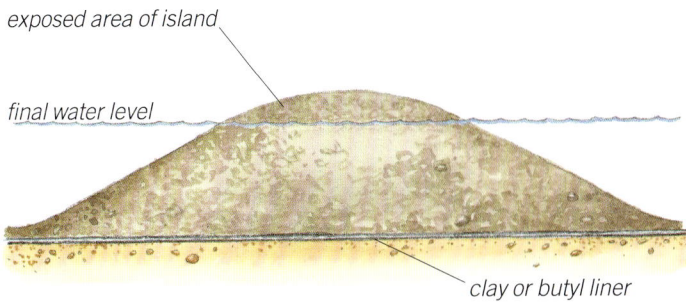

2 Build a mound of soil that will be the base of the island over the top of the liner. There is no need to roll the matting over the island. Make sure that the sides slope at no more than 30 degrees, which will keep the banks stable.

3 Keep building the island up with soil until it is 60–100cm (24–40in) above the water line. This will give the pine tree plenty of water-free root room in which to grow. There is no need to shape the mound at this stage.

Below: A good example of a well-shaped Japanese black pine on a rocky islet. The island is suggestive of a turtle, with the upright stones to the right of the island representing its head.

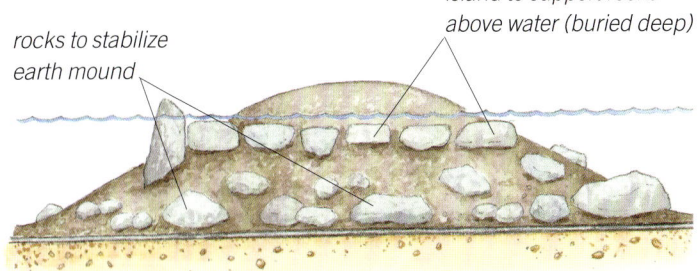

4 Bury rocks deeply all over the mound, from the base up to just below the water line. These will be the foundation for any rocks above water.

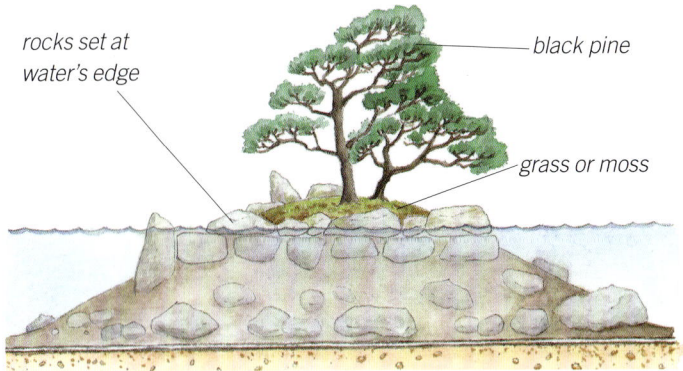

5 Build up an arrangement of rocks on top to imitate a rocky island. Shape the mound to look naturalistic. Add more soil between some of the rocks and use one of these crevices to plant a pine tree. Scatter grass seed over the soil areas in the autumn or spring and water well. Plant some ornamental grasses between one or two of the rocks.

Building a waterfall

Waterfalls were an important feature of Heian pond gardens. They were regarded as the abode of Fudo, an important personification of the Buddha, while the two main supporting stones were considered to be the Buddha's attendants. As a plentiful, natural, life-giving source, water was regarded as sacred, and waterfalls therefore tended to be well camouflaged in the landscape. The *Sakuteiki* says "There are many ways to make a waterfall, but no matter what, they should always face the moon, so that falling water will reflect in the moonlight."

Above: *The sound of a trickling waterfall can create as much atmosphere as a torrent. A stone is often placed at the bottom, at the point at which the water falls, to make a feature of the sound. A notable example of this is the stone at the Dragon Gate cascade in Kinkaku-ji.*

First choose the "waterfall stone", the one that the water actually spills over. This will determine the height of the fall. You may decide to build a series of falls, but remember that a large amount of water does not necessarily mean a better effect. A small waterfall falling from a height of 1m (40in) into shallow water or on to a carp stone, a tumbling cascade or a plain sheet of water can be just as effective. Always follow the "desire" of the stones and the way they want to direct the water. If you are using a recycling system with an electric pump, try to minimize the amount of water that will be lost through splashing.

WATERFALL PRACTICALITIES

Spillage Use a butyl liner to contain any potential water spillage.

Sound When planning, think of the sound effects as well as appearance.

Security Bed the base stones well into concrete to make a secure beginning.

Flow Test the water flow as you place stones using a hose to see the effect.

Control Be patient and flexible, water is difficult to manage when it is in freefall.

Flow rate The waterfall will change character if the flow rate is changed. If you are using a pump, make sure you buy one with a variable flow valve so you can manage the water flow to suit your waterfall.

You will need
- a good selection of large rocks to suit the shape of the proposed waterfall
- a spade
- a crowbar
- a large sheet of butyl rubber to fit the dimensions of the waterfall (note that you need to lay wider than the fall itself)
- a strip of liner sealing tape (optional if pond is clay lined)
- concreting sand and cement
- a wheelbarrow
- a concrete mixer (optional)
- machinery, such as a sack truck or skid loader for moving rocks if they are too heavy and awkward to move by hand (see moving rocks on page 70–71)

HOW TO CONSTRUCT A WATERFALL

1 First make an outline sketch of how you would like the waterfall to look. Then mark out the proposed position on the ground. If you have already made a selection of rocks, these will help to decide the design; otherwise, select special rocks to suit the intended shape of your cascade.

2 Dig out an area three or four times wider than the waterfall itself. This will give you plenty of room to work and to spread out a large sheet of butyl liner. The liner will lie under the whole structure of the waterfall so that any splashes and leakages will find their way back into the pond.

The liner is laid wider than the waterfall

Stones to weight down liner

The waterfall liner overlaps the pond liner, creating a sealed joint

3 If the pond has a butyl liner, lift up the edge of the liner and tuck it under the waterfall liner. The pond liner should be well above the pond water level. Seal the two liners together with the sealing strip. If the pond is clay lined, let the waterfall liner drop under the waterline.

4 Make a firm concrete base for the first foundation stones. These may be the two main supporting stones or simply the base from which you can build up a series of stones for a cascade-style waterfall.

5 Measure where you expect the water to fall and erect the main stone. Seal the joints between it and the main supporting stones.

6 You will need to build a header pool, even if the waterfall is being fed by a stream. The header pool will help to keep the flow of water constant.

7 Add more rocks to the sides and above the header pool to make a naturalistic setting and to help retain the soil on the steep sides. Make provision for some soil pockets to plant sedges, ferns and other waterside plants. Make sure all concrete joints are skilfully disguised.

8 Allow the waterfall base to open up by positioning a number of smaller stones and cobbles there. Having observed the flow of the water, place a "carp stone" at the base to receive the water, which will spill over and around it.

BUILDING A STREAM AND WATERFALL SYSTEM

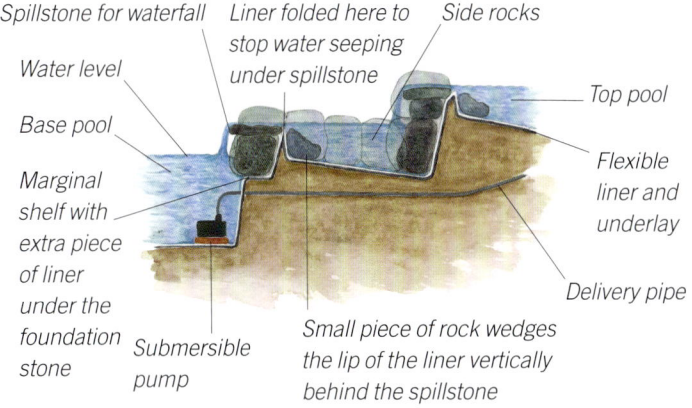

Below: *With a natural water course and interesting contours, you can recreate the effects of a mountain stream. The Tully Japanese Garden has carefully observed the rocks and flow of natural streams.*

The dry garden style

The dry garden is the most contemplative of all the Japanese garden styles. It is also the most abstract. You do need a fairly good understanding of the origins of this style to make one that is truly effective. Have a look at photos of the famous dry Zen gardens of Japan, and see if you think that your site would be suitable. You will also need to keep it tidy, so it's not an ideal choice for a large family garden. Dry gardens are especially well suited to courtyards and small enclosed spaces – even those areas that are inhospitable to plants.

Above: *Dry gardens use gravel and rocks to suggest the flow and expanse of water in its different forms.*

ELEMENTS OF A DRY GARDEN

As its name suggests, a dry garden's essential elements are dry materials in the form of sand and gravel, which are often raked into patterns, and carefully chosen and strategically placed rocks. Another important element is a flat site, as the extensive use of sand and gravel means that a level surface is highly preferable to a slope.

Sand and gravel

The "dry" aspect of the garden consists of sand or gravel spread to represent an expanse of water, either in the form of the sea or a lake. Dry gardens might also contain a dry "stream" and a dry "waterfall", although these are not essential. The use of all this dry material means that dry gardens need very little maintenance: the occasional raking of the gravel (and the trimming of any shrubs that might be included) is all that is required.

The sand and gravel will usually be contained within a rectangular frame. (In Japan, they are found in rectangular courtyards in Zen temples.)

Rocks

Once you have established that your garden is suitable, the key to a successful dry garden is in the arrangements of the rocks. There are many arrangements to choose from, for example a Buddhist grouping, where a central stone represents the Buddha or the sacred mountain Mount Shumisen; a grouping that represents different aspects of the Mystic Isles of immortals; or an arrangement simply placed with intuition and instinct – you will have to try this one out by moving your rocks until you are happy with the effect. All of these arrangements should be designed with a sense of the tranquil, and should avoid any excessive forms in shape or size.

Plants

If rocks are difficult to obtain, or you have decided not to use them, interesting arrangements can also be made with groups of plants clipped to the shape of distant hills or to represent sacred sites.

Left: *Mirei Shigemori, in his finest work at Tofuku-ji, used bold groups of rocks and stylized gravel raking, to illustrate the ancient Chinese myth of the Mystic Isles.*

Left: *Most dry gardens are designed in courtyards, where the rectangular shape in a sense represents the frame of a painting, while the spread of sand represents the white "unpainted" canvas. Despite this, they can be equally effective and suggestive in more naturalistic surroundings, such as this example in Kew Gardens in England, although it is more difficult to play with the sense of scale.*

Below: *Rocks set near the edge of an expanse of gravel can suggest a river or lakeside. Well-placed rocks need simple plantings to enhance their form: these rocks at Kew are set against a plain wall with a dramatically pruned pine.*

THE DRY GARDEN STYLE 159

Garden plan: a dry garden

The best place for a dry garden is a courtyard enclosed by walls or fences. This contains the garden so it can be seen as a painting "hung" within its frame, and protects it from the elements. The deeper Zen meaning of these dry gardens is one of emptiness of mind – a goal of Zen meditation. The whole garden should possess an air of restraint and be a calm and spiritual place of sand, rocks and maybe a few plants.

TOPIARY IN THE DRY GARDEN

The use of topiary to represent a landscape can be seen in some of the great dry landscape gardens such as the Ryoan-ji or Shoden-ji. A weathered pine might suggest a mountain or a seaside landscape, and groups of clipped plants could symbolize a range of distant hills.

1 Make a sketch of the site and draw an outline of the landscape you want to reproduce. This kind of design typically incorporates *shakkei* (borrowed landscape), so look outside your garden to see if there is anything you could integrate. Get further inspiration by looking through a book on Chinese landscape painting. You may want to reproduce a favourite landscape that is familiar to you.

2 Decide whether to buy small, young plants, which are cheaper and easier to establish, but will take time to grow, or larger plants for a more instant result. Use plants that will be different sizes, as a variation in heights is effective. If you cannot obtain large azaleas, you should be able to buy large plants of cheaper unclipped boxwood, which you can clip to your own shape. Other evergreens could be used, such as varieties of camellia, photinia or osmanthus.

3 If the soil on your site is poor or of the wrong type for azaleas, which prefer acid soil, dig out generous holes for each plant. Make sure that the area is well drained or put some gravel in the bottom of the holes, then fill with the soil mix you require and plant your specimen plants.

4 Spread the gravel and sand for the raked "dry water" effect (see pages 168–9 for notes on gravel and drainage).

Above: *The interplay between the breaking waves of sand against the tiled "frame".*

Right: *Black bamboo is suitable as it does not get too big or spread around.*

Right: *Mossy mounds may need frequent watering in order to keep them fresh and green.*

Right: *Clipped azaleas can have the same solid presence as standing rocks.*

GARDEN PLAN: A DRY GARDEN 161

How to make a dry garden

Dry gardens are generally best sited on level ground, unless you intend to include a dry waterfall, but even this can be built up in one corner of the garden. A garden called the Daisen-in in the Daitokuji Temple in Kyoto portrays an entire mountain landscape and has almost all the elements of a dry garden: rocks and bent pines, dry streams, a dry waterfall, a natural stone slab bridge and even a block of stone "floating" on the sea of sand. Here is a suggestion for a dry garden design that incorporates these key features, all contained in a defined rectangular area. The planting is restricted to a pine and some bamboo, interspersed with stones and rocks and surrounded by raked gravel. The three stages of creating this garden are shown in the following pages: positioning rocks, placing edging stones and improving drainage.

Above: *While dry gardens are popularly known as Zen gardens, the Japanese name is* kare-sansui, *which translates as "dry mountain water", with sand or gravel representing water and the rocks the mountains.*

Above: *This dry garden was made on the site of an old barn with little or no soil. This factor, combined with the old walls and level site, made a dry garden the natural choice.*

TYPICAL FEATURES OF A DRY GARDEN

A dry garden should be a rectangular level courtyard within three walls, the fourth side used as a viewing platform and including the following:

• a rectangle of edging stones or tiles to frame the garden;

• rocks of interesting shapes;

• gravel, preferably a light silvery grey;

• moss around the bases of rocks to make them look like islands;

• stepping stones and lanterns;

• bent pines and small-leaved evergreens to tuck around the rocks;

• clipped azaleas to imitate hills;

• dry waterfalls and landscapes with dry streams and bridges.

PLANNING AND VISUALIZATION

Before you start you must have a good idea of the elements you want to introduce and be certain that you can get all of them to the site. Rocks are especially difficult to move in narrow confines, but mini-diggers can get through openings of around 1m (1yd) wide, which might be sufficient. If you are contemplating growing plants in your dry garden, make sure the soil is right for them. If there is no soil on site or the drainage is poor, you can build up planting areas between rock arrangements or dig trenches to improve the drainage.

ROCKS, EDGING AND GRAVEL

The first priority is to get the rocks in place as this will be the most awkward and messy job. After this, you can frame your "picture" with edging stones that will contain the area of gravel and will set off both the gravel and the rocks. In Japan these edges are often quite elaborate, using a combination of tiles, strips of granite, and a row of cobbles that doubles up as a drainage channel. Even if you are using a more contemporary design, unconfined in an open space, it will still be necessary to build an edge to contain the gravel or sand.

The gravel will need to be spread around 5–6cm (2–2½in) deep if you intend to rake it into patterns (see pages 78–79). It can be less deep if you want the gravel to be a practical element that can be walked over. However, the spiritual, Zen quality of a dry garden is more effectively achieved by the creation of elements for both viewing and contemplation.

Positioning rocks

Rocks are seen as important natural symbols of strength. They are used in many Japanese gardens, with the order and positioning seen as key to the balance of the garden. They can vary from monumental sizes that need digging in and cementing to stabilize them, to smaller rocks that can be moved by hand. Rocks should always be placed in a naturalistic manner, so that they look balanced in relation to each other. Traditional Japanese gardeners, attributing a living spirit to rocks, described this as "following their desire".

Above: *Rocks with interesting grain patterns and markings are ideal for dry gardens.*

The placing of rocks is a crucial aspect of Japanese gardening. You may choose to employ professional landscapers, but with some guidance it is possible to organize it yourself, so that you understand the process, from hiring the right equipment to all the safety issues. Once you have established how you are going to move them, you will need to know how to position them both safely and artistically. Establish the rough weight of the rocks so that you can be advised on the right size of machinery and correct gauge of lifting straps. See also pages 70–71 on moving rocks.

You will need
- two people to carry the rock
- protective clothing (e.g. hard hat, gloves and boots)
- strong straps (from a hire shop)
- a scaffolding pole and shackle
- a spade and a crowbar
- smaller propping stones
- a fencing stake
- a sledgehammer
- loose soil for backfilling

ROCK PRACTICALITIES

Finding rocks It may be hard to find rocks that match your artistic intentions exactly, so be flexible when arranging them.

Buying rocks Allow yourself one or two extra ones to give more choice.

Placing rocks Move back from time to time to a different vantage point. The rocks must look right from all possible viewing angles.

Adjusting rocks Take your time to make sure the rocks feel right. It may seem like hard work, but large rocks will be very difficult to move later, once the garden is established.

Leaving rocks Once you have set the rocks and finished the garden, it will be virtually impossible to move any of the bigger rocks without considerable disruption.

1 Decide which way round and up you want the rock to be. Then measure the amount of rock that will show above ground and how much needs to be buried. Tall upright rocks will need to be buried deep to ensure they are stable. The more angled you want the rock to be, the deeper the hole should be.

2 Draw a line with a piece of chalk to indicate ground level on the rock. Measure again so that you know how deep to dig the receiving hole, taking into account the extra 4–6cm (1½–2½in) of gravel that will be laid over the area.

3 Dig the hole, and lay a fencing stake, with a spirit level on it, across the top, raised to the height of the finished gravel.

4 Check the hole has been dug to the right depth. Digging too deep may make the soil loose below the rock and cause it to "settle" too much. Allow for plenty of room each side for packing and adjusting the angle of the rock.

5 Using a digger, lower the strapped-up rock very slowly into the hole. Two people should be in place to help to guide the rock as it is lowered, twisting it so that it is angled correctly.

6 With the rock safely strapped up and attached to the lifting gear, try out different angles and positions until you are satisfied that it is placed where you want it.

7 Keeping the rock still strapped up and attached to the digger, support the undersides and sides of the rock with smaller stones. These can also be used to wedge between two rocks for support.

8 Use a sledgehammer to ram the stones tightly into place. Then test the rock for its overall stability. The rock should be in a "rock solid" position even before you start to pack around it with soil.

9 Backfill the hole with a loamy or clay soil. Sandy soil will not pack well and is far too loose. With the butt end of a fencing stake, ram the soil between the stones.

10 Ram the final layers of soil firmly around the rock with a sledgehammer.

11 Rake the surrounding soil until it is level. Set the accompanying rocks in place. In this case they are smaller and lower, and therefore don't need such a deep and solid foundation.

12 The final stage of the process is to water the soil in around the rocks to remove all air pockets and to help compact the ground.

MOVING ROCKS

There are various practical considerations to bear in mind when positioning rocks:

- move large rocks with a mini-digger (see pages 70–71);
- use tough nylon/canvas fibre straps to minimize damage to the rock;
- so you can calculate the foundation depth, decide which part of the rock will be visible in the finished garden;
- dig the hole slightly deeper than you need so you have the flexibility to adjust the position later;
- try the rock in different positions and angles before removing the straps;
- check the rock for stability and fill in tightly with soil.

Placing edging stones

Most dry gardens are set within a framed space, whether it be in the open with a fenced area or in a courtyard with existing walls surrounding the space. This framing serves both to contain the dry sand or gravel and to make the garden look more like a painting hung within a frame. In all the famous dry gardens, you will notice the considerable care that is taken in choosing the edging materials and how they are laid. Long pavers of granite or dark blue tiles, or both, can be used with a channel of cobbles between them as an aid to drainage.

In your own garden, you can use any native materials. For this project lengths of stone made of the same local sandstone as the rocks have been used. These edging stones are fairly uniform but by no means perfect rectangles. These stones are being used to separate a border of cobbles against the surrounding wall from the dry sea of gravel.

Above: *Edging stones not only help to separate planting areas from gravelled areas but can also make decorative features of their own, such as this raised area in the Tully Japanese Garden. The Japanese pay close attention to detail in all parts of the garden.*

You will need
- a hand-picked selection of stones
- builder's twine and pegs
- a tape measure
- a spirit level
- a pick
- concreting sand and cement
- a shovel
- a rubber-headed hammer
- a brick-laying trowel
- weed-suppressing fabric
- scissors
- cobbles
- a rock to break up the uniformity of the edging (optional)

EDGING MATERIALS

The following materials can be used for framing areas of the dry garden:

- local or salvaged materials;
- old, slightly misshapen bricks;
- old granite setts;
- old roofing or floor tiles set on edge;
- charred wooden post tops.

1 Set up a builder's line parallel to one of the walls and mark the level of the outside of the edging stones, using a tape measure to check that it is an equal distance from the wall at both ends. On a flat site, use a spirit level to check the line is level. On a sloping site, set the line up tightly at either end of the edging run. Dig out a trench for the edging stones, a little deeper and wider than the stones themselves, always keeping an eye on the line. Lay out your row of edging stones so that they are easily reached.

2 Make a concreting mix using soft or sharp sand mix, eight parts sand to one part cement (most cement will have mixture recommendations on the bags). Small amounts of concrete can be easily mixed in a wheelbarrow with a spade but larger amounts might require a concrete mixer. Towable concrete mixers, both electrical and petrol-powered, can be hired from plant hire depots. Shovel a small amount into the trench, enough to set 1m (1yd) of edging stones at a time.

3 Set one of the edging stones on to the cement bed so that it sits slightly higher than the builder's line.

4 Using the hammer, tap the stone firmly until it becomes level with the line. Repeat with the other stones until the path edge is complete. The stone ends should be close enough to prevent sand and gravel slipping between them.

5 Shore up the edging stones with the concreting mix, making sure that the mix will not show above the finished gravel.

6 Spread some soft sand between the edging stones and the wall. Remove any stones or blocks of earth that are still protruding.

7 Measure, cut and lay weed-suppressing fabric over the layer of soft sand and tuck in the edges well.

8 Spread a layer of cobbles over the fabric, keeping the level of the cobbles below the top of the stones.

9 For an unusual touch, place a natural rock, one that can be easily moved using a sack truck, into a pre-measured gap. Scoop out 6–10cm (2½–4in) of soil and spread a layer of 4cm (1½in) of sharp sand, then lay the rock directly on to the bed of sharp sand.

Improving drainage

Drainage requirements must be carefully considered in the early stages of planning a dry garden, especially if you are intending to grow plants. Dry gardens are most frequently created on level sites, and often close to buildings, where heavy machinery and ground works may have caused compaction of the natural texture of the soil. This is especially true of gardens built on clay soils or on a concrete base. In such situations, flexible drainage pipes may need to be laid to improve the drainage.

Poor drainage will kill plants and may cause damage to buildings and walls. If a dry garden is constructed over badly drained heavy clay soil, the water will stay on the surface after heavy rain once the rocks and edging stones are in place. To remedy this, the best solution is to lay a network of feeder drains and a main drain to ensure that the water can flow away naturally.

Above: *On some level sites you will need to make allowance for drainage. This can be set around the edge of the dry garden and made into a design detail of its own. A trench filled with large gravel or cobbles may be enough to disguise such areas.*

You will need
- 10cm- (4in-) diameter flexible perforated drainage pipe
- angled joints
- a sharp knife
- a spade and shovel
- a wheelbarrow
- a hose
- 10–20mm (½–¾in) pea gravel
- crushed stone with stone dust (known as scalpings or hoggin)
- coloured gravel or sand
- a roller or wacker-plate
- a rake

1 Mark the layout of the drains with marker paint. Then dig the main drain to a depth of at least 45cm (18in) and the feeder drains, closer to the surface, at 30–35cm (12–14in) deep. The trenches should slope to give a fall of at least 10cm (4in) per 20m (20yd).

2 Spread a layer of pea gravel (small, smooth, rounded stones) 4cm (1½in) deep in the bottom of the trench.

3 Lay the flexible drainage pipe in the trench and check that the slope allows an effective fall of water by filling with a hose at the top end. Cover the pipe with at least a further 10cm (4in) of gravel. Leave uncovered in places where the feeder pipes will join it.

4 Cut the main pipe at the places where the feeder pipes (from the planted areas) will join it. (The perforated drainage pipes can easily be cut with a sharp knife.)

5 At the junctions of the feeder drains to the main drain, you will need to fit angled joints. These joints are often designed to take different sized pipes; cut out the size that fits your chosen pipe sizes. Once again, cover over all the pipes with gravel.

6 Spread a 5–7.5cm (2–3in) layer of crushed stone/stone dust mix over the entire area of the dry garden where the raked sand or gravel will eventually be.

7 Spread the layer until it is level, filling in potholes and making sure the drainage trenches are filled in. The roller will not be able to firm in narrow trenches so these should be compressed with your feet. This will help to avoid any subsidence later on.

DRAINAGE PRACTICALITIES

Soak-away You will need to check for the nearest point for collecting storm water. If this is at some distance, you should construct a soak-away or French drain to collect the drain water.

Location Check the location for all services, such as sewerage pipes, electric cables, gas pipes and mains water pipes, before you dig any trenches and before you decide where to lay the main drain.

Flow Check how the drainage levels will work. The principle to follow is that the main drain must be dug to the lowest level, so that all the drains on the site can feed into it. This can be done by eye and by feeding a hose into one of the drains to check for flow, or by using levelling equipment for more precise measurements.

Fall The fall for a drain should be no less than 10cm (4in) in every 20m (20yd).

Capacity On large sites, a larger main drain of 15cm (6in) diameter may be required.

8 Using the mechanical wacker-plate or a roller, compact the surface. If any subsidence occurs in this process, fill in any depressions with more crushed stone and roll again, until the whole surface is perfectly level.

9 Spread the gravel or sand over the surface to the required depth and rake it level. For sand that will be raked in patterns the depth should be at least 6cm (2½in).

Right: On this site, the subsoil was of solid clay so a drainage pipe was laid around the perimeter of the garden. Additional drains feed from the planting holes into the main drain.

IMPROVING DRAINAGE

The tea garden style

This type of garden is characterized by pathways and thresholds, and represents a journey to a more spiritual world. You enter a tea garden through a covered outer gateway, or *sotomon*. Inside, the garden is divided into two halves: an outer area, where a small waiting room can be placed, and an inner area, where the tea house will be found. Linking the two areas is the path, or *roji*, which leads the visitor past shelter seats and through a stooping gate to reach the ultimate goal: the tea house itself and the host within who waits to welcome the guests.

Above: *Water basins and lanterns were originally set alongside the tea paths of Japanese gardens as part of the tea ceremony.*

ELEMENTS OF A TEA GARDEN

There are four important elements that make up a Japanese tea garden: the tea house, the path or *roji* (dewy path) and garden around it, lanterns to line the path, and a water basin.

Tea house

A tea house is traditionally a rustic building set within a tea garden. It can be quite small and hidden away in a secluded place, but in later Japanese gardens it became a more open building placed with a view over the garden. This makes it more like a tea arbour, or a gazebo. The original essence of the tea house was as a "mountain place in the city", a secluded rustic hermitage and retreat from busy lives.

Path

The path, usually a stepping-stone path, will pass by the waiting room and through a small "stooping gate" – encouraging visitors to be aware of the world they are leaving behind and the wilderness and realms of higher

Left: *Reaching the tea house is the ultimate goal of a tea garden. The route typically consists of gateways that mark significant stages of the journey, and the tea house itself can often not be viewed until the final stage.*

consciousness ahead. The wilderness does not need to be literal – it can be suggested by "mountain" plants, usually glossy-leaved evergreens such as camellias and aucubas, planted under a canopy of maples.

Lanterns and water basins
The path and the area around the main water basin should be lit by carefully positioned lanterns, originally because tea ceremonies were often held in the evening. The water basin is an important feature representing the need for cleansing before entering the tea house.

Right: *The veranda pillars at Hosen-in frame the scene from the tea house.*

Below: *Shelter seats are placed alongside the tea path for guests to wait in comfort before they are summoned to the tea house.*

THE TEA GARDEN STYLE 171

Garden plan: a tea garden

The principles of making a tea garden can be adapted to almost any space. The main feature is the path of stepping stones inside the main gate that leads to the tea house via a waiting room, past lanterns and water basins, and through intervening gates. The garden should become wilder as the path approaches the tea house. This, as in so many of the Japanese arts, is achieved symbolically rather than literally.

THE MIDDLE CRAWL-THROUGH GATE
This gate is placed halfway through the tea garden between the inner and outer *roji*. In leaving the everyday world for the spiritual world, the guest is forced to bow their head, either under a low lintel or, as in the style of gate described below, by pushing their way under it.

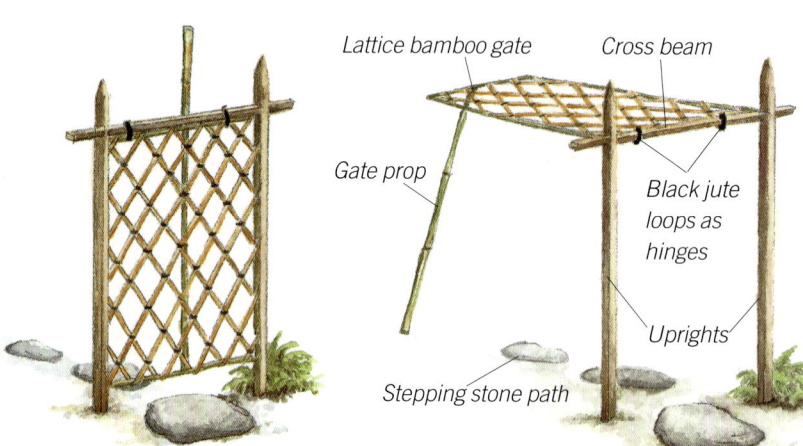

1 Using the gate as a guide, mark where the two upright posts will be. They should be 7.5–10cm (3–4in) square or round and 2.5m (8ft) long.

2 Dig holes 60–70cm (24–28in) deep for the posts. If the soil is firm, simply firm the two posts in around the bases. In loose ground, you should concrete the base of the two posts.

3 Measure the height of the gate, and trim off the tops of the two posts to the right height.

4 Fix the cross beam (which should be the same width as the posts and 1m [1yd] long) on top of the posts, creating mortise-and-tenon joints, by drilling holes for a piece of dowelling and pushing it through, or by screwing the crossbeam down with two 15cm (6in) screws on to each post.

5 Hang a lightweight bamboo gate, 1.5–2m (5–6½ft) high, on to the cross beam using some thick black jute for hinges.

6 Attach a bamboo pole 4cm (1½in) in diameter and 2.5m (8ft) long to the base of the gate. This pole will be used to prop the gate open.

Left: Guests rest in a waiting room before the host invites them to go into the tea house itself.

Left: *A fence and gate along the tea path divide the garden into two halves. This one is a hinged bamboo gate, but could equally be a middle crawl-through gate.*

Left: *The* tsukubai, *or "crouching basin", is always accompanied by a lantern.*

Plant list
1 *Enkianthus perulatus*
2 Clipped azalea
3 Autumn-flowering camellia (*Camellia sasanqua*)
4 Sedge (*Carex*)
5 Domestic bamboo (*Nandina domestica*)
6 Red pine (*Pinus densiflora*)
7 Japanese black pine (*Pinus thunbergii*)
8 Japanese maple (*Acer palmatum*)
9 Fern (many species)

GARDEN PLAN: A TEA GARDEN 173

How to make a tea garden

The art of creating a Japanese tea garden is not just in placing the features: it requires some understanding of the philosophy behind the tea ceremony. Once familiar with this, you can combine the elements of the stepping-stone path, lanterns, water basins and plants into a style that is both unified and unique to your own tastes and culture. The tea garden adapts well to small areas: the essential wandering path can be as short as 5m (around 16ft), though in a large garden it could be 30m (100ft) or more. The practical sequences that follow you will show you how to create the main features of a tea garden: arranging a *tsukubai*, setting a lantern and laying a stepping-stone path. The example shown below combines all the elements; there is room for a tea house, but the path will lead to a "tea room" in the house itself.

Above: *A tall water basin of this type would commonly be found next to a veranda in a courtyard garden, or as a self-contained unit on the "spiritual" journey to the tea house through the tea garden.*

Camellia japonica

Lantern

Bamboo clump

Fern

Gravel sea

Stone water basin

Fore stone

Moss

Ophiopogon

Stepping stones

174 CREATING A GARDEN

Right: *Using a sea of cobbles around a* tsukubai *arrangement aids drainage when the water spills out of the basin; this feature has also become a core aspect of the design.*

PLANNING AND VISUALIZATION

Once you have established the goal of the tea path (i.e. the tea house or tea room), you will want to work out an intriguing journey for the path to take. At some point on the path, look for a suitable place to create the *tsukubai* arrangement – the combination of the water basin and lantern. If your tea garden is large, you might want to divide the garden into two halves – an inner and outer *roji* – placing a waiting room in the inner garden and a middle crawl-through gate (see page 172) to divide them. Build up the planting to suggest a wilderness, with rocks informally placed at the sides of the path, using ferns and sedges and also including other plants tucked in among them.

Even if you have only a very small space, try to place all the elements to create the sense of a journey that leaves the busy world behind, so that you and your guests can feel you are entering a place of spiritual purity.

TYPICAL FEATURES OF A TEA GARDEN

In addition to the tea house or tea room, the following are usual elements:

- an entrance gate;
- a winding stepping-stone path;
- a water basin with cobbles around it;
- lanterns to light the path and basin;
- a waiting room or bench for guests;
- a middle crawl-through gate;
- woodland planting of camellias, maples and bamboos, and low planting of ferns and sedges around rocks.

WATER BASIN

The simplest system is to source an attractive basin and fill the basin by hand, as you would a bird bath. But if you want your water basin to be constantly topped up, you will need to build a reservoir under the basin to receive the spillage. The water can then be drained to a soak-away, a pond or a mains drain, or be recycled by a small pump placed in the base of the reservoir (see pages 112–113). If you use an electric pump, and if you want an electric lantern, you will need a source of electricity that is both safe and fully weatherproofed.

Arranging a *tsukubai*

The *tsukubai* is one of the key ingredients of the tea garden. The term *tsukubai* means a low crouching basin that guests use to wash their hands and face, a spiritual cleansing before they enter the teahouse. It has also come to refer to the whole arrangement of the low water basin and its accompanying lantern, the paving stone that the guests stand on when they use the water basin, and the sea of gravel and cobbles around it. The paving stone, or laver stone, on which visitors stand, results in the lowering of the body before water, indicating humility.

The water basin is replenished with fresh water each time the tea guests arrive. This can be done either by manually emptying the basin and refilling it with a jug (pitcher) – the easiest method – or by a having a constantly dripping flow of water fed from a tap or natural spring via a bamboo pipe, which then overflows into the reservoir below, where the water is either drained away or recycled by an electric pump.

Above: *Water can be fed to the basin through a bamboo pipe. Allowing a tap to drip slowly but steadily at the source will ensure that you keep a constant supply of fresh water in the basin. Cleanliness and purity are viewed as sacred, and are crucial aspects of the Japanese tea ceremony.*

SETTING UP A *TSUKUBAI*

The elements that accompany the *tsukubai* are as important as the water basin itself for an authentic setting.

Rocks Place two or more flat-topped rocks on either side of the *tsukubai*. These are useful to stand a lantern on and for guests to place their personal effects on while they are washing themselves.

Cobbles Arrange a sea of cobbles around the *tsukubai*. While not essential, this makes an attractive surrounding for the basin as well as helping to keep the surface area around it dry.

Ladle Keep a bamboo ladle near or laid over the basin for guests to scoop up water to wash with. The ladle will need to be kept clean, as bamboo becomes mouldy quickly when it is left damp; alternatively you can place it by the basin only when guests are expected.

Drainage Provide a drainage outlet for larger basins (see pages 112–113).

You will need
- a spade
- a wheelbarrow
- a reservoir kit (optional; see page 112)
- a water basin
- rocks
- a flat stepping stone
- large-diameter gravel or cobbles
- a bamboo spout (optional)

1 Having selected the position of your *tsukubai*, first dig a hole with a spade to accommodate the reservoir you have chosen. The hole should be made deep enough in order to leave the rim of the reservoir approximately 4cm (1½in) proud of the soil level.

2 Place the reservoir in the hole, check that it is level, backfill with sand and then firm it in place.

3 Level the surrounding soil for the area that will represent the "sea". If you are not recycling water from the reservoir (see pages 112–113) you could use a large plastic pot that can be filled with gravel to help with drainage. If you do this you will need to make sure there are adequate holes in the base of the pot for the water to drain through.

4 Spread a layer of sharp sand 4cm (1½in) deep over the soil area, so that it lies level with the rim of the reservoir. The sand will help both to keep the site clean and to act as a free-draining medium on to which to lay the cobbles. Place the metal grill over the reservoir and then lay a piece of fine plastic mesh over that. The mesh should be fine enough to prevent debris, soil or sand falling into the reservoir; this is especially critical if you intend to use a recycling pump, which can easily become blocked by debris.

5 Place a few cobbles to secure the mesh in place and lower the water basin on to the middle of the grill.

6 Spread a layer of cobbles or large gravel over the area to a depth where there is no soil, sand or mesh visible.

7 Collect the cobbles around the basin. Place your stepping stone next to the basin and firm it in so it is surrounded by cobbles or gravel.

8 Place the surface layer of cobbles by hand, arranging them so that they fit snugly together and lie in an attractive but natural manner.

Right: *Plant some ferns, sedge or ophiopogon close to the basin as well as around the surrounding rocks.*

ARRANGING A TSUKUBAI 177

Setting a lantern

Lanterns are integral to any Japanese tea garden. Originally they were found only outside Buddhist temples, but they were later introduced to the tea garden as the tea ceremony became influenced by Zen Buddhist symbolism. The lamps were lit as an offering to the Buddha, and early ones accommodated an oil lamp. Lanterns were also needed to light the tea path, as tea ceremonies often took place in the early evening. The stone lantern is an important connecting factor in the Japanese garden, as both a raw material and a manmade element.

Above: *Although most lanterns are placed as sculptural features in the tea garden, they are sometimes lit. This light is often very subdued.*

Once you have placed the *tsukubai*, you will need to choose a position for the stone lantern. If only one lantern is used in a tea garden, this should be placed to accompany the water basin, ostensibly to light the *tsukubai* arrangement and the path. In many Japanese gardens these lanterns are rarely lit – they are designed more for their artistic and sculptural quality. We have chosen the Oribe-style lantern, with a carved image of the Buddha on the pillar. This lantern is both easy to assemble and easy to install by burying the base of the pillar in the ground and securing it with concrete.

You will need
- a lantern set
- a spade
- a spirit level
- concreting sand or aggregate
- cement
- a shovel
- water for concrete and cleaning
- mastic (optional)
- low-voltage electrical supply (optional)

2 Dig a hole to accommodate the base of the lantern. This should be 15cm (6in) wider than the base of the pillar and 10cm (4in) deeper than the height of the pillar that is to be buried.

1 Lay out all the parts of the lantern to show the correct sequence of assembly. This lantern arrived from the supplier with pencilled-on numbers. Notice the rough granite base on the main lantern pillar: once the lantern is buried, this rough area will be covered.

3 If the base of the lantern is small, for example just 15cm (6in) deep, you will need a wider concrete base to make it more secure. Prepare a concrete mix made up of one part cement to six parts of concreting sand or aggregate. Add enough water to the mix to make a firm concrete. (A sloppy, wet mix will make it difficult to level the pillar base.) Place a shovel or two of the concrete mix in the hole.

4 If you are intending to light the lantern, thread an electric wire through the base before you lower the pillar into the hole. With the pillar in the hole, stand back and check that the front of the pillar is facing in the right direction. Using a spirit level, check that the pillar is standing vertically straight. If not, adjust it before the concrete sets.

5 Now check that the pillar is level horizontally by placing the spirit level across the top. After making any adjustments to the pillar position, check the level once again both vertically and horizontally until you are happy that it is straight.

6 With a concreting trowel, smooth concrete around the base, making sure it slopes away, and that no concrete will show once you have levelled the soil around it.

7 Leave the concrete mix to set for at least six hours before you add the remaining parts of the lantern. It is vital that the base is held firm before more weight is added.

8 Add each remaining part of the lantern in turn. Their weight gives them stability, but for absolute safety, secure the individual parts with some mastic.

9 Once the main box for the light is in place, position the two final elements: the roof of the lantern and the carved top.

LANTERN PRACTICALITIES

The following information will help you create an effective lantern feature:

- pick predrilled granite lanterns so an electric light can be inserted easily;
- ensure that you have a safe source of electricity (preferably low-voltage);
- LED lights consume little electricity.

Right: *In time, this lantern will weather and develop a surface of algae and moss.*

Laying stepping stones

The popularity of stepping stones in all Japanese gardens comes as a result of their introduction into the tea garden centuries ago. The stones themselves can vary in size and shape but are mostly natural and very thick, sometimes even whole rocks buried with just their tops showing. You can add formal paving, millstones or the occasional large stone beside the *tsukubai* or in any good place to stop and look around. Very large stones can lie on the ground just on a bed of sand, while smaller stones may need to be more firmly installed on a bed of concrete.

Above: *Stepping stones in Japanese gardens are often very thick and substantial, and are designed to sit proud of the surrounding area of gravel or moss.*

When planning a stepping-stone path, avoid using very smooth stones, as these can become slippery and dangerous, especially in damp shady areas. Naturally riven paving is safer and much more attractive to look at. Growing moss between the paving stones is the best approach for a Japanese garden to give the stone a distressed, timeworn quality, or alternatively you can try growing a few ground-hugging plants such as dwarf ophiopogon or ajuga to soften the paving edges.

You will need
- sharp sand
- a wheelbarrow
- a shovel
- a rake
- paving stones
- a sack truck
- cement (optional)
- a concreting trowel
- a rubber-headed hammer
- a spirit level
- a stiff broom

PATH DESIGN

Design your stepping-stone path as a weaving line of stones. This will add mystery to the garden as the path leads through the wilderness, past shrubs, trees and hills, towards the tea house itself.

1 Choose the line that your tea path will take and remove a layer of topsoil at least the depth of your stones. Collect some sharp sand in a wheelbarrow and pile it along the path. Use a generous amount – the eventual depth needs to be 4–7.5cm (1½–3in).

2 Spread the sharp sand along the path, ensuring it is flat, and even it out. Move the paving stones into place at the side of the path, preferably using a sack truck. You may need two people to handle any heavy, awkward stones.

3 Lay out the pattern of stepping stones before you finally set them. Stand well back from the pattern to assess the effect. In fact, it is advisable to leave them for an hour – even a day – and come back to look at them afresh. Then walk along the path to check that it is an easy and interesting route. Stones should be laid no more than 20cm (8in) apart, and at a regular distance from each other.

4 Heavy stones can be set directly on to the sand, but lighter stones will need a cement base. Make up a dry mix of eight parts sharp sand to one part cement. A dry cement mix is easier to use. Make four or five piles of the mix, 4–6cm (1½–2½in) higher than the desired height of the base of the stone.

5 Lower a paving stone on to the piles of cement. With the rubber hammer, tap the stone down until it is in position. Thin stones can easily break if not well bedded down. Repeat with the remaining stones.

6 The edges and corners of the stones are the most liable to break and tip over because they will take the pressure if the stone is unevenly supported, so shore up any hollow corners with some wet mix.

7 On a flat site, check the level of each stone, or if you are aware of the overall fall of the path, make allowances for this. If you don't have a spirit level, use builder's string laid along the length of the path, or you can simply lay a long length of timber down to make sure there are no snags that could trip someone up. Check the level from one stone to the next.

8 Brush sharp sand between the stones and wash the path down. This helps to eliminate air pockets, settle the sand and set the mix.

Right: Plant around the paving or spread fine gravel or cobbles. To encourage moss, spread a thin layer of sharp sand, 2cm (¾in) deep, and press firmly into the soil.

LAYING STEPPING STONES 181

The stroll garden style

A stroll garden, just like a pond garden, should be set around a pond as its main feature. The pond is usually stocked with fish and circled by a winding path. The garden should be designed to be seen from various vantage points along this path, where special views are composed. These views can be of a single well-placed pine tree or of a whole scene of the pond with small hills beyond it, maybe with trees that act both as a backdrop and to frame a "borrowed view" or *shakkei* (using elements outside the garden).

ELEMENTS OF A STROLL GARDEN

A stroll garden is made up of many of the elements of pond gardens, dry gardens and tea gardens: a pond, a dry area, lanterns, buildings, fences or statues and decorative planting.

Pond

The pond should have a pond with a varied outline, or one that might correspond to a Chinese ideogram for water or heart. The inlet to the pond may include an area for water irises.

Dry area

An area between the main building and the pond can be made of sand, rocks and clipped shrubs. It can also include a tea arbour, stepping-stone paths, lanterns and water basins.

Above: *Stroll gardens usually had large ponds as the focus of the garden. Fishing pavilions such as this one would have been used for boating parties. It would also have given attractive views of the pond from the paths around the garden.*

Below: *Stroll gardens evolved in the Edo period, and incorporated many aspects of earlier styles. Paths circulate around the garden arriving at points with specially contrived views.*

Above: *Paths can be narrow or broad, cobbled or gravelled and may pass groups of trees.*

Right: *Most stroll gardens circle around ponds that are crossed by bridges, such as this one made with a curved stone.*

Lanterns
These can also be placed on the side of slopes or beside the pond – wherever makes the most pleasing composition.

Structures and statues
A rustic wisteria arbour, handsome stretches of bamboo fences, pagodas and statues of Buddha may all feature.

Plants
The planting can be varied and have something for every season. Many stroll gardens include a grove of cherries, but if space is limited, a single tree will do.

Garden plan: a stroll garden

A stroll garden can be made in a relatively small space. If you start with a flat site, small hills can be built up using the soil dug out when the pond is made. The path can wander around these hills and by the edge of the pond. The weaving path will lure the strolling visitor to arbours and vantage points to view cherry groves, waterfalls or iris beds, or to entice them over a natural stone bridge.

HOW TO BUILD NATURAL STONE STEPS

Steps can be created from naturally found rocks or large stones. When building the steps, always start from the bottom and work uphill. Design your steps to follow the natural shape of the garden, allowing them to change direction from time to time. Over long stretches, add the occasional platform or bench as a resting place.

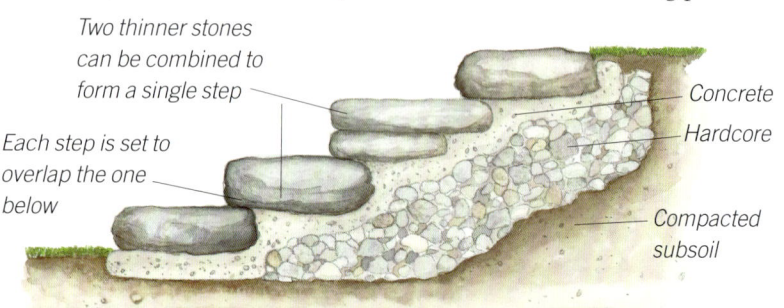

Two thinner stones can be combined to form a single step

Each step is set to overlap the one below

Concrete
Hardcore
Compacted subsoil

Hexagonal thatched arbour

Clipped hedge

Stepping-stone path

1 Measure the vertical and horizontal distances that you need the steps to climb. If you take the average of each stone you have available you can work out the number you will need. The steps should be flat, and the ideal dimensions are 10–15cm (4–6in) risers and 40–100cm (16–40in) treads. With Japanese-style steps these dimensions can vary with each step to make them appear more natural.

2 Dig out to a depth of 10cm (4in) below the lowest step, and lay a 10cm (4in) thick layer of concrete (one part cement to six parts concreting aggregate). Lay the first stone on this concrete slab.

3 If the ground is solid and the hill is not constructed artificially, you may not need the concrete mix, but you will need to firm the soil well as you go. On made-up ground, dig out all the loose soil to a depth of at least 30cm (12in) and backfill on to the compacted subsoil with hardcore, leaving enough room to add the 6–7.5 cm (2½–3in) depth of concrete for each step. Make sure the hardcore is rammed solid.

4 The front edge of each of the stones that you add should rest on the back of the previous one. This will ensure greater stability and will also appear more natural.

5 Set one step at a time, but be careful not to stand on them as you build the next one. For a long stretch it is advisable to build five or six steps at a time, then leave the concrete to set over two days before continuing. If you are building without concrete this will not be necessary.

Above: Lanterns may be placed on promontories as the watchful symbol of the lighthouse.

Above: Recycled materials (mitate) such as these millstones make beautiful stepping stones.

Right: Waterfalls and pond inlets in stroll gardens are built with naturalism and artistry.

Left: There are many styles of bridge in wood or stone. A single slab of stone looks very natural.

How to make a stroll garden

The stroll garden evolved as a style to combine many aspects of the tea garden, dry garden and pond garden. The central feature is usually a pond, with a gravel path that weaves around it, wandering through the garden and reaching vantage points to view specially composed scenes. Stroll gardens can range dramatically in size from park-like gardens to relatively small spaces; in small gardens, it may be possible to increase the sense of space using the technique of *shakkei* (see page 30). The layout shown below is suitable for a reasonably large garden. A gravel path leads to a tea house, then over some stepping stones to a planted area almost surrounded by the pond. A wisteria has been trained over an arbour here and the trailing purple flowers reflect attractively in the water. The process of making this garden is shown in the following pages.

Above: *A path's "flow" is linked to the quality of the surface. Smooth gravel or neat granite pavers will enable easier movement than uneven, narrow paving stones. But the latter can contribute to the atmosphere of the garden.*

Wisteria arbour   Natural stone steps   Japanese red pine

Tea house

Stepping stones

Pond

Iris ensata   Lantern   Rocks around the edge   Ferns   Gravel path   Hydrangea

Right: *Tully Japanese Garden in Ireland has many features typical of an authentic Japanese stroll garden: a circular path, a pond, a tea arbour and a wisteria-clad arbour.*

PLANNING AND VISUALIZATION

To plan a stroll garden you need some kind of vision of a scenic landscape so that you can sketch out the general contours and outline of the pond. From the house you may also compose a scene that will be framed by a window or an arbour. In a stroll garden you may have some open grassy areas, some hills, a bridge and one or two good vantage points from where a variety of scenes can be viewed. Ponds should have some shady, deeper areas for fish to shelter from the heat. Paths can be made in any style but the main strolling path should be surfaced in gravel and wide enough for two people to be able to stroll side by side.

THE POND AND PLANTING

The main challenge is how to keep the pond water healthy. Unless you are lucky enough to have a natural stream, you will need to circulate the water with a pump. Drainage will be necessary to collect the overflow. You will need to be sure you can keep an adequate water supply going so that the water will be well aerated, so get advice on the size of pump required. Otherwise you might have a stagnant, half-empty pond by midsummer.

Make sure that your site is large enough to spread out the soil that is removed when you dig out the pond. This soil can be used to construct small hills, making the site more interesting and intriguing for people using the main gravelled path to wander around visiting tea houses and arbours.

Any fairly open site with good soil, some sunshine and good access can be used. Shady areas can be adapted to grow azaleas and hydrangeas, but cherry trees need an open aspect to grow and flower well. Wisteria too needs at least half a day in full sun to flower abundantly.

TYPICAL FEATURES OF A STROLL GARDEN

- a pond;
- a stream and cascade or waterfall;
- stone or wooden bridges over the stream or to an island on the pond;
- rocks among the plants on pond edge;
- small hills with dwarf or pruned pines;
- a strolling path in gravel or paving stones;
- gates into the tea garden;
- stepping-stone or paved tea paths;
- a wisteria arbour;
- a waiting room or bench;
- a tea house or tea arbour for viewing;
- fences surrounding the garden and bordering the tea path;
- shakkei, or "borrowed scenery";
- lanterns;
- water basins near tea house and on path;
- a dry garden near the house or in an enclosed courtyard;
- extensive plantings including: groves of cherries, plums and maples; groups of clipped azaleas, bamboo and hydrangeas; evergreen trees, especially pines, cryptomeria and hinoki cypress; herbaceous plants such as grasses, anemones, tricyrtis, platycodon, asters.

Making a pond with a flexible liner

The versatility of flexible (butyl) liners has made them the most popular of materials for a variety of applications for holding water, such as lining ponds and streams, and for backing around waterfalls. They certainly provide the greatest scope for small pond design. (For larger ponds, you will need to use a clay or synthetic clay liner; see pages 152–153.) They can also be used with natural stone, concrete or walling blocks to stabilize the sides of an excavation and have the advantage that they will not dry and become brittle if the water level should drop in dry weather.

Above: *When laying out a pond with a butyl liner, make sure that the liner is not visible, especially around the edges of the pond.*

To calculate the liner size, measure a rectangle to enclose the pool. After measuring the length and breadth, measure the depth and add twice that measurement to each dimension.

The measurements for length and width represent the minimum of liner required. Add about 30cm (12in) to each measurement to provide a small overlap of 15cm (6in) on each side. For brimming pools, where the surface of the water has to be level with the edge, add a little more than the width of the paving or bricks that will edge the pool to provide enough liner to extend beneath and behind (the end of the liner will finish by being held vertically behind the edging material).

One rectangle of liner can be used for a variety of pool shapes, including designs with narrow waists. Where the wastage would be excessive for narrow sections, smaller joining pieces of some types of liner can be welded together or taped together on site using proprietary waterproof joining tapes. Large creases in the corners of rectangular pools or sharp curves in informal shapes are inevitable, but they can be made to look less conspicuous if the liner is carefully folded before the pond is filled.

You will need
- a garden hose, rope or sand
- a spade
- plastic sheet
- a rake
- a spirit level
- a straight-edged piece of wood
- sand or underlay
- flexible liner (calculate the dimensions as described above)
- bricks or heavy stones as temporary weights
- large scissors
- paving for the pool surround
- ready-mixed mortar
- a mortaring trowel

1 If the pond is to be sited in a lawn, remove the turf by stripping off the grass to a depth of 5cm (2in) in squares of 30cm (12in) and stack the turf upside down for later use. Dig out the hole to a depth of 23cm (9in), angling the sides of the hole slightly inwards. The soil from the top 23cm (9in) can be stored on a plastic sheet nearby if it is to be used for any new contouring of the surrounds. Rake the hole base to a rough level finish after the first layer of soil has been removed and mark with sand the position of any marginal shelves around the sides.

2 The inner or deeper zone, avoiding the marginal shelf outlines, can now be dug out to the full depth of the pond. The soil from this deeper zone will be subsoil and can be used later if it is placed underneath any fresh topsoil. It should not become mixed with the freshly excavated topsoil. Marginal shelves around the sides of the hole should be 30cm (12in) wide and be positioned where you anticipate having the shallow water plants.

3 Rake the bottom of the pool to level the surface and remove any sharp stones, protruding roots or sharp-edged objects. Gently firm the surface by patting. Line the pool with about 1cm (½in) of damp sand – it should stick to the sides if they slope slightly. If the soil is stony, drape a piece of underlay across the hole and shelves, to overlap the edge of the pool by about 30cm (12in).

4 Lay the flexible liner over the sand or underlay. Once you have done this, place temporary weights, such as bricks or heavy stones, on the edges of the liner to keep it securely in place. Make sure that there is enough liner width above the edge of the pool all the way round. Then use a hose to start filling the pond with water.

5 Wait until the water has almost filled the pool, then remove the bricks or stones temporarily holding the edges of the liner. Replace any turf you want around the edge, and complete any edging finishes before the water is filled to the final level. Trim the surplus liner only when you are completely sure that the water level and edging are working satisfactorily.

6 Cut away the surplus liner and underlay, leaving an overlap around the edge of about 15cm (6in) to be covered by the paving.

7 If you want edging paving, bed the paving on mortar, covering the edge of the liner. The paving should overlap the edge of the pool by about 2.5cm (1in). Finish off by pointing the joints with mortar using the mortaring trowel.

8 If there is ample surplus liner, features such as bog gardens can be made around the sides. When a kidney-shaped pool is created, a small bog area can be achieved using the corner piece of a rectangular liner. Instead of cutting off the surplus, place soil on the liner and prevent it from spreading into the main pool water by a small submerged retaining wall of inverted turfs, rocks or walling stones.

Right: *This small pond is surrounded with gravel and provides a home for koi carp.*

Making a gravel path

The Japanese stroll garden is specially designed for taking a walk around the scenic environment and for this you will need a suitable path. A gravel path may seem simple to make, but it must be done properly or all sorts of problems will ensue. The edging of gravel paths is vital, as it prevents the gravel from drifting on to beds, grass or mossy areas. In Japanese gardens this edging is often made of stone or granite blocks. When choosing suitable blocks you should always aim to achieve a balance between the natural and the artistic.

The most common mistake made by gardeners is to dig out a trench and fill it with pea gravel. However, deep gravel is very spongy, making it awkward to walk on, and almost impossible to push a wheelbarrow or wheelchair over. For a successful path, follow the guidelines below.

Above: *The minimum width of a path for two people to stroll side by side is 1.5m (1½yds). As well as this practical role, paths also play an important part in linking garden elements and creating fluidity in the design.*

You will need
- a spade
- a shovel
- a rake
- a wheelbarrow
- edging stones
- concreting sand and cement
- a concreting trowel
- a rubber-headed hammer
- weed-suppressing landscape fabric
- scissors
- "scalpings" or a mix of crushed stone and stone dust
- gravel
- a roller or motorized wacker plate

1 Mark out the edges of the gravel path you are planning. Using a shovel, dig out the area of the path down to a depth of 10–15cm (4–6in) and remove the soil. Lay out the edging stones informally.

2 Position the stones so that you can see what they look like before you actually fix them in place.

3 Fix the edging stones in place using a concreting mix of one part cement to eight parts sand. Firm them in place with a rubber hammer and check that they are level.

4 The concrete mix on the inside edge should fall below the stones by at least 4cm (1½in). Allow the concrete to set for a day before proceeding. Collect some soft sand in a wheelbarrow and bring it to the path.

5 Lay a thin layer of soft sand over the path area. This will protect the landscape fabric from being punctured by small stones.

6 Lay out the landscape fabric so that it tucks in around the edging stones. Cut the fabric to shape with sharp scissors.

7 Spread a layer of "scalpings" or crushed stone/stone dust mix to a depth of 10–12cm (4–5½in), raking it evenly so that the top level is 2–4cm (¾–1½in) below the top of the edging stones. Do not roll this layer.

8 Spread a single layer of gravel over the "scalpings" base, and rake it out evenly.

9 Roll the single layer of gravel so that it is pressed well into the base layer. Now spread another single layer of gravel over this pressed surface and roll again. (Do not spread more than 4cm (1½in) of gravel in total. You can always top it up later.) Test the surface for firmness and comfort before adding any more gravel. Rake out the gravel around the edges of the path so that it works in nicely around the edging stones.

GRAVEL OPTIONS

Type of gravel	Advantages	Disadvantages
Very fine gravel	Easy to deal with, attractive to look at	Can get caught in the soles of shoes and can easily be kicked around the garden
Sand/stone mix	Gives a firm, well-drained finish	Expensive
Stone chippings	Attractive and interesting to look at	Can be uncomfortable to walk on in soft-soled shoes
Pea gravel 10–20mm (½–¾in) in diameter	Ideal for general use, beds down well and tends to stay in place	Will need raking and topping up from time to time

Below: *Gravel paths should be raked and brushed regularly to keep an even layer of gravel.*

Making a wisteria arbour

The native Japanese wisteria, *Wisteria floribunda*, can be seen cascading out of trees on hillsides and valleys in some parts of Japan. Wisteria is ideal for festooning wooden arbours, constructed so that the long scented flower racemes hang down between the rafters. The pendulous flowers look especially wonderful when reflected in water, so arbours are often constructed near to or even leaning out over ponds. In Japan, wisteria arbours are very simple constructions that can be easily assembled from round poles or branches with the bark still on them.

Although rustic poles are ideal for an arbour, it is sometimes difficult to find ones of sufficient strength. (Indeed, some arbours are built using concrete "logs".) This project gets around this problem by using square posts and beams locked together using mortise-and-tenon joints that are fixed by a dowelling peg. The rafters can then be made of rustic poles laid across the beams or lighter-weight poles can be simply fixed in place with screws.

Above: *The two most popular species of wisteria are* W. floribunda, *the Japanese species with very long racemes, and* W. sinensis, *the Chinese species whose flowers are half the length. You will need to allow plenty of headroom in an arbour for these trailing flowers to hang.*

You will need
- posts and beams, 10–14cm (4–5½in) square, made of green oak, cedar or treated softwood
- rafters, 7.5–10cm (3–4in) in diameter, made of rustic poles
- a post-hole digger
- a crowbar
- a spade
- concreting aggregate and cement
- metal post fixers (optional)
- a hammer and chisel to make mortise-and-tenon joints for the upright posts
- 10mm (½in) diameter dowelling
- an electric drill and 10mm (½in) wood drill bit for dowelling
- 7.5cm (3in) screws

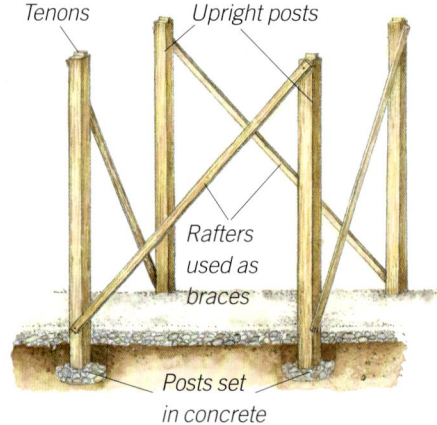

4 Set the posts in a concrete mix of one part cement to six parts concreting aggregate. The rafters should ensure that the arbour stays square as the concrete sets. This process requires precision.

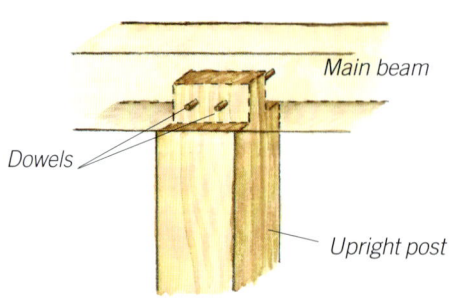

5 Lay the main beams on the mortise-and-tenon joint uprights (at the top of the posts). From the side, drill twice through the beam and the tenon of the post, and hammer in two lengths of dowelling.

6 The dowelling should be tight but it will swell up and tighten more once it gets wet. Set the holes around the posts in the same concrete mix that was used in step 4, ensuring the joints line up snugly, and leave the structure to set for at least 24 hours. You may need to adjust the joints during this time, especially if you are using green oak, which can warp quickly. Once the concrete is set, further bending of the oak will add to the pergola's natural charm.

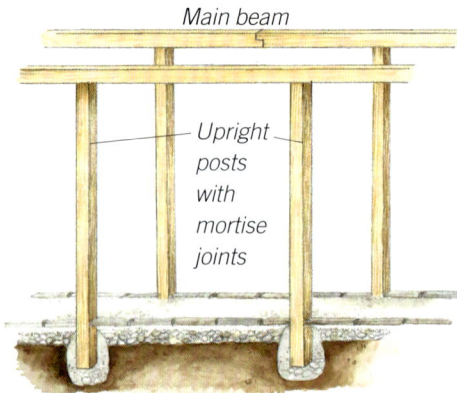

1 Mark on the ground where the arbour posts will be placed, making sure they are square.

2 Dig the post holes 25cm (10in) wide and 4cm (1½in) deeper than the post will be. The posts should be set at least 45cm (18in) deep if set in concrete. Make sure the posts are upright and in line.

3 Lightly nail the rafters at an angle from one post to another to make the structure secure.

7 Remove the brace rafters. Rest the rafters on top, across the main beams. They can be notched to fit over the beam to hold them in place. One or two screws drilled from above down into the main beams should fix them. The arbour is now ready as a structure over which wisteria can be planted and trained.

ARBOUR DESIGN

Timber A mature wisteria plant has twisting stems that can exert a stranglehold on any structure, so any timber you use must be of sufficient strength and thickness to withstand its grip. Green oak is both strong and long-lasting.

Height Japanese wisteria flowers can be more than 50cm (20in) long, so the roof of the arbour should be high enough for a person to stand in comfort beneath the flowers – a recommended 2.5m (8ft).

Posts Set the posts no more than 2m (6½ft) apart along the sides, and at least 1.5m (5ft) apart across the width of the path.

Fixings You could construct an arbour using screws, bolts and nails, but it may not last as long as a mortise-and-tenon jointed construction.

Joinery You may be able to ask a timber merchant to cut the pieces of wood for you and to make the mortise-and-tenon joints. It will then be simply a case of assembling the arbour.

Above right: *This sturdy wisteria arbour draws the viewer into the garden. Arbours are best placed at transition points in a garden.*

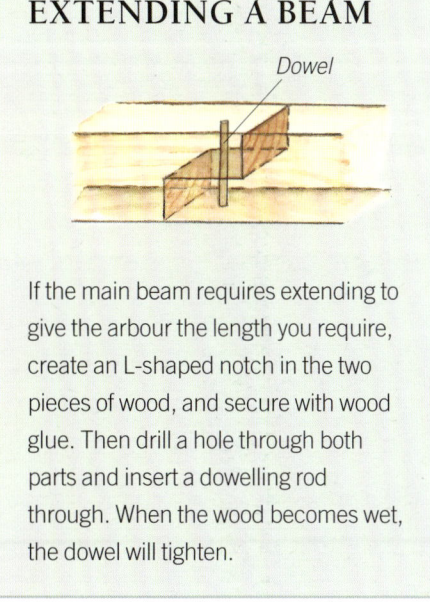

EXTENDING A BEAM

If the main beam requires extending to give the arbour the length you require, create an L-shaped notch in the two pieces of wood, and secure with wood glue. Then drill a hole through both parts and insert a dowelling rod through. When the wood becomes wet, the dowel will tighten.

MAKING A WISTERIA ARBOUR 193

The courtyard garden style

The form of a courtyard garden has many variations. The main criterion is that it is a small, sometimes minuscule, space contained within a building or the narrow passage that leads from a street to the main door of the house. The courtyard might be viewed from more than one room, so it should look good from more than one angle and is an excellent opportunity to experiment in miniature landscapes or with abstract design, mixing the many elements that make up the various styles. You may find this style of garden in a Japanese restaurant, a hotel or even a temple garden.

ELEMENTS OF A COURTYARD GARDEN

Most courtyard gardens are dry gardens, often laid out with a spread of gravel, sometimes with a stepping-stone path crossing over it. Although the space is limited, there may be room for a very small pond, but in courtyards where no soil is available and light is poor, a purely "dry" garden is ideal. Lanterns and water basins, along with minimalist planting, are key features.

With enough space, you could combine rocks and plants, a waterfall and a small pond, but more often a courtyard may have only enough space for an island of greenery in the middle, decorated simply with a few rocks, ferns, a water basin and lantern.

Above: *A chequered pattern of moss and gravel on the Brunei Gallery roof garden in London evokes the one used by Mirei Shigemori at Tofuku-ji in the 1930s.*

Below: *Dry gardens suit roof gardens well, where the weight of soil and invasive plant roots might damage the building. This dry courtyard garden contrasts natural rock forms with carved blocks.*

Lanterns and water basins

Most courtyard gardens include a lantern and water basin arrangement, similar to that found in a tea garden. A taller water basin, or *chozubachi*, can also be placed where it can be easily reached from the veranda of a nearby room or passage, and where the eaves of the house help to protect the water.

Plants

In a very shady courtyard, some plants do not grow well, and you will have to choose shade-loving plants such as aucuba, camellia and bamboo. With more light, a single pine tree or cherry tree might provide a point of focus and possibly some welcome shade in the heat of summer.

Left: *These raised paving stones give a sculptural quality, as well as leading up to the veranda.*

Below: *Courtyard gardens can be made in almost any enclosed space. They are typically bordered by the walls of the house.*

Garden plan: a courtyard garden

Courtyard gardens, or *tsubo-niwa*, can be made in the most unpromising sites, in narrow passages or in places where little light can reach. They often include elements from other garden styles, such as sand and rocks from the dry garden, or stepping-stone paths, lanterns and basins from the tea garden (with careful consideration of the miniature scale). Plants could include a clipped pine, an azalea, bamboo and a few ferns. The gardens are usually enclosed within walls or fences.

CREATING A *SHUKKEI*

The art of *shukkei*, which literally means "concentrated view", is most often found in courtyard gardens, especially in the form of a *kare-sansui* (dry-mountain-water) design made up of stones, gravel and clipped plants. The aim is to reduce an entire landscape scene to a miniature scale.

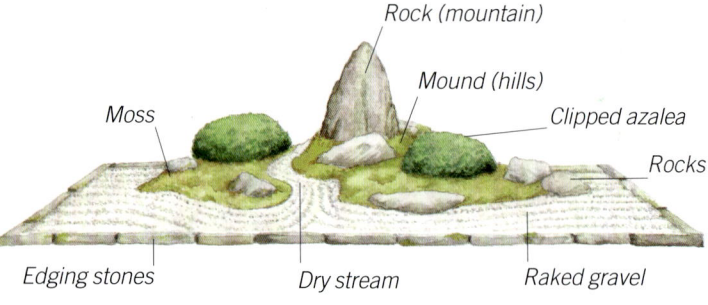

Rock (mountain) — *Mound (hills)* — *Moss* — *Clipped azalea* — *Rocks* — *Edging stones* — *Dry stream* — *Raked gravel*

1 When choosing and planning your location note that *shukkei* should be laid out over a level site. The scenery can then be built up using small amounts of soil and rocks to suggest mountain and hill ranges. To do this, make small mounds of earth into which you will "plant" your rocks. Choose rocks that have credible mountain shapes. Some of these rocks can be almost buried, leaving exposed areas to look like escarpments.

2 Re-work the soil after placing the rocks to create a realistic undulation of hills and valleys, leaving indentations around the edges at ground level where you might expect seas and rivers to have eroded the natural forms.

3 Plant azaleas or boxwood, which can be clipped into mound or hill shapes, around the rocks and on the mounds. You can also add a wizened old pine to suggest an open weathered mountainside. Plant the earth with pieces of moss if you can find some, or with dwarf "dragon's beard" (*Ophiopogon*).

4 Spread gravel and sand around the level area to suggest an area of sea or a lake, drawing some of the sand into the scenery you have created where rivers might flow.

Above: Sleeve fences are used to deflect or to help frame a view.

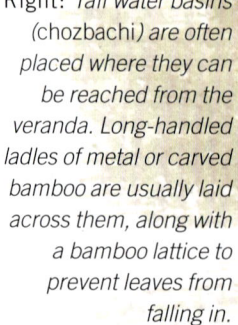

Right: Tall water basins (chozbachi) are often placed where they can be reached from the veranda. Long-handled ladles of metal or carved bamboo are usually laid across them, along with a bamboo lattice to prevent leaves from falling in.

GARDEN PLAN: A COURTYARD GARDEN

How to make a courtyard garden

The courtyard garden is any small area in an enclosed space that incorporates traditional features found in other Japanese garden styles. Some are dry gardens with just a spread of sand and one or two rocks, while others might include elaborate paths that cross over the space, using plantings that evoke a distant but miniaturized landscape. Here is a suggestion for a courtyard garden in a level space. A mound (middle back), which represents a hillside, is planted with a dwarf Japanese red pine, ferns and *Ophiopogon japonica*. The space itself is walled on one side and has a bamboo screening fence on two other sides. Crossing the space is a semi-formal stone path leading from a door in the house to a side gate. Like most courtyard gardens, this one also includes a lantern and a water basin – elements borrowed from the tea garden. The process of making this garden is shown on the following pages.

Above: *Defined as a closed-off external area, the courtyard garden is an excellent style to use for controlled drama. The minimalism and simplicity of this design, a view from a Japanese restaurant, creates an attractive, peaceful pictorial composition of the enclosed garden beyond.*

198 CREATING A GARDEN

Above: *This courtyard garden was designed to be viewed from more than one angle and to act as a passage to a back gate. The path then becomes an intrinsic part of the design.*

COURTYARD GARDEN: TYPICAL FEATURES

The following features would normally be found in a courtyard garden:

- sliding screens, small fence panels and bamboo blinds for private areas;
- dry-garden elements with one or two rocks and a "pool" of raked gravel;
- stone paving bordered by lanterns;
- stepping stones;
- clipped evergreens such as azaleas, mahonias, nandinas and bamboos;
- glossy evergreen shrubs, such as aucubas, fatsias and camellias, as well as shade-loving ferns, bamboos and farfugiums;
- a carpeting of moss;
- lanterns, basins and small bridges.

PLANNING AND VISUALIZATION

Before making a courtyard garden, you need to think carefully about your design. If you want to include a number of features, then you must have an overall composition that is coherent. Is your garden going to act as a path from one room to another, or is it simply going to be viewed from one or two points?

Your next consideration is a question of scale. A *shakkei*, or condensed landscape, for example, should not have too many features, as this might make it appear too busy. Make a plan, and stand back from time to time to check the view over the garden as you construct it.

As courtyards are, by their very nature, enclosed, access to them can be tricky, so make sure you can get all the materials into the space (some may have to come through the house, which could be difficult). Also, being so close to a house, the space may have water, electricity and gas services crossing underneath, so check before doing any excavation. Generally, deep excavation is not necessary in courtyard gardens except to ensure that the site is well drained before planting anything.

Courtyards may not have a great deal of light, so plants should be carefully chosen to suit the amount of light available. Remember that you will need a source of water to irrigate the plantings, to maintain any water feature and to keep the space clean. Electricity may be required for lighting or for any water pumps, but neither of these is essential for a successful courtyard garden.

Building a bamboo screen fence

The design and construction of bamboo fences in Japan has developed into a highly specialized and elaborate art, and if you are interested in developing the skills to make your own traditional fence, there is no shortage of information available. If you prefer a more instant solution, however, you can buy sections of these beautiful bamboo fences ready-made from specialist suppliers. In this project, rolls of bamboo canes, held together with wire and supported with a frame, were used, which required a fence on two sides that would act as a screen.

Above: *A detail of bamboo fence supplied in a roll. This economical form of fencing is often used, even in authentic Japanese gardens. Bamboo of this type will usually need replacing after five to ten years, depending on the weather and how well it is cared for.*

When using bamboo in rolls, you will need to build a suitable frame against which to support the bamboo. Every one of the timber elements in the frame should be made of durable hardwood or treated softwood. You should also remember to apply an additional coat of preservative to the parts of the posts that are going to remain underground.

You will need

- 10cm (4in) square posts, 2.5m (8ft) long
- a 5 x 7.5cm (2 x 3in) supporting baton, ideally just one length measuring the length of the fence
- temporary supporting batons to hold posts in position
- 4 x 5cm (1½ x 2in) cross batons, in 1.5m (5ft) lengths
- capping timber 14 x 4cm (5½ x 1½in), the length of the fence
- vertical strips 2.5 x 7.5cm (1 x 3in) and 2m (6½ft) long for facing boards to hold the fence in place
- a roll of bamboo fencing, 2m (6½ft) high – these are usually available in 3m (10ft) lengths
- a wood saw
- an electric drill
- 6cm (2½in) screws
- a screwdriver
- a spirit level
- concrete mix of aggregate using 1 part cement to 6 parts aggregate
- a chisel
- a shovel
- a wheelbarrow
- thick black jute twine

1 Identify your fence line with builder's twine. Mark out the position of the posts, around 1.5–2m (5–6½ft) apart. Dig holes for the posts up to 45–50cm (18–20in) deep by 20cm (8in) wide. Stand the posts upright in the holes. Screw on the lower supporting baton, which should be 4cm (1½in) off the ground and perfectly level. This will help to keep the posts square.

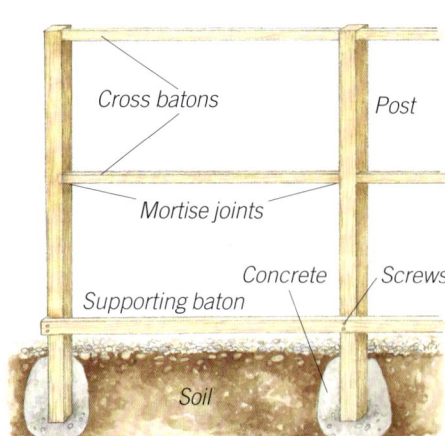

4 Once all the posts have set, remove the temporary supporting batons. Chisel out shallow mortises in the uprights to receive the cross batons (see mortise-and-tenon detail shown on page 192). The cross batons, and therefore the joints, should be positioned half way up the posts and at the top of the posts. From the side, drill through and screw the mortise-and-tenon joints into the posts.

2 For extra stability, erect some temporary supporting batons to help hold the posts perfectly upright while the concrete sets.

3 Make up a mix of concrete and fill the holes, tamping it in firmly around the posts. Using a spirit level, check again that the posts are in line, and are square and upright. Leave the concrete to set for at least 24 hours.

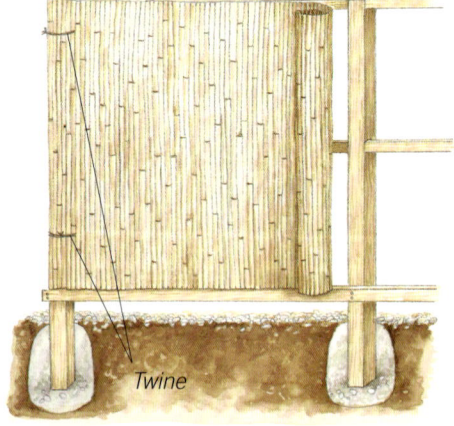

5 Stand the roll of bamboo fencing on the lower supporting baton, temporarily attaching one end of it to a post with some twine. Unroll the fence, attaching it to the cross batons with twine as you go and as necessary to hold it in place. You can leave the twine in place attaching the bamboo roll to the cross batons as additional support, particularly if you weave it in a way that makes it an attractive addition to the design.

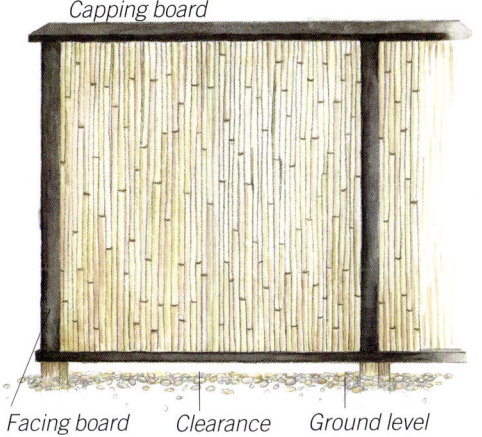

Capping board
Facing board *Clearance* *Ground level*

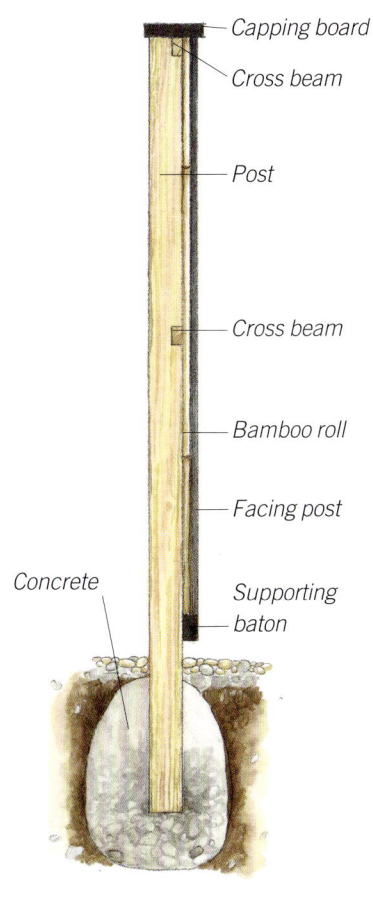

Capping board
Cross beam
Post
Cross beam
Bamboo roll
Facing post
Concrete
Supporting baton

6 To hold the bamboo roll securely in place, screw facing boards on to the posts. Cut off the tops of the posts so that they are level with the top of the bamboo fence roll. Lay the capping boards over the tops of the posts and then screw them down on to the posts. Either stain all the exposed timbers ash black or leave them to weather naturally.

Below: *The neutral colour and quality of bamboo fences make them excellent backdrops to many styles of Japanese garden.*

MAINTAINING THE FENCE

If you maintain your bamboo fence well, it will last much longer. Bamboo will eventually become brittle and attract mould if left untreated, so, every year or two, scrub off the mould and apply either some light teak oil or a matt varnish diluted 1 part varnish to 3 parts white spirit. (There are special wood preservatives formulated for willow and hazel fences that would be equally effective on bamboo.) To make maintenance easy, make sure that you attach the bamboo roll to the fence in such a way that it will be easy to remove. For example, don't use heavy nails as these will be hard to pull out without damaging the frame.

Note that some bamboo rolls are made of heavier cane than others – the larger the cane, the longer they will last.

Left: *Cross-section of a bamboo fence.*

Laying a paving-stone path

There are many styles of stone path to choose from in the Japanese garden (see pages 120–121 on path styles), but they almost all use natural materials in a combination of formal and informal shapes. Your choice of design may be determined by the availability of materials. This courtyard garden uses a combination of local paving stones, most of which have at least one straight edge, and large cobbles from a local quarry. Using the straight edge to act as a border to the path, the cobbles are set out to weave a thread through the path, unifying the design.

Above: *A randomly paved path makes a bold entrance to the Huntington Botanical Gardens. The guardian dogs are a Chinese inspiration.*

It is advisable to lay a path with a complex design such as this on a level site over a concrete base. You should make sure that the surface allows rainwater to drain off, because stones that stay wet will become slippery and therefore dangerous.

To keep the stones clean, lay them on a dry mix of cement and moist sand, rather than using a wet cement mix. This mixture can also be easily brushed into joints between the stones. The mixture will then set either from the moisture in the sand or from rain. If the weather remains dry, hose down the paving stones with water after they have been put in place to make sure that the cement sets properly.

There is a danger of the stones becoming stained by the cement while laying. For any persistent stains, use a stain remover, such as muriatic acid, which will dissolve cement. Always follow the manufacturer's instructions carefully when using chemicals.

You will need
- hardcore for the base
- a wheelbarrow
- a sack truck
- different sizes of natural paving stones
- large rounded cobbles or smooth, flat-topped stones
- marker paint or powdered lime
- white chalk
- concreting sand and cement
- a shovel
- a tape measure
- a bricklaying trowel
- a rubber-headed hammer
- a stiff broom
- stain remover (muriatic acid)
- old rags
- builder's twine

1 Prepare a level site with a solid hardcore base and lay out the stones and cobbles on the ground to establish the pattern you want. Mark out the outline of the path with marker paint. This type of paint comes in spray cans, and is available from most builders' merchants. Alternatively, sprinkle a line of powdered lime which will dissolve after a few days.

2 Number or code each stone with white chalk so you remember which stone goes where in the path. Then remove all the paving stones to one side of the path. Obviously some variations may occur when you replace the stones, but try to keep the main dynamic of the design within the marked eges of the path.

3 Dig out the base to a depth of 10–16cm (4–6¼in), allowing 5–7.5cm (2–3in) for the concrete mix and 3–5cm (1¼–2in) for the paving thickness, and 2–4cm (¾–1½in) for the gravel. If you want the paving to sit proud of the ground, reduce the depth to allow for this.

4 Make a mix of 1 part cement to 8 parts sand. Lay the paving slabs first, spreading this mix (dry or wet) to a depth of 5–7.5cm (2–3in).

5 The mixture should be heaped up in the corners so that each stone is laid higher than its intended level, as its weight will press the mix down.

6 Once the stones have been laid and the mortar mix is set, fill in over the mortared areas with a dry mix of 1 part cement to 8 parts sand and brush it level. Tamp the stones down gently with the handle of a hammer. Use a spirit level to check that the stone is level.

7 Lay out the cobbles on top of the dry mortar mix, push them down and tamp them into position. Here, the cobbles sit proud of the mortar mix, which has hardened from the ambient water and some rain.

8 Once the stones and cobbles have nearly set, apply some water to the surface to check it flows away from the path. Brush or scrape out any excess mortar that may be preventing water from draining off the surface of the path.

9 After two or three days, wash off any stains from the path using stain remover and a rag.

Right: *The deep-set pointing of the path will encourage moss to grow after a few years, particularly in dark, damp areas. You can encourage it by adding leaf mould or compost in the gaps and keeping it damp, but it is best to keep the stones themselves clean and dry – otherwise they may become slippery with algae.*

Building a mound

Courtyards are often contained on level sites within buildings or compounds where there is little or no soil, and where a complex web of underground services may be running beneath the garden. In this courtyard garden, building up a mound of earth answered this practical issue, and also added to the artistry of the garden, because the mound of earth takes on the representation of a landscaped hill, or even a mountain. Planted with a dwarf Japanese red pine, and laid with rocks, the garden has the feeling of a condensed landscape.

Above: *Mounds of moss represent the Mystic Isles in this courtyard garden. Rocks in a large expanse of raked sand complete the picture. The mounds form dramatic shapes in the space and give structure and balance to the created landscape.*

As moss can be tricky to establish in many climates, planting the lower level with dwarf ophiopogon helps to give the appearance of a grassy hillside, while ferns soften the outline of the rocks. Finally an authentic Japanese touch is achieved by placing both a lantern and a water basin just off the paved path that crosses the courtyard to the gate.

You will need
- 2–3 tonnes of screened topsoil
- a wheelbarrow
- a shovel
- a selection of small rocks
- a sack truck to move rocks
- plants: a dwarf Japanese red pine, a clump of *Ophiopogon japonicus*, a *Camellia sasanqua*, two *Polystichum setiferum* (ferns)
- a planting trowel
- a paving stone
- sharp sand
- a rubber-headed hammer
- a water basin
- a lantern
- gravel
- a rake
- a broom

PRIOR PLANNING
- Assess the site access before ordering materials such as soil and rocks.
- If you are building a mound on a rooftop, ask a building engineer to assess the load that the building can carry.

1 Add a heap of screened topsoil to the area, surrounding it with a ring of stones to prevent soil spilling on to the gravel. The stones can be moved later, so put them into temporary positions for now. Then start shaping the mound so that it has natural contours.

2 Plant large shrubs first. Placed at the highest point, the dwarf Japanese red pine anchors the mound, accentuates the shape of the hill and gives a central feature. Place more rocks on the banks of the mound to create the escarpments and rocky outcrops.

3 Partly bury the rocks so that only a third remains exposed. Simply placing rocks on top of the soil will look unnatural. Reshape the mound and build up soil behind the rocks for planting pockets and to create a more uneven shape. Stand back to check the result.

4 If you already have a clump of ophiopogon or have bought a large pot, you can divide the plant up by simply pulling it apart. Firmly gripping the base of the plant, tease it apart gently, taking care not to break too many of the roots.

5 Plant your ophiopogon divisions around the slopes of the mound at a distance of approximately 15cm (6in) apart, tucking them under the rocks. The plants will spread until they knit together eventually to form a carpet. Plant the ferns underneath the pine.

6 The next stage is to lay a well-shaped paving stone on to which you will place the water basin. The paving stone can be simply laid on a bed of sharp sand, without any cement. Spread the sand out evenly and then raise it up in small ridges.

7 Lay the stone on the sand base. Tamp the stone down with a rubber-headed hammer.

8 Place the water basin on the stone. Leave space at the side for a ladle, for guests to drink from and clean themselves.

9 Follow the step-by-step guide to installing a lantern on pages 178–9. Place some more rocks artistically around the lantern and in other places on the flat area.

10 Spread an even layer of gravel over the entire flat area to create a dry garden effect. Clean the paving and brush out any gravel that has strayed into the joints of the paving.

Below: *The underplanting of Japanese mondo grass (*Ophiopogon japonicus*) will knit together to form a solid carpet over the next few years.*

BUILDING A MOUND 205

PLANT DIRECTORY

The Japanese have planted beautiful trees and shrubs ever since they first started making gardens. Although initially many plants were brought over from China, gardeners soon harnessed the potential of the native plants. Japan has exceptional and enviable flora, including many species of cherry, azalea, camellia and magnolia, which blossom in the mountains in spring, while in the autumn, maples and oaks give a display of fiery reds, yellows and oranges. Evergreen trees such as cedars and pines are considered symbols of longevity and resilience.

Wisterias, peonies and hydrangeas feature in many Japanese gardens, in natural groupings or massed in orchard-like groves rather than in formal beds. Herbaceous and bulbous plants, such as platycodons, lilies, hostas or Japanese anemones, are usually planted naturalistically with ferns in individual clumps near the base of a rock, in a carpet of moss, or scattered in small groups. Irises are grown in swampy areas or in formal beds near the inlet of ponds, while sedges and ferns are used to soften the edges of streams. This chapter will show you many of the best plants to use, along with seasonal highlights and care instructions.

Above: *The stunning autumn foliage of* Acer palmatum *'Sango-kaku'*.
Left: *Wisteria is a classic plant in Japanese gardens*.

How plants are named

All living things are classified according to a system based on principles that were devised by the 18th-century Swedish botanist, Carl Linnaeus. The method used a two-name method of classification, where all plants were given two Latinized names to determine their relationship to all other living things. This system states that a particular plant genus (plural: genera) is a group of plants containing similar species. Beyond that there may be plants that are simply a slight variation of a species, or are a hybrid (cross) of different species or variations.

Above: *Camellia sasanqua* is a species native to Japan. It starts to flower in late autumn, with more flowers opening throughout the winter.

SCIENTIFIC NAMES

Under this internationally adopted system, plants have botanical names, which are often Latin but are also derived from other languages that consist of the genus name (for example, *Prunus*), followed by the name that denotes the particular species (for example, *serrulata*). Some genera contain a number of species that may include annuals, perennials, shrubs and trees, while others contain just one species. While all members of a genus are assumed to be related to each other, this is not always visually obvious.

A species is defined scientifically as consisting of individuals that are alike and tend naturally to breed with each other. Despite this system, botanists and taxonomists (the experts who classify living things) often disagree about the basis on which a plant has been named. This is why it is useful for a plant to retain its synonym (abbreviated to syn. in the text), or alternative name. Incorrect names often gain widespread usage, and in some cases, two plants thought to have separate identities, and with two different names, are found to be the same plant.

VARIATIONS ON A THEME

Genetically, many plants evolve over time to adapt to a changing environment. In the wild, natural random mutations will survive and reproduce only if they are well adapted. The average garden is a controlled environment, so variations can be grown within a species that have small but pleasing differences such as variegated leaves and double flowers. The terms for these variations are subspecies (subsp.), variety (var.), form (f., similar to variety and often used interchangeably) and cultivar (cv.). A cultivar is a variation that would not occur in the wild but has been produced by deliberate cross-breeding. Cultivars are given names in single quotes, for example *Prunus mume* 'Beni Chidori'.

HYBRIDS

When plant species breed with each other, the result is a hybrid. Rare in the wild, crossing is very common among plant-breeders, and is done to produce plants with desirable qualities such as larger or double blooms, variegated foliage and greater frost resistance. A multiplication sign (x) is used to indicate a hybrid, and the name will often give a clear idea of the origins of the hybrid.

GROUPS

A plant group is a grouping of similar variations. Their names do not have quotation marks, for example *Tradescantia* Andersoniana Group.

Callicarpa japonica

Deutzia

How to use the plant directory

Within the plant directory, the plants are split into sections relating to seasons and particular types of plants, such as Spring Trees and Shrubs, Autumn Foliage or Evergreen Shrubs. Each main entry within these sections features the botanical name, the Japanese name, the common name and the plant's family. This is followed by a general introduction to that genus with a description of the plant, including the leaves, flowers and growth habit. There are also brief notes on methods of propagation, flowering time, average size, preferred conditions, as well as a guide to the plant's hardiness. Entries in the directory often also suggest a selection of closely related species that may fulfil a similar role in the garden.

Paeonia suffruticosa

Genus and species name
This is the internationally accepted botanical name for a group of related plant species. This starts with the current botanical name of the plant, and this can refer to a species, subspecies, hybrid, variant or cultivar. If a synonym (syn.) is given, this provides the alternative name(s) for a plant. A common name may be given after the botanical name.

Japanese name
The Japanese name for each plant is given.

Common name
This is the non-scientific, vernacular name, so it is different in each language.

Propagation
This gives the best method of producing more plants by seeds, cuttings, grafting or other methods.

Flowering time
This indicates the season of flowering, where applicable.

Size
The average expected height and spread of a genus or individual plant is frequently given, although growth rates may vary depending on location and conditions. Metric measurements always precede imperial ones. Average heights and spreads are given (as H and S) wherever possible and appropriate, and more consistently for perennials and bulbs, although it must be noted that dimensions can vary a great deal.

Paeonia suffruticosa
Botan, moutan
Tree peony
Family: Paeoniaceae
The tree peony flowers at exactly the same time as the wisteria, and both are associated in Japan with beautiful women. There are many cultivars of *Paeonia suffruticosa*, known as the "flower of prosperity" and the "king of flowers" because of its luxuriant blooms. It is not easy to cultivate in Japan, and the flowers are too gorgeous and blowsy for the subtle refinement of most of their gardens, so it is usually grown in pots. The most prized colours are white, pale pink and red. It is often represented on painted screens with lions, tigers and bamboo plants.
Propagation grafted
Flowering time late spring
Size shrub to 2.1m (7ft)
Pruning by removing over-long and crossing shoots in late winter
Conditions full sun or partial shade; deep, rich soil
Fully hardy/Z 4–8

Photograph
A large number of entries feature a full-colour photograph that makes identification easy.

Caption
The full botanical name of the plant in question is given with each photograph.

Family
This shows the larger grouping to which the plant belongs and can reveal which plants are related to each other.

Pruning
Indicating the most effective method of pruning and at which time of year this should take place.

Conditions
This section gives the level of sun or shade that the plant either requires or tolerates, with advice on the best type of soil in which they should be grown.

Plant hardiness and zone
A plant's hardiness and zone are given at the end of this section. Zones give a general indication of the average annual minimum temperature for a particular geographical area in the USA. The smaller number indicates the northernmost zone it can survive in and the higher number the southernmost zone that the plant will tolerate. In most cases, only one zone is given. (See page 256 for details of hardiness ratings, zone entries and a zone map.)

HOW TO USE THE PLANT DIRECTORY 209

Spring trees & shrubs

The first signs of spring are a cause for celebration throughout the temperate world, but especially in Japan. In spring gardeners enjoy the bright green of new buds and the blossoms of the azaleas. Camellias and some azaleas are evergreen; some varieties flower very early, and they lend themselves well to being clipped. Kerria has been grown in Japanese gardens since the 11th century and often flowers early, as do many species of magnolia, some of which are native to Japan. You will also find many varieties of rhododendron in full bloom.

Above: *The red flowers of* Chaenomeles japonica, *the Japanese quince, open almost as soon as the winter ends.*

Camellia japonica
Tsubaki
Camellia
Family: Theaceae
This evergreen shrub, native to the warm temperate coasts of Japan, is planted in gardens together with species and hybrids from China. *Camellia sasanqua* has smaller, narrower leaves than *C. japonica*, and the pale pink single flowers appear sporadically through winter before dropping when spent.

Camellias are now common, but in the past they were found mainly in Buddhist temples. The simpler, paler coloured, single-flowered forms with glossy foliage, known as *wabi-suke*, were planted in tea gardens. Two types of camellia can be grown as hedges: the dense, glossy foliage of *C. japonica* or the tea plant *C. sinensis*, with smaller leaves than other species and white flowers in autumn, often clipped to give a compact, dense shape.
Propagation semi-ripe leaf cuttings
Flowering time mid- to late spring
Size shrub or small tree to 10m (30ft); keep to 2m (6½ft) by restricting the roots in a tub, or by regular stem pruning
Pruning by thinning out stems after flowering
Conditions light shade and away from early morning sun; moist, acid soil
Fully hardy/Z 6–7

Chaenomeles japonica
Boke
Japanese quince, japonica
Family: Rosaceae
The Japanese quince, or japonica, is loved for its early spring flowers, which range in colour from the deepest scarlet to pale pink and white. They appear before the leaves, clustered close to the bare, spiny stems. It can be pot grown, when it tends to take on a wizened habit of growth.
Propagation semi-ripe cuttings
Flowering time spring
Size shrub to 1m (3ft)
Pruning by cutting back hard after flowering to encourage a compact habit, or training against a frame or wall
Conditions sun or partial shade; well-drained, slightly acid soil
Fully hardy/Z 5–8

Kerria japonica
Yamabuki
Jew's mallow
Family: Rosaceae
A deciduous shrub native to Japan, kerria has been grown in gardens since the 11th century. Its simple, five-petalled, orange-yellow, star-like flowers are a welcome sight in spring. The double-flowered form is most common in the West, but Japanese gardens tend to use the single form, usually planted as part of a broad scheme.
Propagation hardwood cuttings
Flowering time mid- to late spring
Size shrub to 2m (6½ft)
Pruning by thinning out old stems after flowering
Conditions full sun or partial shade; any soil
Fully hardy/Z 5–9

Camellia japonica

Kerria japonica

Magnolia

Magnolia spp.
Mokuren
Magnolia

Family: Magnoliaceae

Native magnolias have been planted down the centuries and include the deep purple-pink, lily-flowered *Magnolia liliflora*, known as mokuren; the familiar white, star-flowered *M. stellata*, hime-kobushi; and its taller close relative, *M. kobus*, kobushi. The large *M. obovata*, to 15m (50ft), is a hardy, deciduous tree with highly scented, cream-coloured flowers in midsummer. In more recent years the bold American evergreen species, *M. grandiflora* (bull bay), growing to 18m (60ft), has proved popular, with its large, cream-coloured flowers appearing in late summer. Magnolias are usually planted in large stroll gardens.

Propagation seed and grafted
Flowering time mid-spring to midsummer
Size large shrub or small tree, 3–12m (10–40ft)
Pruning by removing over-long shoots in late winter; best left unpruned
Conditions partial shade; rich, acid soil
Fully hardy/Z 5–9

Paulownia tomentosa
Kiri
Foxglove tree

Family: Scrophulariaceae

Although strictly a native of China, the foxglove tree has been cultivated in Japan since the 9th century. Planted as specimen trees in the courtyard gardens of aristocrats, they became associated with the military leader, Hideyoshi. Paulownias have two notable features: the fabulously large leaves and the beautiful, lavender-blue, foxglove-shaped flowers. It may take a few years and some mild winters before a *Paulownia* will establish a strong stem, but once a trunk has been developed, the tree will form a handsome and perfectly hardy crown.

Alternatively, the stems may be coppiced in spring to encourage the production of massive leaves, up to a metre (40in) wide. This eliminates the flowers, but when combined with bamboos, palms and cycads, it has a bold, tropical look.

Propagation seed
Flowering time mid- to late spring
Size tree to 12m (40ft)
Pruning none needed unless grown as a pollard
Conditions sheltered position in full sun; any soil
Fully hardy/Z 6–9

Rhododendron spp.
Satsuki (small-leaved); hirado (large-leaved)
Rhododendron, azalea

Family: Ericaceae

Evergreen and deciduous azaleas belong to the genus *Rhododendron* (Tsutsuji), of which 50 species are native to Japan. The two main kinds of azalea are the kirishima (*R. obtusum* type) and the slightly later flowering satsuki (*R. indicum*). There is also the large-leaved azalea, called hirado. Most of the thousand or more hybrids are of mixed parentage and have flowers that span the colour spectrum from purple to pink, salmon and white. Flower sizes vary, as does the growth.

Azaleas, most of which flower after the cherries and wisterias, have no symbolic significance in the Japanese garden. Kirishima azaleas have been grown in gardens since the 11th century, though they are often seen on treeless mountainsides in drifts and mounds. This natural habit has made azaleas the perfect subject for clipping for centuries; they lend themselves to being rounded into mounds that imitate hills, trimmed down to echo the shape of a stream, or used in a clipped form with rocks or at the edge of small pools to add shape and contrast. The clipping also reduces the number of flowers, which, to the Japanese, is a bonus because too much colour over-stimulates the senses. Left unclipped, their flowering is so profuse that the leaves are completely obscured.

The art of *o-karikomi* (similar to the representational forms of topiary) is often practised on blocks of azaleas and camellias. In the garden at Shoden-ji, three groups of clipped azaleas have been planted as part of a dry landscape (*kare-sansui*).

Propagation seed, softwood cuttings
Flowering time spring to early summer
Size shrub 1–3m (3–10ft)
Pruning by shaping after flowering and, if necessary, again in the autumn
Conditions full sun or shade; moist, acid soil
Fully hardy/Z 6–9

Paulownia tomentosa

Rhododendron

Spring blossom

The end of winter is signalled by the plum blossom (mume) whose flowers, appearing as the last snows melt, are regarded as brave and resilient. The delicate pink flowers of the peach tree (momo) are the next to open after the plum, but it is for the sakura or cherry blossom that Japanese gardens have become famous the world over. Indeed, their first flowers entice people out to celebrate spring. Cherry trees are relatively shortlived and are only lightly pruned, while the longer-lasting plum is tolerant of hard pruning.

Above: *The kikuzakura (chrysanthemum cherry), flowering in late April/early May, has as many as one hundred petals per blossom.*

Prunus mume
No-ume

Japanese plum or Japanese apricot
Family: Rosaceae
Like the European sloe (*Prunus spinosa*) and the damson (*P. damascena*), the deciduous Japanese plum has a pure white blossom, which may open in some areas while snow is still on the ground. The earliness of the blossom makes it one of the most popular flowers in Japan. The flowers of some forms are pale or deep pink, covering whole valleys with a haze of colour. The round fruit is often pickled or candied.

Prunus mume

Unlike cherry trees, which are relatively short-lived and resent being pruned, venerable plum trees may be pruned hard. Old trees with their branches covered in lichen are revered more than vigorous young trees; the gnarled trunks might need to be propped up and bandaged like an old soldier, with ropes, jute and hessian, and should still bear a few branches with blossom.

The festivals of plum-blossom in Japan lack the boisterous aspect that you often find later in spring under the boughs of cherry blossom. Plum blossom appears when the weather is often quite cold and is viewed with quiet solemnity, touched with a hint of sadness. A symbol of purity and hope, it is revered as the prophet of spring. *Prunus mume* is also seen as the epitome of integrity and fidelity, "as virtuous as a true gentleman", and its resilience marks it out as one of the "three excellent plants" that bear the winter so bravely (the others are pine and bamboo). It was said to be a courageous tree, releasing its scent from leafless branches while the last of the winter cold persists, which is why it was popular with warriors, who might carry sprigs of plum blossom into battle. According to Japanese legend, when a warbler (the equivalent of a nightingale) sings in the branches of the plum tree, the two join together to become the spirit of the awakening spring.

The most common variety of *Prunus mume* in cultivation in Western gardens is the deep pink form called 'Beni Chidori', which is sweetly scented. It is an upright shrub to 3m (10ft). The variety 'Omoi-no-mama' is white. Suitable substitutes for damsons include *P. cerasifera* (cherry plum, myrobalan), which grows to 10m (30ft) and has white flowers in early spring (but avoid the purple-leaved form, 'Nigra'); *P. cerasifera* 'Princess' is suitable for a small garden. *P. glandulosa* is a shrub, to 1.5m (5ft), with white to pale pink flowers followed by red fruit.
Propagation budded or grafted
Flowering time early spring
Size small tree to 9m (9yd)
Pruning by thinning out old stems after flowering
Conditions full sun; any soil
Fully hardy/Z 7–9

Prunus persica
Momo

Peach
Family: Rosaceae
The deciduous Japanese peach is the next flowering tree, after the plum, to be honoured in spring. Peaches were planted in great numbers on the sides of Kyoto's Momo-yama (Peach mountain) as an emblem of longevity and perfection. It was on this same mountain that the great shogun Hideyoshi built his Fushimi castle in the late 1500s; his reign was later referred to as Momoyama.

Prunus persica

Peach blossom is a soft, vibrant pink, and the flowers appear just as the leaves unfurl. The peach was thought to win over the spirits of the dead, and was also a sign of new life. Concoctions of peach were taken at the first sign of pregnancy and were administered as a cure for morning sickness. Peach blossom festivals, originating in China, are still celebrated at the beginning of March. They are a special favourite with children, especially girls, who decorate themselves and their dolls in silk and lacquer.

Peach trees are generally rather short-lived (as little as 15 years) and are prey to a number of pests, including the disfiguring peach leaf curl.
Propagation budded or grafted
Flowering time early spring
Size tree to 8m (25ft)
Pruning by removing dead, diseased and damaged branches in midsummer
Conditions full sun; rich, well-drained soil
Fully hardy/Z 7–9

Prunus serrulata
Sakura
Japanese cherry
Family: Rosaceae

It is for the sakura, or cherry blossom, that Japanese gardens have become famous the world over. Their first flowers bring people out in celebration, and there are huge spring festivals for three weeks in April. The length of Japan, "The Land of the Cherry Blossom", friends gather in gardens and public parks to have picnics and sip sake well into the night, as the ephemeral clouds of blossom float above them. People also tie red paper lanterns in the branches, while children run around in the early evening, clapping to the music of drums and *shamisens*, a lute-like instrument.

The classic Japanese cherries mostly date from the late 19th-century Meiji period. These trees often have fully double and profuse blossoms that derive from the Japanese hill cherry, *Prunus serrulata*. The best-loved forms are those with white flowers and dark, unfurling leaves that are revealed as the petals fall.

Before the 19th century Japanese gardeners mainly grew the species *P. incisa* (Fuji cherry), *P. serrulata* (the Japanese hill cherry) and *P. jamasakura* (formerly *P. serrulata spontanea*), when their more subtle elegance was in keeping with the aesthetics of the times. These trees were the object of veneration and celebration, their short-lived blossom being viewed by the samurai as a reminder of their own fragile mortality, and a symbol of chivalry and loyalty to their lords and masters.

The first of the cherries to flower, from late autumn to spring, is *P.* x *subhirtella* (Higan cherry, rosebud cherry). Its weeping forms, 'Pendula Rosea' and 'Pendula Rosea Plena', are very popular in Japan, the cascading branches being propped up by cedar poles and bamboo frames. *P. incisa* flowers soon after, just before its leaves appear, and makes a small, spreading, attractive tree to 8m (25ft), ideal for the smaller garden.

The next to flower is the hybrid *P.* x *yedoensis* (Yoshino cherry), which is named after Mount Yoshino. The white flowers appear just as the leaves break from their buds, and the spreading tree has a lovely, weeping form, 'Shidare-yoshino'. Around the Arishyama district of Kyoto and the gardens of the Tenryu-ji, hundreds of Yoshino cherries have been planted and admired for over 800 years. The foliage of *P. incisa* also turns beautiful shades of yellow, orange and red in autumn.

In the last 200 to 300 years, especially during the early 19th century Edo period when plant breeding became very popular in Japan, innumerable hybrids and forms of *P. serrulata* were raised. These have become known as simply "Japanese flowering cherries" or Sato zakura (literally "domestic cherries").

Japanese flowering cherries are very easy to grow in almost any soil type that is neither too wet nor too dry. The roots are often very shallow, sometimes lifting to the surface. In general they are short-lived trees, some living less than 50 years. They do not flower all at the same time, so it is possible in a large garden to make a selection from these hybrids and the other species that extend the flowering season from very early spring to late spring.
Propagation budded or grafted
Flowering time early to late spring
Size tree 3–8m (10–25ft)
Pruning only by removing dead, diseased and damaged branches in midsummer
Conditions full sun; rich, well-drained soil
Fully hardy/Z 7–9

Prunus x yedoensis

OTHER CULTIVARS OF CHERRY OFTEN FOUND IN JAPANESE GARDENS

'Amanogawa'

'Shirofugen'

'Ukon'

- 'Amanogawa', a columnar tree with dense clusters of lightly fragrant pink flowers. This is ideal for the small garden or town garden as the tree only spreads to 2m (6½ft) wide and grows only to 8m (26ft) high. Flowers in mid- to late spring.
- 'Beni-yutaka', with semi-double disc-shaped flowers of a unique sugary pink with a dark central eye. Flowers in early to mid-spring.
- 'Hanagasa' (Pink parasol), a tree with a broad spreading habit that bears heavy clusters of long-stemmed blooms in pale pink surrounding a crown of green. Flowers in mid-season.
- 'Ichiyo', a tree with ascending branches with double shell-pink flowers set against bronze green unfurling leaves. Flowers in mid-season.
- 'Kanzan', a classic broad vase-shaped tree often seen in Western gardens, with its densely double, deep purplish-pink flowers. The colour of this popular tree would be too strong for most Japanese garden settings.
- 'Kiku Shidare Sakura' (Cheal's weeping), a charming small weeping tree whose branches cascade vertically down. The flowers are double rose-pink and held in dense clusters.
- 'Pink Perfection', a strong growing vase-shaped tree with bronze unfurling leaves that contrast with the rose-pink flowers. A very dwarf form of this variety called 'Little Pink Perfection' would be perfect for the small garden or even for growing in a pot.
- 'Shirofugen', one of the oldest and still one of the very best varieties. It makes a vigorous wide spreading tree with large double white fragrant flowers that open late in the season.
- 'Shirotae' (Mount Fuji cherry), another very old variety that almost went extinct in Japan but was rescued by an English plantsman 100 years ago and reintroduced to cultivation. This tree has remarkable branches that spread out almost horizontally and slightly weeping. The very large single and semi-double white fragrant flowers burst in drooping clusters amid soft green emerging foliage. Mid- to late season.
- 'Taihaku' (the Great white cherry), a stunning hybrid that makes a vigorous spreading tree with very large white flowers. Mid-season.

'Taihaku'

- 'Ukon', an unusual tree for its clusters of pale yellow to sulphur-green flowers that hang from wide spreading branches. Mid- to late season.

Hybrids from some of the other species also have particular properties that are worth considering:

For the small garden:
- *P. incisa* (Fuji cherry) 'Kojo-no-mai', with curious zig-zag growth, and *P. nipponica* var. *kurilensis*, brilliant colour with large open pink flowers.

For autumn colour:
- *P.* 'Amanogawa' (Japanese flowering cherry), *Prunus avium* 'Beni-yutaka', *P.* 'Taihaku' (Great white cherry), *P. sargentii* (Sargent cherry) and *P. incisa*. *P. sargentii* turns bright red while the others turn a mix of orange, yellow and red.

Prunus sargentii

Late spring & summer trees, shrubs & climbers

As the last of the cherry blossom falls, the wisteria unravels its pendulous, perfumed flowers. Alongside the wisteria, the tree peony unfurls its fabulous frilly petals. This is a plant with sumptuous flowers, which was highly regarded by the Chinese long before the Japanese introduced it to their gardens. Other plants are grown for their shape and foliage as much as for their flowers, and small trees such as *Styrax japonicus* (Japanese snowbell) continue their blossom season into the summer. Clematis are popular in Japan but are mostly grown in pots.

Above: Deutzia gracilis. *This small shrub is smothered with flowers in late spring and has an attractive fine texture.*

Clematis spp.
Tessen
Clematis
Family: Ranunculaceae
Some species of large-flowered clematis, such as *C. patens*, are native to Japan. Although rarely grown as climbers over arbours as they are in Western gardens, the very colourful hybrids of *C. patens* are often planted in containers and placed near the main house entrance.
Propagation seed, all cuttings, layers
Flowering time summer
Size climber up to 4m (13ft)
Conditions sun and part shade
Fully hardy/Z 4–9

Clematis patens

Cornus kousa
Mizuki
Japanese flowering dogwood
Family: Cornaceae
A handsome deciduous large shrub or small tree up to 10m (33ft), native to Japan and China, with wide spreading tiered branches that carry flowers with four white bracts in early summer. They open green and steadily change to pure white, or pink in the variety 'Satomi'. The best form is *Cornus kousa* var. *chinensis*, which freely bears larger and whiter flowers than the straight species. *Cornus kousa* and its forms are outstanding plants, not only because they are very hardy and can be grown in most soil types, but also because they flower in midsummer when few other trees or shrubs are blossoming. There are some hybrids between this species and the American flowering dogwood, *Cornus florida*, which flower earlier in the spring.

Cornus kousa

Cornus kousa and *C. florida* both turn tones of red and purple in the autumn, keeping their display for up to a month.
Propagation grafted, layers, seed or softwood cuttings
Flowering time early summer
Size small tree to large shrub, up to 10m (33ft)
Conditions sun or part shade
Fully hardy/Z 5–8

Deutzia spp.
Unohana, utsuki
Japanese snowflower
Family: Philadelphaceae
The Japanese grow many species and forms of deutzia in mixed plantings. The shrub's white or pink flowers are borne later than those of other spring-flowering shrubs and can be used to bridge the gap before the summer. *Deutzia crenata* and *D. gracilis*, both native to Japan, have clusters of star-shaped white flowers.
Propagation stem cuttings
Flowering time late spring to early summer
Size shrub 1m (3ft)
Pruning by cutting out old flowering stems after flowering
Conditions full sun; any reasonable soil
Fully hardy/Z 5–9

Paeonia suffruticosa

Paeonia suffruticosa
Botan, moutan
Tree peony
Family: Paeoniaceae
The tree peony flowers at exactly the same time as the wisteria, and both are associated in Japan with beautiful women. There are many cultivars of *Paeonia suffruticosa*, known as the "flower of prosperity" and the "king of flowers" because of its luxuriant blooms. It is not easy to cultivate in Japan, and the flowers are rather too gorgeous and blowsy for the subtle refinement of most of their gardens, so it is usually grown in pots. The most prized colours are white, pale pink and red. It is often represented on painted screens alongside lions, tigers and bamboo plants.
Propagation grafted
Flowering time late spring to early summer
Size shrub to 2.1m (7ft)
Pruning by removing over-long and crossing shoots in late winter
Conditions full sun or partial shade; deep, rich soil
Fully hardy/Z 4–8

Sophora japonica
Enju
Japanese pagoda tree
Family: Papilionaceae
Sophora japonica belies its name. It is not native to Japan, but, like so many garden plants, was introduced from China around 1,000 years ago. This fine stately tree, growing ultimately to 20m (65ft), has elegant pinnate leaves and produces large panicles of small white flowers in late summer.

In Japanese gardens you will often see the weeping form *S. japonica pendula*, which needs support as even its main stem has a serpentine nature and is unable to form a straight trunk. The tree may become self-supporting, making an umbrella-shaped mound. While hardy, *Sophora japonica* and its forms need hot summers to ripen the wood and flowers.
Propagation seed (weeping form is grafted)
Flowering time late summer to autumn
Size medium-sized tree up to 20 (65ft)
Conditions sun
Fully hardy/Z 7–9

Spiraea nipponica
Shimotsuke
Nippon spiraea
Family: Rosaceae
Several species of spiraea are native to Japan, most small to medium-sized shrubs. They make a round or spreading shape, with arching growth, decked with bunches of tiny flowers. *S. nipponica* has dark green leaves and white flowers.
Propagation semi-ripe cuttings
Flowering time midsummer
Size shrub to 1.2m (4ft)
Pruning by cutting hard back after flowering to remove old flowering stems
Conditions full sun; any soil
Fully hardy/Z 5–9

Sophora japonica

Spiraea nipponica

Stewartia pseudocamellia
Hatsutsubaki
Japanese stewartia
Family: Theaceae
Grown for its small, white-cupped, camellia-shaped flowers (which bloom in mid- to late summer), mottled bark and autumn tints (with yellow, red and purple leaves in the autumn), this small to medium tree is often planted among mixed blocks of evergreen shrubs or as a specimen near a gateway.
Propagation seed
Flowering time midsummer
Size tree to 20m (65ft)
Pruning none needed
Conditions full sun or light shade; moist, acid soil; does not tolerate wind or drought
Fully hardy/Z 5–7

Stewartia pseudocamellia

Styrax japonicus
Storax

Japanese snowbell

Family: Styracaceae

The Japanese snowbell is a small, broad, deciduous tree, with glossy, dark green leaves and masses of small white flowers.

Propagation seed
Flowering time early to midsummer
Size tree to 10m (30ft)
Pruning none needed
Conditions full sun or partial shade; moist, neutral to acid soil
Fully hardy/Z 6–8

Ulmus parvifolia
Akinire

Chinese elm

Family: Ulmaceae

A graceful medium-sized tree, native to both Japan and China. It has relatively small leaves, which are not dropped until well into winter, and hop-like flowers late in the summer. It has given rise to some dwarf forms, such as 'Yatsubusa' and 'Hokkaido', which have extra dense growth and very small leaves and would make ideal companions to other Japanese plants in a very small garden. These dwarf forms could also be pruned to give the appearance of an older, larger tree in a *shukkei*, or "condensed landscape" arrangement.

Propagation seed (dwarf forms from hardwood cuttings)
Flowering time late summer to autumn
Size medium-sized tree up to 20m (65ft)
Conditions sun
Hardiness/Z 4–8

Wisteria spp.
Fuji

Wisteria

Family: Papilionaceae

As soon as the cherry blossom has fallen in mid-spring, the long racemes of wisteria start to unravel. *Wisteria floribunda* is native to Japan, where it can be seen in the wild, tumbling out of tall trees and creating blue cascades on steep hillsides. *W. floribunda* has much longer racemes than its cousin from China, *W. sinensis*, and in the cultivar 'Macrobotrys' (formerly 'Multijuga') the racemes of lilac-blue flowers can reach 1.2m (4ft) long. Wisterias were revered for their longevity and were the only climbing plants to have been cultivated seriously in Japanese gardens. They have been grown through pines since the 1600s, but are now more often planted on frames, arbours and tripods. Wisterias also look terrific when they are draped over a specially constructed bridge, with the long racemes reaching down to the water beneath to meet their reflection. Another wisteria grown in Japan is *W. brachybotrys* 'Shiro-kapitan' (syn. *W. venusta*), which produces attractive, beautifully scented white flowers a few weeks before the leaves appear.

Wisterias may also be trained against a firm stake as standards, to stand alone as specimens, or grown more as a shrub, by simply allowing them to spread along the ground. To keep wisterias within bounds, they need to be pruned quite hard. Pruning is done in two sessions, the first in midsummer, when the long wands of growth are reduced by two-thirds, and the second in midwinter, when growth is further reduced to 10cm (4in) spurs. The plant's tolerance of pruning makes it suitable for pot growing as well as bonsai treatment.

Ulmus parvifolia 'Yatsubusa'

Wisteria

Propagation mostly grafted, seed
Flowering time early summer
Size to 9m (30ft)
Pruning in midsummer and in midwinter
Conditions full sun or partial shade; rich, moist soil
Fully hardy/Z 4–10

SPRING FOLIAGE

Early spring is not just about flowers, because Japanese gardeners try to avoid using too much colour. *Salix babylonica* (weeping willow) has been planted around ponds and lakes in Japan since its introduction from China in the 9th century. The soft green of its unfurling leaves is much admired. The young foliage of *Acer palmatum* is quite varied, with tints ranging from soft green to salmon pink. In general, purple, golden and variegated foliage is not found in traditional gardens, because the colours are too unnatural and detract from the overall design.

Summer flowers

Japanese summers often bring heavy rain, which few flowers can endure. However, hydrangeas continue to flourish in these conditions, and in recent years they have gained in popularity. Apart from hydrangeas, two flowers are often grown as Buddhist symbols of mortality and immortality: the annual morning glory for its fleeting existence, and the lotus, a symbol of purity as it emerges out of the wet mud in ponds. The iris is also planted in or near water, and is a plant celebrated for its power to ward off evil spirits.

Above: *The mop-headed* Hydrangea macrophylla *here grows profusely in a shaded woodland.*

Hydrangea spp.
Ajisai
Hydrangea
Family: Hydrangeaceae
Hydrangeas were first mentioned in Japanese gardens as early as 759, but they did not become instantly popular. The four petals and rather gloomy purple colours were thought to represent death. The common name, ajisai, means "to gather purple". They were also called shichihenge, which meant "to change seven times", alluding to the way in which the flower colour changes through the season.

Three of the most important species of hydrangea are native to Japan, *Hydrangea macrophylla*, *H. petiolaris* (climbing hydrangea) and *H. serrata*. The great round mop-head hybrids originated here and are found in a number of Japanese gardens. Among their useful attributes are their late-summer flowering and their ability to withstand heavy summer downpours. On acid soil with plenty of moisture, the blue varieties are intensely blue. The lacecaps, which come closer to the species in their flower form, are also very elegant and suitable for planting in light woodland shade, where their mysterious beauty can be almost bewitching, especially when the flowers are moist from the rain. Varieties of *H. macrophylla* can be grown in pots, if regularly fed and watered. The other species that is native to Japan is *H. paniculata*, which has cone-shaped flowerheads in late summer. It is ultra-hardy and can be grown in full sun. All these hydrangeas come in a multitude of forms to suit every taste, and they have become very popular in Japan in recent years, with some towns and districts making the hydrangea their special flower.

Propagation semi-ripe and hardwood cuttings
Flowering time mid- to late summer
Size shrub to 2m (6½ft)
Pruning by removing dead and over-long shoots in early spring
Conditions sun or partial shade; moist, rich soil
Fully hardy/Z 4–9

Hydrangea

Ipomoea
Asagao
Morning glory
Family: Convolvulaceae
During the Nara and Heian periods, when poets typically sang of the fleeting condition of human life, they latched on to morning glory as an ideal symbol: as one flower fades after a day of glory, it is quickly replaced by another. But it was in the 18th and 19th centuries that the morning glory became fashionable among the *daimyos*, who helped to create a new array of colours. Morning glory is usually grown in pots over lightweight bamboo trellises and fences. While so many flowers tend to wilt at the onset of summer, the morning glory revels in the heat.

Propagation seed
Flowering time summer to autumn
Size climber to 6m (20ft)
Conditions full sun; any soil
Tender/Z 8–10

Ipomoea

Iris laevigata

Iris spp.
Hanashobu
Iris

Family: Iridaceae

The iris is a great favourite in Japan. *Iris laevigata*, known as kakitsubata, grows naturally in the swamps around the ancient capital of Nara, where it was collected to be made into a dye, its blue colour exclusively used to decorate the robes of the imperial family. In *The Pillow Book*, a novel dating from the 11th century, the author writes of the iris festival when men, women and children warded off evil spirits by adorning their hair and clothes with iris flowers and roots. The festival still takes place in late May and early June.

I. laevigata is cultivated in gardens in swampy, but not waterlogged, ground, often near an inlet to a pond. *Yatsuhashi* or zigzag plank bridges weave over the beds, forcing the visitor to slow down and admire the plants from different angles. The flowers are said to have a "naive neatness" that needs no improvement; they are narrower and smaller than the larger and flatter *I. ensata* var. *spontanea*, known as hanashobu.

Hanashobu is more spectacular than kakitsubata and has been bred intensively. It now comes in all shapes and colours, from white and pink to deep purple, and is often cultivated in large beds in slightly ridged rows or in pots, so that it can be admired as an individual against golden folding screens.

In parts of Japan where they cannot cultivate either of these irises for lack of water, the European *I. germanica* is often grown in the same way, in large beds exclusively devoted to irises. Other irises grown are *I. tectorum* (roof iris) and the shade-loving *I. japonica*, whose wild look is perfect for the tea garden.

Propagation division
Flowering time summer
Size to 80cm (32in)
Conditions full sun or partial shade; slightly acid soil
Fully hardy/Z 4–9

Nelumbo nucifera
Hana-basu
Lotus

Family: Nymphaeaceae

By high summer the glories of the spring blossom have long faded, and it is time for the lotus to bloom. The lotus is the flower most closely associated with Hinduism and Buddhism, and the Buddha is often portrayed in statues and images sitting on a lotus, in his state of perfect enlightenment. The lotus symbolizes the evolution of the human spirit, with its roots in the mud, its growth passing through water and air and into the sun, to open, pure and unsullied. The wheel-like formation of the petals is also said to represent the cycle of existence.

A succession of flowers opens over six weeks, the buds opening at dawn with an indescribable sound. The white flowers of *N. nucifera* 'Alba' have an especially powerful and sweet perfume. Lotus flowers close in the heat of the day and after a couple of days gracefully fall, one petal at a time, leaving their distinctive honeycombed seed pods. The lotus is also an important source of nourishment. The seeds, roots and leaves are all eaten, but varieties grown as food rarely flower. The lotus is not reliably hardy, and some climates are simply not hot enough in the summer to stimulate its flowering. In these circumstances *Nymphaea* (waterlily) is a good substitute, although the flowers sit closer to the surface of the water and are not held on erect stalks, like the tall flower stems of the lotus.

Propagation division
Flowering time summer
Size 1.2m (4ft) above water
Conditions in full sun; in water to a depth of 60cm (24in)
Half hardy/Z 4–11

Iris ensata

Nelumbo nucifera

Autumn foliage

Plants that celebrate autumn with their colourful leaves were known collectively as *momichi*, but in time the term became synonymous with the beautiful tones of *Acer palmatum*, the first entry here. Traditional Japanese gardens do contain other trees and large shrubs, although the *Acer* varieties will always be favourites for autumn colour. Some of these trees and shrubs also turn beautiful colours in autumn, while others are more valued for their glossy evergreen leaves as a foil to the bright foliage of the *Acer* and other plants. A few are scented or bear edible fruits.

Above: Acer palmatum *can be grown as a single or multi-stemmed small tree. In the autumn its leaves turn to shades of scarlet, yellow or orange.*

Acer palmatum
Kaede
Japanese maple
Family: Aceraceae
The Japanese maple is perhaps second only to the cherry blossom in popularity in Japan, and it has become a tradition to take special trips to view the flaming autumn tints of their wild maples. *Acer palmatum* is native to Japan, where it can be seen mingling on hillsides with cedars, bamboos and pines. Although there are hundreds of fancy types of Japanese maple, some with finely cut leaves and others with variegated and purple foliage, the species *A. palmatum* is the chief focus of all the celebrations in gardens and in the wild. *A. micranthum*, *A. tataricum* var. *ginnala* and *A. japonicum* are also native, and all turn beautiful colours, but in November the temples and gardens of Kyoto are ablaze with the fiery red and orange leaves of *A. palmatum*.

Some very beautiful forms of Japanese maple have foliage that is salmon-tinted in spring, while some turn bright yellow rather than red in autumn, and others have bright red or green stems in winter. The dwarf and cut-leaf forms may be more suitable for the smaller garden, but it is better to try and avoid the purple-leaf forms, which tend to distract from carefully composed, harmonious arrangements.
Propagation seed and grafted (all named varieties will need to be grafted, although to raise just one or two plants you can layer them)
Size small tree to 8m (25ft)
Pruning best left unpruned; can cut out over-long stems in late winter
Conditions full sun or partial shade; moist soil; occasionally the young growth can be injured by late frosts or cold winds
Fully hardy/Z 5–8

Other species of maple, native to Japan:

Acer buergerianum
Buerger-kaede
Trident maple
Family: Aceraceae
This small oval tree is often seen in larger Japanese gardens but in a mild autumn holds on to its leaves well into the winter, and will not always colour as reliably as some of the other species. It has a multi-stemmed habit and medium-fine, glossy dark green leaves. The bark exfoliates to expose an orangish under-bark.

Acer cissifolium
Mitsude-kaede
Ivy-leaved maple
Family: Aceraceae
This barely looks like a maple at all with its three-lobed leaves. It is one of the very first to colour in autumn, but keeps those leaves for a remarkably long time as they turn a patchwork of oranges, yellows and reds.

Acer ginnala
Amur-kaede
Amur maple
Family: Aceraceae
An upright but eventually broad spreading small tree that has handsome leaves. The form *A. ginnala* 'Flame' has been selected for the brilliance of its autumn colours.

Acer palmatum 'Linearilobum'

Acer buergerianum

Acer japonicum
Momji
Full moon maple
Family: Aceraceae

Second only in popularity to *Acer palmatum*, *A. japonicum* has much larger leaves. While rarely cultivated in gardens it has produced the two forms of 'Aconitifolium' and 'Vitifolium', bold and fine garden plants which are easily grown, slowly becoming medium-sized trees. 'Vitifolium' has leaves like grape vines while those of 'Aconitifolium' are deeply incised. Both come into leaf very early and turn fiery red in autumn. The golden-leaf form, which turns more or less green in summer, is now classified as *Acer shirasawanum* 'Aureum'. Another form of this latter species is *Acer shirasawanum* 'Ogurayama', with smaller leaves and a more upright habit. *Acer sieboldianum* is similar to both these and makes a small tree.

Acer micranthum
Komine-kaede
Komine maple
Family: Aceraceae

A small-leaved maple that grows in native forests in central Japan with *Acer palmatum*. It forms a delightful small wide spreading tree that colours brilliantly in autumn.

Acer rufinerve
Uri hada kaeda
Redvein maple
Family: Aceraceae

This snake-bark maple has long white striations in the bark and beautiful leaves that turn a mix of yellow and red.

Acer cissifolium

Acer japonicum

Acer palmatum var. *dissectum*

SUITABLE CULTIVARS OF ACER PALMATUM

- *A. p.* 'Chitoseyama' has a hint of purple in the foliage as it unfurls in the spring, and then turns purple-red in autumn.
- *A. p.* var. *dissectum* (Dissectum Viride Group) is a small, rounded shrub with deeply cut leaves and fine autumn colour. There are many purple cut-leaf forms of this type that are sometimes planted in contemporary Japanese gardens but their colour intensity is too distracting for more refined and traditional styles.
- *A. p.* 'Ichigyoji' has bold green foliage similar to the species itself but turns an especially bright yellow in autumn.
- *A. p.* 'Katsura' has bright pink young foliage in spring, which turns red in autumn.
- *A. p.* 'Linearilobum' has deeply cut linear leaves that are bright green in spring and summer, turning rich tones of yellow and orange in autumn.
- *A. p.* 'Omurayama' has finely cut leaves that become elegantly pendulous with age. The leaves turn orange and yellow in autumn.
- *A. p.* 'Osakazuki' is a rounded tree with large leaves that turn bright orange and red in autumn.
- *A. p.* 'Seiryu' is a wide spreading small tree of exceptional beauty and an excellent maple for small gardens or for groups. It has elegant, finely cut leaves which unfurl as a soft green and turn a mix of flame colours in the autumn.
- *A. p.* 'Sango-kaku' has salmon spring tints, and the leaves turn yellow in autumn. The stems are red and stand out well in the winter landscape.

Cercidiphyllum japonicum
Katsura
Katsura tree
Family: Cercidiphyllaceae

Thought to resemble the moon, this medium-sized tree has ascending branches and beautifully rounded leaves that colour up in the autumn. As the leaves fall they give off an aroma akin to burnt, crushed sugar.
Propagation seed
Size tree to 20m (65ft)
Pruning by removing over-long or crossing branches in late winter
Conditions sun or light shade; slightly acid soil
Fully hardy/Z 5–9

Cercidiphyllum japonicum

Diospyrus kaki
Kaki
Persimmon
Family: Ebenaceae
A fine autumn tree with yellow to orange fruits. The most edible of date plums, it is grown for its handsome leaves, which turn yellow, orange-red and purple before they fall. In cold areas this frost-hardy plant is best grown against a wall.
Propagation grafted
Flowering time summer
Size tree to 10m (33ft)
Pruning by removing over-long or crossing branches in late winter
Conditions sheltered position in full sun; rich soil
Fully hardy/Z 4–8

Enkianthus perulatus
Dodan
White enkianthus
Family: Ericaceae
A member of the heather family, this large shrub has clusters of small cream- and pink-tinted bells in spring, but is more often grown for its bright red and golden-orange autumn foliage. When pruned hard it produces few flowers, although judicious pruning can enhance its tiered branching. Grow as a hedge or mix with evergreens. An alternative is *E. campanulatus*.
Propagation semi-ripe cuttings
Flowering time mid-spring
Size shrub to 2m (6½ft)
Pruning by cutting out crossing or over-long shoots in early spring
Conditions sun or partial shade; moist, slightly acid soil
Fully hardy/Z 5–7

Enkianthus perulatus

Ginkgo biloba

Ginkgo biloba
Icho
Maidenhair tree
Family: Ginkgoaceae
The ancient maidenhair tree dates back to the time of the dinosaurs. It is unique with no close living relatives. Its leaves, curiously shaped like webbed feet, turn to shades of bright butter yellow in autumn. Originally native to China, ginkgo is now found all over Japan, especially in Kyoto, where trees can be seen growing to an immense size and the ground under them in autumn is smothered in blankets of yellow. They produce an edible but unpleasant-smelling fruit in autumn. *Ginkgo biloba* 'Annie's Dwarf' would be suitable for smaller gardens or pot culture.
Propagation seed and grafted
Flowering time (catkins) spring
Size tree to 30m (100ft)
Pruning by removing diseased or dead branches in late winter or early spring
Conditions full sun; any soil
Fully hardy/Z 5–9

Nandina domestica
Nanten
Sacred bamboo
Family: Berberidaceae
Native to Japan, the nanten is a close relative of *Berberis*. In midsummer, small white flowers are carried in large open panicles, and they are followed by red berries, which lie above the glossy, pinnate foliage. In a good autumn the leaves turn bright red, especially if the shrub has been planted in full sun, although they are tolerant of some shade. In very cold areas many of the leaves tend to fall by late winter, but the plant is considered to be evergreen.
Propagation seed
Flowering time midsummer
Size shrub to 2m (6½ft)
Pruning by trimming back over-long shoots in mid- to late spring
Conditions full sun; moist soil
Fully hardy/Z 7–10

Stewartia pseudocamellia
Hatsutsubaki
Japanese stewartia
Family: Theaceae
Each leaf of this plant turns a mixture of yellow, orange, green and red. It also has small white flowers in high summer.
Propagation seed
Flowering time midsummer
Size tree to 20m (65ft)
Pruning none needed
Conditions full sun or light shade; moist, acid soil
Fully hardy/Z 5–7

Styrax japonicus
Storax
Japanese snowbell
Family: Styracaceae
This, combined with various cherries, adds lovely shades to the autumn garden. Its leaves are dark green and it bears masses of small white flowers in summer.
Propagation seed
Flowering time early to midsummer
Size tree to 10m (30ft)
Pruning none needed
Conditions full sun or partial shade; moist, neutral to acid soil
Fully hardy/Z 6–8

Nandina domestica

Autumn flowers

The "seven grasses of autumn" have been known and used in Japan since the 11th century. The selection of these seven herbaceous plants has varied over the centuries and from region to region, but in general they are the ones that flower after the summer rains and during the autumn leaf colour season. Included here are some of the original seven, together with a few others that have since gained in popularity. Except for *Miscanthus* none of these are grasses, and the remainder can be categorized as meadow flowers.

Above: *Potted hybrid chrysanthemums outside a Japanese temple.*

Anemone spp.
Shuumeigiku
Anemone
Family: Ranunculaceae
Plants known as Japanese anemones have been developed from the Chinese import *Anemone hupehensis*, which has been extensively hybridized. This tall herbaceous plant with vine-like leaves is often seen in shady gardens, planted in clumps of moss and beside streams. The finest form is the single, pure white *A.* x *hybrida* 'Honorine Jobert', but there are many cultivars, with colours ranging from white and pale pink to a deep purple-pink, some with double flowers. In fertile soil it can be invasive and may need to be kept under control.
Propagation division
Flowering time late summer to mid-autumn
Size perennial to 1.2m (4ft)
Conditions sun or partial shade; rich, moist soil
Fully hardy/Z 5–8

Callicarpa japonica
Murasaki shikobu
Japanese beauty berry
Family: Verbenaceae
Named after the author of the great 11th-century novel *The Tale of Genji*, the Japanese species *Callicarpa japonica* (beauty berry) is a low-growing, arching, deciduous shrub, which bears beautiful purple berries in autumn and winter. It has delicate pink flowers that arrive in the early summer (which precede the purple berries) and simple, medium blue-green leaves. Its larger cousin, *C. bodinieri* var. *bodinieri* 'Profusion', is more frequently planted in Western gardens but is a much larger shrub.
Propagation semi-ripe cuttings
Flowering time late summer
Size shrub to 1.5m (5ft)
Pruning cut back close to ground level in early spring
Conditions sun or light shade; rich soil
Fully hardy/Z 5–8

Chrysanthemum spp.
Kiku
Chrysanthemum
Family: Asteraceae
Almost all chrysanthemums have now been reclassified as members of the genus *Dendranthema,* but most gardeners still use the old name. The plant was long associated with the imperial Japanese family, and its mythological status has made it the subject of fairy stories and legends. Extracts and essence of chrysanthemum were believed to possess miraculous powers for a longer life.

The large, ball-shaped flowers are rarely seen in Japanese formal gardens, but are often grown in pots, outside temples and in domestic gardens. Great pride is taken in the cultivation of the artificial giants, but more modest species are grown in gardens. The related *Leucanthemum* x *superbum* (formerly *Chrysanthemum* x *superbum*, shasta daisy), with white, yellow-centred flowers, like a large marguerite, might flower in late autumn. These, and a number of wild asters, are suitable for the wilderness parts of the tea garden.
Propagation cuttings and division
Flowering time early to late autumn
Size perennial to 1.5m (5ft)
Conditions sheltered position in full sun; rich soil
Fully hardy/Z 4–9

Anemone

Callicarpa japonica

Eupatorium

Eupatorium spp.
Fujibakama

Hemp agrimony (UK)
Joe Pye weed (US)
Family: Asteraceae
The Japanese species *E. chinense* and *E. lindleyanum* are tall herbaceous plants with flattened heads of fuzzy purple or white flowers, which are adored by bees. The subdued colouring and upright habit make them excellent for semi-naturalizing.
Propagation seed and division
Flowering time autumn
Size perennial 1–2m (3–6½ft)
Conditions full sun or partial shade; any moist soil
Fully hardy/Z 4–9

Lespedeza bicolor
Hagi

Shrubby lespedeza
Family: Papilionaceae
The purple-flowered bush clover is a lax and arching shrub, which comes into leaf late in the season. Its purple, broom-like racemes of flowers, up to 15cm (6in) long, appear in autumn at the ends of shoots and side-shoots on wand-like stems 1–3m (3–10ft) long.
Propagation seed and division
Flowering time mid- to late summer
Size shrub to 2m (6½ft)
Pruning by cutting down to ground level in early spring
Conditions full sun; well-drained soil
Fully hardy/Z 4–6

Miscanthus sinensis
Obana, susuki

Fountain grass or Eulalia grass
Family: Poaceae
Because *Miscanthus sinensis* colonizes waste ground in Japan it is rarely used as a garden plant. When it is, it is used with restraint. The silvery plumes, which appear in autumn, reach 2–4m (7–13ft) high. *M. sinensis* 'Yakushima Dwarf' is a low-growing form from Yakushima, the volcanic island off the south coast of Japan, which makes a rounded clump 1m (3ft) high and across. The old flower and leaf stems turn to shades of fawn, persisting into the New Year before being dispersed by the wind. Eulalia grass covers many of the hills in Japan, where it waves elegantly in the wind.
Propagation division
Flowering time autumn
Size grass to 4m (13ft)
Conditions full sun; well-drained soil
Fully hardy/Z 5–9

Platycodon grandiflorus
Kikyo, asagao

Balloon flower
Family: Campanulaceae
From the campanula family, the balloon flower has inflated and pleated flower buds that give the plant its name. The flowers, which eventually open to a wide cup, are mostly blue, but can also be pink or white. This compact, herbaceous plant with blue-green leaves will do well if planted near the edge of a stream.
Propagation seed and division
Flowering time late summer

Lespedeza bicolor

Miscanthus sinensis

Size perennial to 60cm (24in)
Conditions sun or partial shade; moist soil
Fully hardy/Z 4–9

Tricyrtis
Hototogisu

Toad lily
Family: Convallariaceae
The old Chinese name for this plant means the "oil spot plant" because its flowers are freckled with maroon to purple spots. Its Japanese name, hototogisu, is the same as the name for a cuckoo, which has a freckled chest. This genus, known in the West as toad lily, has only recently become popular in Japan, where its wild forms with their modest and mysterious colours are suitable for planting in moist shade beside a tea garden path or near a stream.
Propagation division
Flowering time late summer to mid-autumn
Size perennial to 80cm (30in)
Conditions shade; rich, moist soil
Fully hardy/Z 7

Tricyrtis

Evergreen shrubs

Japan's flora is rich in native evergreen shrubs. Many are grown in and around the gardens of Kyoto. The following selection has been made for the plants' hardiness and general availability. Camellias and azaleas have already been discussed under spring-flowering shrubs (see pages 210–211), but they need to be mentioned again because they form the backbone of most evergreen schemes in Japanese gardens, especially as they can be well pruned and shaped. Many of these evergeen shrubs can be grown in the shade of trees and buildings.

Above: Buxus microphylla *var.* japonica *is a dense evergreen shrub that can be used to form small hedges and topiary.*

Ardisia japonica

Ardisia japonica
Senryo
Marlberry
Family: Myrsinaceae
Seen in many gardens in Kyoto and in the south of Japan, marlberry is a delightful evergreen shrub which is only hardy in sheltered spots. *Ardisia japonica* is a small shrub with white or pale pink flowers, which are followed by red or yellow berries. They last from autumn into winter.
A. crenata (coralberry, spiceberry), which is known as manryo, is a larger shrub, to 2m (6½ft), with white or pink flowers followed by scarlet fruits.
Propagation seed
Flowering time summer
Size shrub to 1m (3ft)
Pruning by removing over-long shoots in mid-spring
Conditions sheltered position in shade; moist, rich, acid soil
Half hardy/Z 4–8

Aucuba japonica
Aoki
Japanese laurel
Family: Cornaceae
The spotted laurels are reliable evergreen shrubs with glossy foliage. They love shade and tolerate the dry soil among the roots of large trees. In the autumn female shrubs bear small clusters of large red berries, so they are sometimes called Japanese hollies. There are forms with yellow-spotted leaves and others with orange or yellow berries, but in Japanese gardens the most popular plant is the species or its narrow-leaved form, 'Salicifolia'.
Flowering time mid-spring
Size shrub to 3m (10ft)
Pruning by removing crossing or over-long shoots in late winter or early spring
Conditions shade or partial shade; any soil
Fully hardy/Z 7–10

Aucuba japonica

Buxus microphylla var. *japonica*
Asama tsuge
Japanese box
Family: Buxaceae
The Japanese box is a small evergreen shrub up to 2m (6½ft) high and wide. It is hardier than *Buxus sempervirens* (the European boxwood), and has longer, narrower leaves and a more compact habit. Many hybrids and forms exist in rounded, dwarf forms, such as 'Compacta' and 'Green Pillow'. It is easily grown in sun or shade. Like all box, this species can be clipped into almost any shape and this makes it an excellent plant for Japanese gardens, especially in soils of high alkalinity where azaleas are not able to grow.
Propagation hardwood cuttings
Flowering time spring
Size shrub to 2m (6½ft)
Conditions sun or shade
Fully hardy/Z 5–8

Cleyera japonica
Sakaki
Japanese cleyera
Family: Theaceae
This slow-growing evergreen shrub with upright rigid growth is sacred to the Shinto religion. Boughs of its scented leathery foliage are presented at special ceremonies and it is often planted near Shinto shrines and in gardens in Japan. *Cleyera japonica* is not fully hardy, so it should be grown in a sheltered spot on an acid soil.
Propagation seed, semi-ripe cuttings
Flowering time early summer
Size to 10m (30ft)
Conditions sun to light shade; moist, well-drained acid soil
Half hardy/Z 8

Daphne odora
Jinchoge
Winter daphne
Family: Thymelaeaceae
This small evergreen shrub carries its deliciously sweet-scented, pink-white flowers in late winter to early spring. It is most often seen in gardens in the form 'Aureomarginata', which has gold-edged leaves, and is a lovely plant to include in a mixed planting, but is not very long-lived. Note: it is highly poisonous.
Propagation seed or semi-ripe cuttings
Flowering time late winter to early spring
Size shrub to 1.5m (5ft)
Pruning best left unpruned
Conditions sun or partial shade; rich, moist, slightly acid soil
Fully hardy/Z 8–10

Elaeagnus x ebbingei

Daphniphyllum macropodum
Yuzuri-ha
Family: Daphniphyllaceae
A handsome large-leaved shrub, bearing long strap-like leaves with red leaf stalks. This Japanese native plant, which can be grown in almost any moisture-retentive soil in sun or part shade, makes a good substitute for rhododendrons on alkaline soils where bold foliage is required. It will grow into a large shrub. While its flowers are insignificant they release a pungent scent.
Propagation seed, semi-ripe cuttings
Flowering time spring
Size shrub to 8m (26ft)
Pruning after flowering, if necessary
Conditions sun or shade
Propagation hardwood cuttings or seed
Fully hardy/Z 7–8

Elaeagnus spp.
Gumi
Silverberry
Family: Elaeagnaceae
Popular species of elaeagnus include *Elaeagnus pungens*, *E. glabra* and *E. macrophylla*, but the most common green-leaved form is the hybrid *E. x ebbingei*, with dusty green leaves, which are silvery beneath. In autumn small, creamy-white, bell-shaped flowers are borne in the leaf axils, almost out of sight, but their scent can carry far.

This is a wonderful evergreen for mixed hedges, when it can be pruned to maintain a neat shape, and as a general evergreen backdrop. Variegated forms are available, but are not appropriate for a Japanese garden. The growth of *E. x ebbingei* can be a bit rangy and will need some tidying.
Propagation semi-ripe cuttings
Flowering time autumn
Size shrub to 4m (13ft)
Pruning by cutting back over-long shoots in mid-spring
Conditions full sun or partial shade; any soil
Fully hardy/Z 7–9

Euonymus japonicus
Mayumi
Japanese spindle tree
Family: Celastraceae
A handsome and cheerful evergreen, native to Japan, euonymus is often planted

Daphniphyllum macropodum

in coastal areas owing to its resistance to salt-laden air. It is a variable shrub up to 4m (13ft) tall that has produced many variegated forms, but also a large-leaved variety called 'Macrophyllus' and a dwarf form with minute leaves called 'Microphyllus'. This dwarf form would be suitable for smaller gardens but is on the tender side and may need the shelter of other plants. As with most of this species, *Euonymus japonicus* is easily grown on most soil types. A similar species, *E. fortunei*, is much hardier and has given rise to countless cultivars, many of which, like *E. fortunei* 'Coloratus', can be used as ground cover in dry shady areas.
Propagation hardwood cuttings
Flowering time insignificant
Size shrub to 3m (10ft)
Conditions sun or shade
Pruning in autumn or late winter as a shrub or in midsummer if grown as a hedge
Fully hardy/Z 6–8

OTHER NATIVE JAPANESE EVERGREENS

• *Leucothoe keiskei*, which is a small shrub, to 60cm (24in), with slender, glossy, dark green leaves. It must have acid soil.

• *Nandina domestica* (sacred bamboo; see page 222), which is evergreen in mild areas. It is an upright shrub, to 2m (6½ft), with white flowers in summer and bright red fruit.

Fatsia japonica

Fatsia japonica
Yatsude
Japanese aralia
Family: Araliaceae
Native to the forests of Japan, the Japanese aralia has distinctive large, glossy, divided leaves. The flowers, which resemble those of ivy, are like small explosions; they are initially pale cream-green but turn almost black. A hybrid between *Fatsia* and *Hedera* (ivy), *Fatshedera lizei* (tree ivy), is a rather sprawling but smaller plant, to about 2m (6½ft).
Propagation seed, cuttings
Flowering time autumn
Size shrub to 4m (13ft)
Pruning not needed
Conditions sheltered position in full sun or partial shade; slightly acid, humus-rich soil
Fully hardy/Z 7–9

Ilex crenata

Ilex crenata
Inu tsuge
Japanese bush holly
Family: Aquifoliaceae
The Japanese holly, which can grow up to 6m (20ft) high and as wide, looks more like a box than a holly, especially as its leaves are small and spineless. Like box it can also be clipped into almost any shape. *Ilex crenata* is hardier than both *Buxus sempervirens* and *B. microphyllus*, so could be grown as a substitute for these and azaleas in very cold regions. The species, when unclipped, will grow into a large wide shrub with long narrow leaves, but is highly variable when grown from seed. There are a number of selected forms, such as 'Convexa' with small leaves and a low bushy habit, and 'Helleri' with very small leaves and a dense and flattened habit. The berries are black and not as attractive as those of many holly species.
Propagation seed, semi-ripe cuttings
Flowering time spring
Size shrub to 5m (16ft)
Conditions sun or shade
Propagation hardwood cuttings
Fully hardy/Z 5–8

Ilex integra
Mochi-no-ki
Japanese tree holly
Family: Aquifoliaceae
There are a number of *Ilex* species native to Japan that appear in gardens as part of a general mix of background evergreens. *Ilex integra* (mochi-no-ki) is a large shrub with spineless broad leathery leaves that carries red berries in autumn, while *I. rotunda* (see above right) has rounder leaves. In Western gardens, *Ilex aquifolium* 'J.C. Van Tol' would be a suitable substitute as it also has spineless leaves and red berries. *Ilex* x *altaclerensis* 'Camelliifolia' is another variety of holly with more rounded and very glossy leaves, reminiscent of camellia foliage, and would make an ideal tall background evergreen for larger gardens. These species and varieties can also be clipped as hedges.
Propagation seed, semi-ripe cuttings
Flowering time spring
Size shrub to 7m (23ft)
Conditions sun or shade
Fully hardy/Z 5–8

Ilex rotunda
Kurogane-mochi
Japanese tree holly
Family: Aquifoliaceae
Propagation seed, semi-ripe cuttings
Flowering time spring
Size tree to 23m (75ft)
Conditions sun or shade
Fully hardy/Z 7–8

Ligustrum japonicum
Nu-zhen-zi
Japanese privet
Family: Oleaceae
A rounded bushy shrub with very shiny and black-green leaves. In late summer, like many other privets (if not clipped), it produces pyramidal panicles of small white flowers with a strong, sweet fragrance, which some people find disagreeable. Despite this, the Japanese privet is a useful dense evergreen that in cold areas will need some protection from hard frosts and cold winds. It could form a part of the evergreen mixed plantings used as a background in stroll gardens. *Ligustrum japonica* 'Rotundifolium' has very dense blunt foliage that is thick and leathery, and this is often found in Japanese gardens.
Propagation hardwood cuttings
Flowering time summer
Size shrub to 4m (13ft)
Conditions sun or shade
Fully hardy/Z 6–8

TOPIARY AND HEDGES

- Mixed groups of camellias, azaleas, pieris and photinias as well as evergreen oaks and hollies are often clipped into *o-karikomi*, the Japanese equivalent of Western topiary (see pages 88–91).
- These plants can also be grown as hedges. Low hedges of *Camellia sinensis* (tea plant) are often planted in tea gardens; tea plants have much smaller leaves and flowers than the more ornamental camellias and they are less hardy.

Magnolia grandiflora
Taizen-boku

Evergreen magnolia

Family: Magnoliaceae

While this evergreen species of magnolia is native to the USA, it was introduced to Japan by the end of the 19th century and has been extensively planted in gardens. It suits the larger Japanese-style garden due to its bold and glossy foliage. In summer it produces huge creamy white cupped blooms that yield an intoxicating fragrance.

Propagation seed, semi-ripe cuttings, grafted
Flowering time summer
Size tree or large shrub to 10m (30ft)
Pruning best left unpruned; cut back in late winter if necessary
Conditions sun
Fully hardy/Z 7–8

Mahonia japonica
Bealei

Japanese mahonia

Family: Berberidaceae

An erect, pinnate, holly-like plant related to berberis, this mahonia has a strong, architectural shape, and bears spikes of sweetly scented yellow flowers in winter and early spring. When it becomes too woody and overgrown, prune the plant hard, removing the old stems first, immediately after flowering.

Propagation semi-ripe cuttings
Flowering time late autumn to early spring
Size shrub to 2m (6½ft)
Pruning by cutting back over-long shoots after flowering
Conditions sheltered position in partial shade; any reasonable soil
Fully hardy/Z 6–8

Osmanthus fragrans

Mahonia japonica

Osmanthus fragrans
Kinmokusei

Tea olive

Family: Oleaceae

A popular shrub in Japan, the fragrant olive or sweet tea is famed for its creamy autumn flowers, but it is not very hardy. A hardier species, *O. fortunei*, is more suitable for most gardens, or try *O. heterophyllus*, known as hi-ragi, a broad, holly-leaved shrub.

Propagation semi-ripe cuttings
Flowering time autumn
Size shrub to 6m (20ft)
Pruning by cutting back to maintain shape in mid-spring
Conditions sheltered position in sun or partial shade; any reasonable soil
Fully hardy/Z 8–9

Photinia glabra
Kaname-mochi

Red-leaf photinia

Family: Rosaceae

Photinias are mostly handsome, broad-leaved evergreen trees and shrubs, often planted to create a backdrop or shade. White flowers are carried in loose panicles from spring to summer, followed by the rosy-red flush of young foliage, evident in hybrids such as 'Red Robin' and 'Birmingham'. Photinias are pretty hardy and can be kept at a manageable height through pruning. They can also be grown as a hedge.

Propagation semi-ripe cuttings
Flowering time late spring to early summer
Size shrub to 5m (16ft)
Pruning by cutting out crossing and badly positioned stems in early spring
Conditions full sun or partial shade; any moist soil

Photinia glabra

Fully hardy/Z 7–8

Pieris japonica
A-sebi

Japanese Andromeda

Family: Ericaceae

A-sebi means "horse-drunk", relating to its poisonous effects on animals. This compact shrub is reasonably hardy, with pendulous clusters of white lily-of-the-valley-like flowers in early spring. The young growth is tinted pink. The Chinese species, *P. formosa*, has brilliant red-bronze young growth but is not as hardy. The American species, *P. floribunda*, is hardy. Pieris prefers acid soil and plenty of humus but can withstand quite dry conditions in late summer. More commonly seen as a large shrub, it can grow into a small tree. Small-leaved and dwarf forms include 'Green Heath', which grows to 60cm (24in).

Propagation seed, semi-ripe cuttings
Flowering time late winter to spring
Size shrub to 3m (10ft)
Pruning remove dead shoots after flowering
Conditions full sun or light shade; acid soil
Fully hardy/Z 6–8

OTHER NON-JAPANESE EVERGREENS

- *Arbutus unedo* (strawberry tree), a spreading small tree or shrub, to 8m (26ft), with creamy white flowers followed by red fruits.
- *Ilex meserveae* (blue holly), a vigorous shrub or small tree, to 5m (16ft), with sharply spined, glossy, blue-green leaves.
- *Prunus lusitanica* (Portugal laurel), a dense shrub or tree, to 20m (66ft), with large, glossy, dark green leaves.

Evergreen trees & conifers

The general Japanese name for conifers is *shohaku-rui*, and the tall, straight pines in particular were said to draw the gods down to Earth, while the Shintoists beat wooden planks to attract them. Such evergreen trees have been regarded in Japan as symbols of chastity, consistency and loyalty. The Hinoki cypress and Japanese cedar are two of Japan's most important timber trees, their naturally resilient wood being used in many of their buildings and garden structures. Two of the native species of pine are the most popular of conifers in Japanese gardens.

Above: Cryptomeria japonica *has a dense habit and thick, spreading branches. The foliage is scaly and finely dissected.*

Cephalotaxus harringtonia

Cephalotaxus harringtonia
Inu-gaya
Japanese plum yew
Family: Cephalotaxaceae
C. h. drupacea is known as the Japanese plum yew or cow's tail pine. It is a medium shrub up to 3m (10ft) high with a dense compact habit. Its short upright needles are quite soft and form a V-shape on the upper side of the branches. As they age, the plant develops into a large mound with elegant drooping branchlets. *C. h.* 'Fastigiata' is quite different with its stiffly upright habit that bears a striking resemblance to the Irish yew.
Propagation seed or hardwood cuttings
Flowering none
Size tree to 10m (30ft)
Conditions sun or part shade
Fully hardy/Z 6–8

Chamaecyparis obtusa
Hinoki
Hinoki cypress
Family: Cupressaceae
Often planted in forests alongside the Japanese cedar, the Hinoki cypress is a valuable timber tree. It is more commonly seen in gardens in its dwarf forms: *C. obtusa* 'Nana Gracilis' grows to 3m (10ft) high and *C. obtusa* 'Pygmaea' reaches only 1.5m (5ft) high. These smaller versions have more character than most cypress-like trees, with their twisted whorls of vivid young growth. Exceptionally hardy, all these plants can tolerate exposed situations. They can also be successfully clipped into hedges and topiary-style (*o-karikomi*) shapes.

Chamaecyparis obtusa

Propagation hardwood cuttings
Size tree to 20m (66ft)
Pruning not needed, but remove dead or diseased branches
Conditions full sun; slightly acid soil
Fully hardy/Z 4–8

SACRED PINES

Pines (*matsu* in Japanese, which means "waiting for a god") were regarded as the king of trees in Japan and are an important image in Japanese poetry. One of the most famous natural Japanese landscapes is Matsushima Bay, in northern Honshu, which is dotted with more than 800 pine-clad islands.

There are few Japanese gardens that do not contain a pine tree. Together with azaleas and maples, they are one of the fundamental ingredients. Many hours of loving care are spent plucking their needles and pruning their boughs, creating shapes that deliberately evoke trees bent by the winds on mountains and seashores. Pine boughs are often draped with decorations for the moon-viewing celebrations, weddings and New Year.

Chamaecyparis pisifera

Chamaecyparis pisifera
Sawara

Sawara cypress
Family: Cupressaceae
This handsome "false cypress" makes a large tree with spreading branches and flattened sprays of dark green foliage. Its main attribute, however, is the number of sports and varieties that have derived from it. The thread cypress, *C. pisifera* 'Filifera', with its long drooping whip-like shoots and broadly shrub-like growth is planted widely in Japanese gardens. In contrast, *C. pisifera* 'Squarrosa' has soft sprays of dark green foliage, and it has a number of dwarf forms such as 'Intermedia' which forms a dense mound of congested bluish foliage. This is an easy tree or shrub to grow in most soil types and will tolerate a certain amount of shade, especially under the canopy of large deciduous trees.
Propagation hardwood cuttings
Flowering none
Size tree to 20m (66ft)
Conditions sun or shade in any well-drained soil
Fully hardy/Zones 4–7

Cryptomeria japonica
Sugi

Japanese cedar
Family: Taxodiaceae
After the pine, the most important and sacred conifer in Japan is the Japanese cedar. This is capable of living for more than 2,000 years and is often planted as a sign of virtue and as a guardian at the entrance of Buddhist and Shinto shrines. Cryptomerias are planted in most of the commercial forests in Japan, as it is an easily worked timber and is used extensively in the building industry. Its aroma makes the wood prized for sake casks. The cryptomeria is a towering, conical tree, with finely dissected, scaly foliage. It is often coppiced in gardens, and the new growth is pruned into tiers with shaped, pompom-like foliage at the ends. It can also be planted on its own or as part of a mixed hedge. There are many cultivated varieties of *C. japonica*, but most are merely curiosities.
Propagation seed, hardwood cuttings
Size tree to 25m (82ft)
Pruning not needed
Conditions full sun or partial shade; deep, moist, slightly acid soil
Fully hardy/Z 6–9

Juniperus chinensis
Ibuki

Chinese juniper
Family: Cupressaceae
The Chinese juniper is a popular subject for clipping into "cloud pruning". It is a highly variable species that has given rise to one particular form, 'Kaizuka', which is popular in Japan and the USA, where it is also called 'Torulosa'. Its unusually angular branches, clothed in dense clusters of bright green foliage, give it a special picturesque outline

Cryptomeria japonica

Juniperus chinensis

that is ideal for creating a windswept look. *Juniper chinensis* and all its cultivars are very hardy and easy to grow in almost any soil type, even tolerating salt-laden winds, and are best planted in full sun.
Propagation hardwood cuttings
Flowering none
Size tree to 20m (66ft)
Conditions sun
Fully hardy/Z 5–8

Pinus densiflora
Aka-matsu

Japanese red pine
Family: Pinaceae
A fine tree with pinkish-red bark and a rounded head, the Japanese red pine is often pruned to accentuate its soft crown

Pinus densiflora 'Umbraculifera'

Pinus densiflora

and show its elegant, branched structure. *P. densiflora* 'Umbraculifera', known as tanyosho, is a compact, rounded or flat-topped bushy tree, reaching only 2–3m (7–10ft). This dwarf pine can be planted in groves over small hills, giving the impression of a larger landscape.
Propagation seed, grafted
Size tree to 20m (66ft)
Pruning needs little pruning to develop a strong structure
Conditions full sun; any well-drained soil
Fully hardy/Z 3–7

Pinus parviflora
Go-yo-matsu
Japanese white pine
Family: Pinaceae
Native to Japan, the Japanese white pine has shorter, grey-green needles and is slower growing and more manageable than either *P. densiflora* or *P. thunbergii*, but it will eventually make a large, multi-stemmed, mounding tree. There are many dwarf forms, including 'Glauca Nana' and 'Hagaromo Seedling', which are suitable for small gardens.
Propagation seed, grafted
Size tree to 20m (66ft)
Pruning needs little pruning to develop a strong structure
Conditions full sun; any well-drained soil
Fully hardy/Z 4–7

Pinus thunbergii
Kuro-matsu
Japanese black pine
Family: Pinaceae
More rugged and darker in leaf and bark than *P. densiflora*, the Japanese black pine is generally pruned into more horizontal and dramatic windswept shapes. It is the most popular pine for bonsai.
Propagation seed, grafted
Size tree to 25m (82ft)
Pruning during the early growing season
Conditions full sun; any well-drained soil
Fully hardy/Z 6–8

Podocarpus macrophyllus

Podocarpus macrophyllus
Kusamaki
Maki
Family: Podocarpaceae
Although most *Podocarpus* species are not very hardy, this one is fully hardy down to -20°C (-4°F). It forms a distinctive shrub or small tree with very long leaves up to 18cm (7in) long, which are bright green above and pale beneath and arranged in dense spirals around the stems. It is grown both in China and Japan as a rather unusual hedge, but is only suited to acid soils. There are many fancy forms of it in Japan, but the straight species is sufficiently interesting to be grown in its own right.
Propagation seed for species and hardwood cuttings for special forms
Flowering none
Size tree to 15m (50ft)
Conditions sun
Fully hardy/Z 7-8

Pinus parviflora

Pinus thunbergii

POPULAR PINES IN JAPANESE GARDENS

- *Pinus densiflora* (red pine)
- *Pinus thunbergii* (black pine)
- *Pinus sylvestris* (Scots pine), especially *P. sylvestris* 'Watereri'
- *Pinus mugo* (dwarf mountain pine), which grows to only 3.5m (11ft) high and is suitable for very small gardens

Sciadopitys verticillata

Thujopsis dolabrata

Sciadopitys verticillata
Koya maki
Japanese umbrella pine
Family: Pinaceae
This is a most distinctive conifer, usually forming a perfect cone shape and retaining its bright green foliage right to the ground. Its most unusual feature is the cool leathery feel to the long pine-like leaves, which stand out from each other like the spokes of an umbrella. It grows very slowly when young, enjoying a moisture-retentive acid soil but tolerating a neutral soil. Although it will grow in light woodland shade, in full sun it is more likely to keep its perfect shape. It is very rare in the wild but in Japan it is found in temple gardens, especially high in the mountains.
Propagation seed for species and hardwood cuttings
Pruning
Size tree to 20m (66ft)
Conditions sun or part shade
Half-hardy/Z 4–5

Taxus cuspidata
Ichii
Japanese yew
Family: Taxaceae
Taxus cuspidata is hardier than *T. baccata*, the common European yew that is popular for hedging. There are numerous forms of the Japanese yew and hybrids between it and *T. baccata*; some, like 'Hicksii', are quite upright, while others like 'Minima' and 'Nana', which form small dense shrubs, could be planted and clipped in *o-karikomi* style.

Propagation seed or hardwood cuttings
Pruning
Size tree to 15m (50ft)
Conditions sun or part shade
Fully hardy/Z 5–8

Thujopsis dolabrata
Hiba
Japanese elkhorn cypress
Family: Cupressaceae
Thujopsis dolabrata, with its shiny dark green flattened scaly fronds that are silvery on the reverse, is the most interesting of a group of conifers including species of *Thuja*, *Calocedrus* and *Chamaecyparis* that share many similar characteristics. All these evergreens form medium to large trees that are ideal as background planting, for screening or as individual specimens. They all thrive on most soil types and are very hardy. Some have given rise to dwarf forms, such as *Thujopsis dolabrata* 'Nana', which would be more suitable for the smaller garden.
Propagation seed, hardwood cuttings
Pruning
Size tree to 20m (66ft)
Conditions sun or part shade
Fully hardy/Z 6–8

Tsuga
Tsuga
Hemlock
Family: Pinaceae
A genus of elegant, large trees with fine soft-needled foliage. Although there is a Japanese species, *Tsuga sieboldii* (Southern Japanese hemlock), for gardens there are a number of slow-growing and dwarf forms of the American species, *Tsuga canadensis* (Canadian hemlock). Those with weeping habits such as *Tsuga canadensis* 'Pendula', or smaller dome-shaped varieties such as *Tsuga canadensis* 'Nana', would be very suitable for Japanese gardens.
Propagation hardwood cuttings or grafted
Pruning
Size tree to 10m (30ft)
Conditions sun or part shade
Fully hardy/Z 4–8

Taxus cuspidata

Tsuga

Ferns

Japanese ferns are regarded as excellent, shapely plants for softening the hard edges of groups of rocks and for providing a sympathetic foil to glossy evergreens, which are planted to give a wooded, wilderness effect around the path in tea gardens. Ferns are often found tucked around the *tsukubai* and other water features, where they can take advantage of the extra moisture. Camellias with light pastel colours and simple plants such as aucubas, nandinas and maples combine well with ferns.

Ferns vary from the largest tree ferns to tiny species that creep around in crevices, such as *Blechnum penna-marina* (Alpine hard fern). *Athyrium nipponicum pictum* (Japanese painted fern) is native to Japan, and is unique among ferns for its maroon stalk and fronds with a silvery cast. *Athyrium trichomanes* (lady fern) is a finely cut small-leaved fern for tucking into small spaces.

Above: *Asplenium scolopendrium*, the hart's-tongue fern, has a distinctive leaf shape.

Propagation separated by root division
Size from 4–6cm (1½–2½in) to 10m (30ft)
Conditions most species need shade and moisture, and most like humidity
Hardiness dependent on species/Z 4–9

Onoclea sensibilis

USEFUL NON-JAPANESE FERNS

- *Asplenium scolopendrium* (hart's-tongue fern) has strap-like leaves and thrives in deep shade but must not be allowed to dry out.
- *Dryopteris felix-mas* (robust male fern) and its forms could be used under trees or in gardens which are very dry.

Matteuccia struthiopteris

- *Matteuccia struthiopteris* (ostrich fern), *Onoclea sensibilis* (sensitive fern) and *Osmunda regalis* (flowering fern) are all excellent for ground that is damp or swampy.

Polystichum setiferum

- *Polystichum setiferum* (soft shield fern) is an ideal all-round fern species as it is more or less evergreen. It is best to remove all the old fronds in spring just before the new fronds unfurl. This species will grow in shade and full sun in any reasonable soil as long as it doesn't become too dry. The various forms such as 'Dahlem' with simple plain leaves and 'Herrenhausen' with curly edges to the fronds are excellent for planting along the tea path, and under camellias and aucubas.

Athyrium trichomanes

Bamboo

Most Japanese gardens are cultivated in temperate climates, where plants such as azaleas, cherries and plums grow well, but in more tropical or subtropical climates it is best to grow plants that are better suited to the heat. However, if you want to create a "tropical look" in a temperate climate, there are various hardy plants that can be used, and bamboo is ideal. Bamboos can be highly invasive plants, so site them carefully. The bamboo species listed below like full sun or partial shade and rich soil, unless stated otherwise.

Above: Pleioblastus humilis *or dwarf bamboo. This fast-growing bamboo makes a good low hedge or screen.*

Pleioblastus humilis
Nakai
Dwarf bamboo
Family: Poaceae
A fairly low-growing bamboo with dark green canes and light green leaves. It can be invasive, so contain the roots.
Propagation division
Size to 1.5m (5ft)
Conditions sheltered in sun or partial shade
Hardy/Z 1–3

Pleioblastus pygmaeus
Nakai
Pygmy bamboo
Family: Poaceae
This can be planted as ground cover and clipped down to 5–10cm (2–4in) high. It makes a good substitute for lawns or moss.
Size to 40cm (16in)
Conditions semi-shade or full sun
Hardy/Z 6–11

Pseudosasa japonica

Phyllostachys aurea
Kosan chiku
Fishpole bamboo or golden bamboo
Family: Poaceae
These mid-green canes age to golden-brown. It will spread, so contain the roots.
Propagation division
Size to 10m (33ft)
Conditions moist soil and tolerates drought
Hardy/Z 6–8

Phyllostachys aureosulcata
Ousou chiku
Yellow-groove bamboo
Family: Poaceae
This has brown-green canes, attractively ribbed with yellow.
Propagation division
Size to 6m (20ft)
Conditions full to partial sun
Hardy/Z 5–10

Phyllostachys edulis
Kina mousou chiku
Moso bamboo
Family: Poaceae
This evergreen bamboo is often harvested for its huge stems. In colder climates it will not reach its full growth dimensions, which are only seen in the southern half of Japan. *P. edulis heterocycla* has fascinating tortoiseshell-shaped internodes.
Propagation division
Size to 6m (20ft) or more
Conditions Full sun; medium drought tolerance, intolerant of shade
Hardy/Z 7–11

Phyllostachys nigra
Kuro chiku
Black bamboo
Family: Poaceae
This dramatic bamboo is popular for its polished black stems, especially in the form 'Munro'. The distinctive canes become black with age.
Propagation division
Size to 5m (16ft)
Conditions full sun or partial shade; well-drained soil
Hardy/Z 7–9

Phyllostachys vivax
Madake
Vivax bamboo or Chinese timber
Family: Poaceae
This makes a good alternative to *P. edulis*.
Size to 25m (82ft)
Conditions full sun to light shade; well-drained soil
Hardy/Z 6–10

Pseudosasa japonica
Kishima yadake
Arrow bamboo
Family: Poaceae
A tough and rather invasive bamboo with dark green leaves on pale beige stems.
Size to 6m (20ft)
Conditions requires well-drained soil
Hardy/Z 6–11

Palms

As long as they are grown in sheltered positions, many palms are surprisingly hardy; like bamboos, they can be used for a tropical look in a temperate climate. Their growth is reliable and they are also appealing because they are low-maintenance. Although Japanese gardens tend to be associated more with temperate flora, it is not inappropriate to use palms and other exotic plants, providing that the same design principles are followed. In cold areas, cycads are often wrapped up in winter with straw to protect their leaves and crowns from frost.

Above: Trachycarpus fortunei, *distinctive for its huge fan-shaped leaves, is a very hardy palm and thrives in mild coastal gardens.*

Cycas revoluta
Cycas nana
Sago palm
Family: Cycadaceae
This ancient plant is native to the southern islands of Japan. It is a beautiful glossy evergreen, which looks like a cross between a palm and a fern. It is only marginally hardy, and is rarely seen in gardens north of Kyoto. Even in Kyoto the sago palm has to be wrapped up in winter, and like many other aspects of Japanese gardens, this elaborate wrapping has been raised to the level of an art form.
Propagation seed
Size to 2m (6½ft)
Conditions requires full sun and moist, rich soil.
Half hardy/Z 8–10

Rhapis excelsa
Shuro
Miniature fan palm
Family: Arecaceae/Palmae
Native to China, the miniature fan palm was introduced to Japan in the 19th century. Stockier and spinier than the Chusan palm, but not quite as hardy, it is still a valuable addition to the tropical look in a temperate garden. With shiny dark leaves, the fronds of the miniature fan palm stretch out from an upright furry trunk. The plant can be used as group plantation. It is good for planting in shaded areas.
Propagation sucker division
Size to 5m (16ft)
Conditions requires a sheltered position; light shade and any soil.
Fully hardy/Z 8–11

Trachycarpus fortunei
To-juro
Chusan palm
Family: Arecaceae/Palmae
This hardy palm was originally grown for its yield of fibre, and it has since become naturalized in many parts of the country. It grows quite erect and has fan-shaped leaves. Dwarf forms include 'Compacta' and 'Green Pillow'.
Propagation seed
Size full size to 20m (66ft); dwarf forms to 1m (3ft)
Conditions full sun or shade; any soil
Fully hardy/Z 7–10

Cycas revoluta

Trachycarpus fortunei

Other plants of interest

This selection includes plants that can be placed beside the tea path or grown in shady courtyards. Many of them have hundreds of interesting, even quirky, variations, and they are often specially grown in pots so that they can be highlighted. They are not usually grown for planting out in the garden, where they might disrupt the overall scheme. Hollyhocks, popular in English cottage gardens, originated in the Orient, and are often grown against house walls. Mondo grass is the most popular ground cover in Japan, its glossy leaves forming a dense, impenetrable mat.

Above: *Farfugium japonicum is a perennial native to Japan, grown for its attractive foliage and its autumn flowers.*

Althaea rosea

Althaea rosea
Tachia-oi
Hollyhock
Family: Malvaceae
The hollyhock has been popular in Japan since Heian times and is still common, especially in gardens of small houses.
Propagation seed
Flowering time early to midsummer
Size perennial to 2.4m (8ft)
Conditions full sun; any soil
Fully hardy/Z 6–9

Equisetum hyemale
Tokusa
Small tufted mare's tail
Family: Equisetaceae
In Western gardens this is a pernicious but attractive weed that likes wet soils. Japanese forms are less invasive. The vertical, leafless stems of *E. hyemale* are an arresting sight.
Propagation division
Size perennial to 1.5m (5ft)
Conditions sun or partial shade; moist soil
Fully hardy/Z 4–9

Farfugium japonicum
Tsuwa-buki
Leopard plant
Family: Asteraceae/Compositae
The yellow flowers of this evergreen perennial with scalloped leaves are similar to those of *Ligularia*. Many variegated forms have been developed, the most common 'Aureomaculatum', which has random yellow spots on the leaves.
Propagation division
Flowering time autumn to early winter
Size perennial to 60cm (24in)
Conditions partial shade; moist soil
Fully hardy/Z 7–9

Hemerocallis

Hemerocallis
Kisuge or kanzou
Day lily
Family: Hemerocallidaceae
H. fulva is native to Japan and has given rise to hundreds of varieties. In its natural state its flowers are a buff orange, rising up on stalks in summer from a deciduous herbaceous perennial that will colonize large areas in shade or full sun. Day lily flowers last only one day but a succession are produced over several weeks in mid- to late summer. The species *H. flava* produces a lovely fragrance from its yellow flowers in the spring.
Propagation division
Flowering time spring to late summer
Size 90cm (36in)
Conditions sun or shade in most soil types
Fully hardy/Z 4–8

Hosta
Giboshi
Hosta
Family: Hostaceae
Hostas, or plantain lilies, have been planted in Japanese gardens since Heian times. *Hosta sieboldiana*, one of the hostas with the largest leaves, can be seen growing at 1,000m (3,280ft) at the foot of Mount Fuji. *H. plantaginea* has white, scented flowers, while *H. montana* and *H. tardiva*, both native to Japan, are grown for their handsome foliage. *H. ventricosa* is particularly striking,

Hosta

Houttuynia cordata

Lilium

with beautiful violet flowers and strong, green-ribbed foliage. Hostas were selected for their variety of leaf forms during the 19th century. Plants with variegated and twisted leaves were grown as specimens for display, rather than as part of the garden scheme.
Propagation division
Flowering time summer
Size perennial 25–90cm (10–36in)
Conditions sheltered position in sun or partial shade; moist soil
Fully hardy/Z 4–9

Houttuynia cordata
Dokudami
Chameleon houttuynia
Family: Saururaceae
Houttuynia is grown in many Japanese gardens, especially near water, but it can be invasive. The heart-shaped leaves have a strong odour when crushed, while the small white flowers are picked to make herbal tea. There are a number of variegated forms, but the plain green kind is the most popular.
Propagation division
Flowering time spring
Size perennial to 30cm (12in)
Conditions full sun; moist soil
Fully hardy/Z 5–9

Lilium
Yuri
Lily
Family: Liliaceae
Lilium auratum is the golden-rayed lily of Japan. Its large, white, trumpet-like flowers have freckles and golden streaks inside. It is a fussy plant that needs acid soil with plenty of humus. Hybrids between *L. auratum* and *L. speciosum* are much easier to grow. In Japanese gardens lilies are grown in pots and put out on seasonal display.

The unscented but vibrant *L. lancifolium* (tiger lily), with its orange and yellow, heavily spotted, reflexed flowers, has been grown extensively as a food (where the bulbs are eaten) and is only rarely allowed to flower.
Propagation seed, scales, offsets
Flowering time late summer to early autumn
Size bulb to 1.5m (5ft)
Conditions full sun; acid soil
Fully hardy/Z 4–9

Musa
Musa basjoo
Hardy banana
Family: Musaceae
This will survive frosts as low as -10°C (14°F). Grow it in a sheltered position as its huge leaves tend to get shredded and blackened when exposed to cold winds. In cold areas you can wrap the whole stem up with fleece or straw to protect it in winter. Not really suitable in more "temperate" style gardens, *Musa* could be planted with palms and bamboos for a tropical effect.
Propagation division
Flowering insignificant, may fruit in warm climates
Size shrub to 3m (10ft)
Conditions sun or part shade; sheltered spot
Half hardy/Z 7–9

Ophiopogon japonicus
Ja-no-hige or ryo-no-hige
Japanese mondo grass
Family: Convallariaceae
This leathery, grass-like plant can colonize whole gardens. It has dark green leaves, which curve over. Carpets of it can set off larger plants, such as groups of maples, azaleas and bamboos. The flowers are white or pale blue, followed by small black berries. The dwarf, tufted *O. japonicus* 'Minor' is better in small gardens.
Propagation division
Flowering time summer
Size perennial to 60cm (24in)
Conditions full sun or partial shade; slightly acid soil
Fully hardy/Z 6–10

Ophiopogon japonicus

OTHER PLANTS OF INTEREST 237

Care & maintenance

There is a curious ambiguity about the Japanese garden. As a first impression, one might think that maintaining a spread of gravel, a rock or two, a pine tree and a bamboo would require very little work. However, a dynamic Japanese garden, even on a small scale, carpeted with moss and planted with several trees and shrubs around a pond, can in fact involve a high level of maintenance. What is more, Japanese gardeners are meticulous in the way they keep their gardens, and pay extraordinary attention to small details such as training, staking and pruning.

Even the more naturalistic tea gardens are treated with the same high level of care. Traditionally, the work involved in looking after a garden has been seen as spiritually valuable in itself, but it is important to be realistic when creating your design, and think about the time you will have available. On the following pages we look at the main activities to ensure the upkeep of the garden: weeding, pruning, raking, sweeping, tidying, as well as repair and maintenance work.

Above: *Most tree work can be dangerous and should be carried out by professionals who have safety certificates and insurance.*

Below: *The twisting stem of a weeping* Sophora *has been carefully propped up and bound with jute.*

Opposite: *This pine tree was in poor health with the resin bleeding from the bark, so as a precaution it has been bound with hessian.*

Left: *Gardeners at Kenroku-en in Kawazawa, Japan, tie boughs with rope to protect the old pine trees from breaking branches in the snow.*

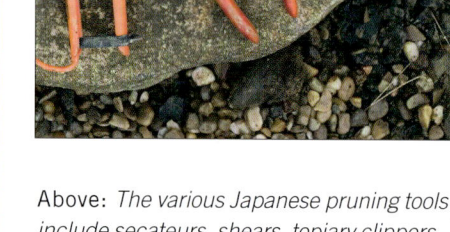

Above: The various Japanese pruning tools include secateurs, shears, topiary clippers, pruning saws and sharpeners.

WEEDING

While Japanese gardens do not have flower borders, they do need regular weeding. Weed-suppressing matting and weedkillers could be used – Western recreations of Japanese gardens routinely use at least the former under gravel – but Japanese gardening is meant to be meditative and calming, and the process of weeding is therefore part of the experience.

Weeding tools

Some of the tools used in Japanese gardens are less well known in Western gardens, but they can be useful for weeding and cultivating in naturalistic garden settings. There are various small choppers and chisel-like planting tools for working between plants and rocks, and a right-angled, short-handled hoe or cultivation tool that is ideal for working in tight spaces. Hand scythes or sickles are used for controlling ground cover plants and for cutting grass in hard-to-reach places or on sloping sites that are unsuitable for lawnmowers. You can also use nylon-line trimmers.

PRUNING

In Japan, teams of professionals descend on public and private gardens once or twice a year to carry out the

Above: The weeds that break up the smooth surface of the grass at Kenrokuen Garden in Honshu are broken loose with a hand sickle, and then carefully collected in baskets.

specialized job of pruning. Most shrubs and trees can be tackled in early to late autumn, but some plants, such as plums, require pruning immediately after flowering in the spring. Pruning is vital because plants in the Japanese garden are used for their structural qualities as well as the beauty of their flowers and foliage, and so their growth must be kept in check. Because Japanese gardens are often quite densely planted, you need to decide how much light should fall on the ground between shrubs to encourage the growth of moss, mondo grass or other ground cover plants. Too much light and some plants will burn in the sun; too much shade might stunt or kill plants, leaving the earth exposed, dusty and brown. Aim for an attractive dappled shade and a green surface.

The term *niwaki* in Japanese means "garden trees", and also applies to a technique of pruning a tree to achieve some very striking effects. Trees may be made to look older than they really are by encouraging a broad trunk supporting gnarled branches; they may also be made to imitate windswept or lightning-struck trees in the wild.

Other pruning techniques include *tama-mono*, the art of creating simple semi-spherical shapes of azaleas, shapes that are often combined with rocks and carefully pruned trees, such as a windswept pine. Another technique called *hako-zukuri* is designed to create box shapes that complement and echo architectural elements within a garden.

Trimming and shaping tools

Japanese gardeners use a wide range of tools which are designed to shape, prune and clip shrubs and trees.

For large hedges, or gardens with a large number of shrubs, powered trimmers (though obviously not traditional) are the easiest option, but large-leaved plants such as camellias should be pruned by hand using secateurs (pruners) to avoid shredding the foliage. Small, shaped shrubs are also best trimmed by hand for accuracy.

Many trimming tools are similar to those used in topiary, and indeed some Western topiary artists favour Japanese tools because of their diversity and suitability for carrying out intricate tasks. For example, as well as a range of standard anvil and bypass secateurs or pruners, there are also special long-

Above: *Gardeners use bamboo structures to prune the leaves of topiaries in Suizen-ji Park, Kumamoto, Japan.*

bladed, narrow-nosed cutters that are used to shorten the new growths or "candles" on pine trees and to thin the bundles of needles. This kind of tool is useful for precision shaping and trimming individual twigs in topiary.

Individual tree branches are often trained to achieve the desired shape and angle using bamboo canes and galvanized or plastic-coated training wire. You can use ladders to reach taller trees, but you may find long-handled or telescopic pruners, loppers and pruning saws useful with their longer reach.

Another essential tool for a Japanese garden containing large shrubs and small trees is a small pruning saw with a curved blade that folds or retracts into the handle for safe storage.

Shears with short blades and narrow noses, sometimes sold as "ladies' shears", are perfect for trimming over the rounded or flattened plates of cloud-pruned trees and shrubs and also for shaping azaleas and other evergreens such as box to resemble rounded boulders. For precise snipping and trimming of foliage on a smaller scale you can buy sprung one-handed cutters or "sheep shears", as well as scissor-like trimming tools. So-called sheep shears are not suitable for extended use as they are heavy, and will tire your hand.

PRUNING A DWARF PINE

This step-by-step process illustrates how to improve the general shape of a dwarf Japanese red pine (*Pinus densiflora umbraculifera*), a small rounded shrub that can be used in small compositions, especially those employing *shukkei* or "condensed landscape". The process could also be used on old junipers and boxwood, and other evergreens such as *Osmanthus* and yew. The aim is to give the impression that the tree is older than it is, and to give it a more open and attractive habit. Dwarf pines and many other conifers become very dense and twiggy with age, creating a dull, uninteresting mass. If you remove old growth, exposing the trunk of the tree and clipping excess growth, you can transform a shrub or small tree into a plant of much greater beauty.

2 Prune off the old dead and half-dead wood inside the bush, plus any crossing branches or weak, spindly twigs and branches. Stand back from time to time to get a good look at how the plant is shaping up. Prune the inside of the plant, removing larger branches so that you can see the branch structure.

4 Collect up the dust sheet around the red pine and dispose of the prunings.

You will need
- a pair of secateurs (pruners) or specialist Japanese pruners
- a small pruning saw
- a dust sheet (optional)

1 The specimen to be pruned is a dwarf Japanese red pine and has grown generally dense and lacking in character. If you have one, lay the dust sheet under the shrub. This is to catch all the prunings as they fall.

3 Prune out leading shoots to encourage the growth of side branches. This will give the plant a more balanced shape, and is important if you need to keep the plant contained within a small space. Do not make the plant too rounded but try to work with, and enhance, its innate form.

5 The plant is now more open and shapely. Continue the process each year, and the plant will develop more shape as it matures.

Left: *A saw-toothed rake being used to create a figure-of-eight gravel pattern. Achieving immaculate shapes such as these needs considerable practice.*

Right: *Gardeners raking a high ridge of sand in a Zen garden at the Silver Pavilion Ginkaku-ji in Kyoto.*

RAKING GRAVEL AND SAND

One of the most meditative practices in a Japanese garden is raking gravel or sand in a dry garden (*kare-sansui*). In temple gardens the rhythmic, focused motions of raking are still part of the spiritual practices of Zen monks. The softer and finer the texture of the sand, grit or gravel, the more frequently it will need raking.

Sourcing rakes

Used for making and maintaining patterns in grit, and often sand too, rakes are not easy to get hold of, even from specialist companies. You can buy three- and four-pronged metal hand rakes, but these are not traditionally used in Zen gardens or *kare-sansui*. For such gardens as these you may need to make your own.

You can fashion a traditional Japanese rake from a rectangular piece of wood with broadly cut, saw-like teeth, which can be held with two hands and used at ground level or with a handle attached. Alternatively, you can make a rake from a row of dowel rods fitted into a block of wood.

Look critically at the area to be raked: the tool must be able to fit between rocks and between rock groupings and pathways or boundaries. A wide rake may be unwieldy in a restricted area, but for a large, open expanse of sand, a bigger rake will cover the space more quickly. When making your own rake, adjust the size of the teeth or the thickness of the dowel rods and their spacing according to the grain diameter of sand or gravel. The larger the gravel, the wider the space required.

Making a wooden sand rake

A sand rake can either be a "dowel-tooth" rake, made using wooden dowelling, which looks rather like a small hay rake. The other option is to make a slightly simpler "saw-tooth" rake. Choose whichever is best suited to the size and style of sand patterns you wish to create (see page 79 for pattern suggestions).

To make a dowel-tooth rake, follow the step-by-step method for the saw-tooth rake (see opposite), but use a block of wood that is about 6cm (2½in) wide so that you can drill holes in which to insert the dowelling. Each piece should be 2cm (¾in) in diameter and 10cm (4in) long.

Left: *A Buddhist monk rakes gravel into wavelike patterns in the Zen garden at Zuiho-in Temple in Kyoto.*

Making a saw-tooth rake

Before designing your rake, consider how deep and how wide you want your ripples or waves to be. This will obviously affect how many teeth your rake will need, and how long each tooth should be. You will also need to know how fine your gravel or sand for raking will be, as a fine-toothed rake will not make much impression on coarser gravel.

1 The first stage is to prepare the wood for the saw teeth. Take the block of wood for the rake end and lay it flat. Then make a mark with a pencil on the long edge of the block, 4cm (1½in) from one end and then every 8cm (3in) along the length. The last mark should be 4cm (1½in) from the other end. Trim the timber to fit the measurements (you may prefer to have a wider or narrower rake, or teeth of a different size).

2 Using a set square, make lines at 60 degrees in both directions from each mark that you have already made. Carry on along the length until you have made the zigzag outline of your saw pattern.

You will need
- for the rake end: block of timber measuring 60cm (24in) long, 5cm (2in) thick (6cm or 2½in wide for a dowel-tooth rake) and 15–20cm (6–8in) wide
- for the handle: length of 4 x 4cm (1½ x 1½in) timber 150–200cm (5–6½ft) long
- for bracing the handle: 2 strips of wood, each 2cm x 3cm x 60cm (¾in x 1¼in x 2ft)
- wood screws
- an electric drill
- a cross-cut hand-saw, or electric jigsaw
- a work-bench vice
- an angle-measuring device, such as a set square
- a wood chisel
- a wood rasp and sandpaper

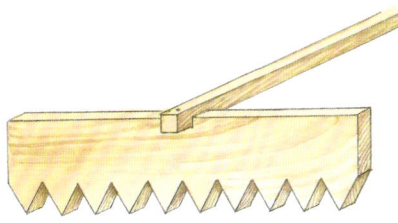

3 Clamp the board in a vice and saw out the teeth. You could use an electric jigsaw, but a fine-toothed cross-cut saw would also be suitable for a small project of this type. If you prefer to saw vertically, then clamp the board in the vice at an angle.

4 Prepare to attach the handle by making a notch in the rake end. The notch needs to fit the exact width of the timber that you have bought for the handle but should be only 2cm (¾in) deep, so that when the handle is placed into the notch, 2cm (¾in) of it will be left proud.

5 Fit the handle into the notch and screw it down into the board.

6 Brace the handle by resting each brace in turn against the handle 45cm (18in) from the rake end, and on the rake end, and mark off the angles. Cut these angles off the braces.

7 Fix the braces by screwing one end to the rake handle, and the other to the rake end.

8 Round off the square edges of the handle along the area where you will be holding the rake with a coarse rasp, then follow this with a good sanding.

BRUSHING, SWEEPING AND TIDYING

In the famous garden of Shisendo, in Kyoto, the surface of the dry garden is covered by light sand, which requires brushing rather than raking. Soft brushwood brooms or besoms made from bundled twigs are used to sweep the sand into patterns. These brooms are also used to sweep debris and leaves off paths and mossy areas.

At the risk of shattering the peace and tranquillity of a Japanese garden, you could also use a powered leaf blower, but in this case take great care not to disturb any raked or levelled areas of sand or fine grit.

You will also need to check paths made of stepping stones are kept clean and free of moss and slimy algae.

Top: *A gardener using a brushwood besom to maintain the gravel patterns in a Zen garden at the Silver Pavilion Ginkaku-ji in Kyoto.*

Above: *A long hand brush is useful for sweeping debris from pathways and removing leaves and blossoms from cobbles and clipped topiary.*

OTHER TASKS

Other occasional maintenance work:
• the repair and re-binding of bamboo fences and gates.
• making or repairing tree supports, elaborate constructs, with black and natural-coloured jute and sisal being used to bind branches to their supports (synthetic black "jute" is available and lasts longer).
• cutting ground cover plants. Some larger Japanese gardens have lawns, but the grass is coarse and cannot be mown too closely. Where spreading dwarf bamboos are used instead of grass, they will need shearing once or twice a year to keep them down to 10cm (4in) at most.
• maintaining water features. Unless you have a natural stream or spring, water gardens will need a certain amount of upkeep. Pump filters must be cleaned and pools dredged to prevent them from silting up and to keep the water clean and fresh.

Left: *The Japanese walk carefully on mossy ground with soft-soled shoes and brush the autumn leaves with twig brooms (besoms).*

Below: *Bamboo fences do not last for many years and will often need repairing. This gardener is tying on new bamboo stays with natural black jute.*

Above: *In cooler areas some plants, such as this cycad, are wrapped and bound with rice straw and twine to protect them from heavy frosts.*

Below: *Elaborate frames are used to extend the weeping boughs of cherries to lift the canopy so that it stretches over walkways and paths.*

Glossary

Amida Buddha the form of the Buddha whose promise of a western Paradise influenced Heian-period garden makers.
Aminoshidate a long pine-clad peninsula on the north coast of Honshu, and one of the five most famous scenic spots in Japan, often symbolically reproduced in gardens.
Aware Lamenting the passing of things, a heightened awareness of fleeting beauty. An emotional attitude to the natural world that infected the sensibility of Heian courtiers.
Bakufu the military bureaucracies that acted for the emperor.
Carp stone a stone placed at the base of waterfalls to represent a leaping fish. Indicates the strivings of humanity.
Cha-niwa tea garden. Garden immediately around the tea house.
Cha-noyu the tea ceremony.
Chonin the merchant class, especially those who enjoyed a period of wealth during the Edo period but were forced to hide it. They made elaborate gardens inside their unobtrusive houses.
Chozubachi taller style of water basin, often placed where it can be reached from a veranda.
Confucius (d. 479 BC) Chinese sage who laid down principles and morals. These were especially popular during the Edo period when Buddhism waned.
Crane island (*tsuru-shima*) part of the Mystic isles myth. Cranes carried the immortals on their backs, and became symbols of longevity. The crane island is portrayed by rocks indicating long necks or an upheld wing.
Daimyo a lord who owned land.
Dyana meditation. The Sanskrit word that is at the root of the word Zen.
Edo period from 1603 to 1867, when the Tokugawa shogunate ruled Japan from its new capital in Edo, now Tokyo.
Eisai the Buddhist monk attributed with bringing both Zen Buddhism and the first successfully transplanted tea plants to Japan in the 13th century.

Enshu, **Kabori** 17th-century garden designer and town planner, whose plans set new standards for garden design, influencing the Katsura palace and many temple gardens.
Fuji-san, **Mount Fuji** ("san" means mountain) sacred mountain whose form can be reproduced symbolically in gardens.
Fuzei taste.
Genji, The Tales of highly influential novel of the Heian period, written by Murasaki Shikobu.
Geomancy Chinese system that brings together many beliefs as to how buildings, cities and gardens should be laid out relative to directions, colours and elements. Also applied in systems of government. Includes such principles as yin-yang and feng-shui.
Go-shintai Shinto term for an area that is considered to be the abode of the gods.
Heian period from 794 to 1185, marking the period from when a new capital was created in Kyoto until the shogunate moved its headquarters to Kamakura.
Hiei-san mountain overlooking Kyoto, views of which were coveted by garden designers. See *shakkei*.
Hojo the abbot's quarters in Zen temples, where most dry Zen gardens were laid out.
Horai the central island in the ancient Chinese myth of the Mystic Isles, often portrayed by a large upright rock.
Immortals inhabitants of the Mystic Isles who possessed the secret of the

Equisetum hyemale

elixir of eternal youth. Mystic Isles were constructed in pond gardens in the hope of luring the immortals to earth.
Ishe-tate-so the "rock-setting priests" of the 14th and 15th centuries, who designed the first *kare-sansui* or dry gardens.
Iwa-kura literally "boulder-seat". Shintoists believed rocks possessed spirits, and certain rocks were given the status of gods, a factor that may well have influenced the way rocks were used in Japanese gardens.
Kamakura period from 1185 to 1392, following the Heian period, when the shogunate moved its headquarters from Kyoto to Kamakura, south of modern-day Tokyo.
Kame-shima see Turtle islands.
Kami the Shinto term for gods.
Kare-sansui the dry landscape garden, where the element of water is represented by sand and gravel.
Kawara-mono the lowest caste in Japan, attributed with having helped to build *kare-sansui* dry gardens during the Muromachi period, especially Ryoan-ji.
Koan Zen riddle to aid emptiness of mind, and a trigger for enlightenment.
Kyoto the most important capital city in the history of Japanese garden design.
Machiya smaller town houses belonging to merchants, which contained small *tsubo-niwa* or courtyard gardens.
Mappo the Buddhist age of "ending law" said to have started in the 11th century. The last of three ages predicted by the Buddha, inducing a sense of pessimism.
Matsushima pine-clad islands off the north-east coast of Japan that inspired reproduction in many gardens.
Meiji restoration the restoration of the emperor as acting head of state in 1868, and the end of the shogunate rule. The emperor moved to the new capital of Tokyo.
Mitate recycled second-hand building materials, such as millstones, incorporated into garden paths and buildings, which show the refined taste of their owner.

Prunus mume

Momoyama period from 1568 to 1603. The era of the generals, especially Totomi Hideyoshi, who unified Japan. The last of the generals was Ieyasu Tokugawa, whose family ruled throughout the Edo period.

Mu nothingness. An aspect of Zen that reveals itself in the empty spaces of sand in some dry Zen gardens.

Muromachi period from 1393 to 1568, when the shogunate returned from Kamakura to Kyoto. Possibly the most intensely creative period in Japanese history, which saw both the dry *kare-sansui* gardens and tea gardens come of age.

Mystic Isles see Horai, Crane island and Turtle island.

Naka-kuguri literally a middle crawl-through gate or stooping gate, a gate that deliberately induced a sense of humility along the tea path before a guest entered the tea house.

Nara period from 710 to 795. Nara was the last of the ancient capitals, standing 50 miles south of Kyoto, before a new capital was built in Kyoto.

Nigiriguchi a small hatch-like entrance to the tea house, whereby the guest entered on hands and knees.

No-da-te an informal tea ceremony conducted outdoors.

O-karikomi the Japanese form of topiary, where plants of many kinds are clipped into abstract shapes.

Pagoda a Japanese or Chinese building that contained relics of the Buddha or his saints. These were often symbolically carved in stone and placed in gardens.

Peng-lai original name for Mount Horai.

Pure Land paradise thought to be in the West, this was the Buddha's abode for the afterlife. Ponds were made to evoke this paradise, especially in the Heian and Kamakura periods.

Rikyu Japan's most famous tea-master, whose influence on the tea ceremony and tea garden is still felt today.

Roji literally "dewy path", the tea path that leads to the tea house.

Roji-mon the entrance gate to the tea garden or roji.

Ryoan-ji the most famous of all the dry Zen gardens in Kyoto, believed to have been built in 1499.

Sakuteiki the first and most influential garden treatise, which was written in the 11th century.

Samurai a soldier in service of a lord (*daimyo*).

Sanzon Buddhist trinity stone arrangements

Sesshu the most influential of Japanese brush and ink painters during the 15th century, who was also a gardener and a Zen priest.

Shakkei literally "borrowed landscape". The inclusion of distant views to become part of the garden scene.

Shibumi is derived from the word meaning "astringent". It describes the minimalist, unpretentious worldly aesthetic of the Edo period that replaced the earlier and more spiritual term *wabi-sabi*.

Shigemori, Mirei the most influential and celebrated Japanese garden designer of the 20th century.

Shiki-no-himorogi sacred areas covered with pebbles.

Shime the binding of artefacts, rocks and trees as part of the Shinto religion. The word *shima*, meaning garden, may have derived from this source.

Shin gyo and *so* an expression to suggest the mixture of formal (*shin*), semi-formal (*gyo*) and informal (*so*) that describes different physical patterns, such as paving, in garden design.

Shinden literally "sleeping hall". The main residence at the centre of the pond gardens of the Heian period.

Shinto the native animistic religion of Japan.

Shishi-odoshi a deer scarer. A bamboo device that repeatedly fills with water, then tips and smacks against a rock.

Shogun military leader. It literally means "barbarian-quelling general".

Shoin architecture the style of architecture developed in Japan during the Muromachi (1393–1568) period that included a study room.

Soan the rustic style of architecture of tea houses.

Sode-gaki sleeve fences. Small sections of bamboo and rush fences that divide up views of the garden from the house.

Sumeru originally a Hindu mountain (Meru) that became Mount Shumisen to the Japanese Buddhists.

Tatami the woven rush matting that was especially favoured for the floor of Japanese tea houses.

Tokonoma the alcove in a tea house.

Tsubo-niwa a courtyard garden.

Tsukubai a low basin found by the path to the tea house, usually accompanied by a lantern.

Tsuru-shima see Crane island.

Turtle island derived from the myth of the Mystic Isles, which were said to float on the backs of turtles. Turtle islands (*kame-shima*) are abstract rock arrangements with flippers and heads suggested.

Wabi-sabi can be literally interpreted as "withered loneliness". An aesthetic term that was originally used in poetry, and later came to describe aspects of the tea ceremony, including its pottery, gardens and architecture.

Yatsuhashi an eight-plank zigzag bridge that crosses over streams and ponds which are often planted with irises.

Yugen literally meaning "too deep to see", suggesting a mystery or depth that goes beyond what can be seen. A quality sought by Japanese artists of all kinds, including garden makers.

Zen Buddhism a form of Buddhism introduced to Japan from China in the 13th century. Zen heavily influenced the arts, especially gardens such as the *kare-sansui* and tea garden.

Useful addresses

SUPPLIERS

AUSTRALIA
Cyclone Industries Pty Ltd
Victoria, Tasmania; Tel (613) 8791 9300
Wide range of cutting tools

Garden Grove
1150 Golden Grove Road, Golden Grove, Adelaide SA 5125; Tel 8 8251 1111; www.gardengrove.com
Nursery and garden supplies centre

Universal Rocks
20 Hearne Street, Mortdale, NSW 2223
www.universalrocks.com.au

CANADA
The Angelgrove Tree Seed Co.
P.O. Box 74, 141 Hart Path Road, Riverhead, Harbour Grace NL A0A 3P0
www.angelgroveseeds.com

Burns Water Gardens
Baltimore, Ontario K0K 1C0
Tel (905) 372-2737
Waterlilies, aquatic plants, ponds

UNITED KINGDOM
UK Bamboo Supplies Limited
Unit 18, Donkin Road, Armstrong Industrial Estate, Washington, Tyne and Wear NE37 1PF; Tel 0191 417 2915; www.ukbamboosupplies.com

Glendoick Gardens Ltd
Glendoick, Glencarse, Perth PH2 7NS, Scotland; Tel 01738 860205
Rhododendrons and azaleas

Japan Garden Company
15 Bank Crescent, Ledbury, Herefordshire HR8 1AA; Tel 01531 630091; Japangarden.co.uk
Lanterns, screens, fences

Japanese Garden Supplies
Millstone, Mill Lane, Worthing, West Sussex BN13 3DF; Tel 01903 691167

Japanese Garden Supplies
Addlestone Road, East Peckham, Tonbridge TN12 5DP; Tel 01622 872403

Jungle Giants
Ferney Hall, Onibury, Craven Arms, Shropshire SY7 9BJ; Tel 01584 856200
Bamboo plants and materials

Junker's Nursery Ltd
PMA Plant Specialists, Lower Mead, West Hatch, Taunton, Somerset TA3 5RN; Tel 01823 480774; www.junker.net

Kenchester Water Gardens
Church Road, Lyde, Hereford HR1 3AB; Tel 01432 270981
Water products, waterlilies and irises

Rockfeatures
Wilton Farm, Marlow Road, Little Marlow, Buckinghamshire SL7 3RR; Tel 01628 533335; www.rockfeatures.co.uk
Fibreglass and cement, imitation rocks

Silverland Stone
Holloway Hill, Chertsey, Surrey KT16 0AE; Tel 01932 570094;
www.silverlandstone.co.uk

www.mudmom.com
full size and table-top Zen rakes

UNITED STATES
Bamboo Gardens of Washington
5035 – 196th Ave NE, Redmond, WA 98074; Tel (425) 868-5166
Bamboos, fences, lanterns and basins

Bamboo and Koi Garden
2115 SW Borland Road, West Linn, OR 97068; Tel (503) 638-0888;
bambookoigarden@aol.com

Cherry Blossom Gardens
Tel (952) 758-1923;
www.cherryblossomgardens.com
Japanese garden ornaments

Japanese Garden
PO Box 3847, Portland, OR 97208; Tel (503) 223-1321;
www.japanesegarden.com
Bells, lanterns, bonsai and ikebana

Japanese Garden Fences Inc.
P.O. Box 2212, Pawcatuck CT 06379; Tel (860) 599-2348
Handcrafted *sode-gaki* fences

Riverside Enterprises
Tel call toll-free on 1-888-773-8769 or call (518) 272-3800; www.wirestore.com

Tatami Room
466 20th Street, Oakland, CA 94612; Tatamiroom@yahoo.com
Blinds, tatami, lanterns and water basins

Above: *St Mawgan Japanese Garden, Cornwall*

SOCIETIES AND JOURNALS

Japan Garden Society
www.jgs.org.uk

Journal of Japanese Gardening
www.rotheien.com

GARDENS TO VISIT

The Japanese Garden Database
www.jgarden.org
Worldwide listing of gardens

AUSTRALIA
Cowra Japanese Garden
Binni Creek Road, Cowra, NSW 2794; Tel 02-6341 2233

Edogawa Commemorative Garden
36 Webb Street, East Gosford, NSW 2250; Tel 2 4325 0056

The Melbourne Zoo Japanese Garden
Elliott Avenue, P.O. Box 74, Parkville, Victoria 3052; Tel 3 9285 9300

BELGIUM
Hasselt Japanese Garden
Gouverneur Verwilghensingel, 3500, Hasselt; Tel 0 11 23 95 40;
www.trabel.com/hasselt-japanesegarden

CANADA
Kurimoto Japanese Garden
Devonian Botanic Gardens, Edmonton, Alberta; Tel (780) 987-3054

Nitobe Memorial Garden, 895 Lower Mall, Vancouver, British Columbia; Tel (604) 822-6038; www.nitobe.org

FRANCE

Citroën Garden
Parc André-Citroën, Quai André-Citroën, 75015 Paris; Tel: 01 40 71 76 07

Jardins Albert Kahn
Musée Albert-Kahn, 14 rue du Port, 92100 Boulogne-Billancourt, Paris; Tel 01 55 19 28 00

UNESCO Japanese Gardens
7, place de Fontenoy, Paris 75007
Tel (0)1 45 68 10 00; www.unesco.org

GERMANY

Bonn Japanese Garden
Rheinaue Park, Nordrhein-Westfalen

Freiburg Japanese Garden
Ökostation Freiburg, Seeparkgelände, Falkenbergstrasse 21b, Freiburg 79100

Karlsruhe Japanese Garden
Stadt Karlsruhe, Gartenbauamt, 76124 Karlsruhe

Augsburg Japanese Garden
Botanischer Garten, Dr.-Ziegenspeck-Weg 10, D-86161 Augsburg

JAPAN

Daisen-in (Kyoto), Kita-ku, Murasakino, Daitokuji-cho, Kyoto-shi, Kyoto-hu

Ginkaku-ji (Kyoto), Sakyo-ku, Ginkakuji-cho, Kyoto-shi

Joei-ji in (Yamaguchi), Miyano-mura, Yoshiki-gun

Katsura Palace (Kyoto), Ukyo-ku, Katsura, Shimizu-cho
Get permission from the Imperial Park Agency, Kyoto Gosho, 3 Kyoto-Gyoen, Kamigyo-ku, Kyoto; Tel 075 211-6348

Jiko-in (Nara), Nara-shi, Nara-ken

Joju-en (Kumamoto), Kumamoto, Kyushi

Kenroku-en (Kanazawa), 1-4 Kenroku-machi Kanazawa-city, Ishikawa I

Koishikawa-Koraku-en (Tokyo), 1-6-6 Kouraku, Bunkyo-ku, Tokyo 112-0004; Tel (0) 3-3811-3015

Koraku-en (Okayama), 1-5 Korakuen, Okayama-shi, Okayama

Motsu-ji (Iwate), 58 Osawa, Hiraizumi-cho, Nishi-Iwai-gun, Iwate

Raikyu-ji (Takahashi), 18 Raikyuji-cho, Takahashi, Okayama

Ryoan-ji (Kyoto), Ukyo-ku, Ryoanji, Goryoshita-cho, Kyoto-shi

Ryogen-in Zen Garden (Kyoto)
Daitoku-ji-cho, Murasakino, Kyoto-shi

Saiho-ji (Kyoto)
Write for permission: Saiho-ji, Nishigyo-ku, Kamigatani-cho, Matsuo, Kyoto

Sanzen-in (Kyoto), Sakyo-ku, Ohara, Raigoin-cho, Kyoto-shi

Shisen-do (Kyoto), 27 Monguchi-cho, Ichijoji, Sakyo-ku, Kyoto-shi

Shugakuin Palace (Kyoto), Sakyo-ku, Shugakuin, Kyoto-shi

Tôfuku-ji Hojo (Kyoto)
15-778 Honmachi, Higashiyama-ku, Kyoto-shi www.tofukuji.jp/english.html

NEW ZEALAND

Waitakere Japanese Garden
Waitakere City Council, 6 Waipareira Avenue, Waitakere; Tel (09) 836 8000

UNITED KINGDOM

Brunei Gallery Roof Garden
SOAS, Thornhaugh Street, Russell Square, Bloomsbury, London WC1H 0XG; Tel 020 7898 4915

Compton Acres
Canford Cliffs Road, Poole, Dorset BH13 7ES; Tel 01202 700778

Heale Garden and Plant Centre
Middle Woodford, Salisbury, Wiltshire SP4 6NT; Tel 01722 782207

Holland Park Gardens
London W8 6LU; Tel 020 7471 9813

Japanese Garden and Bonsai Nursery
St Mawgan, nr Newquay, Cornwall TR8 4ET; Tel 01637 860116

Newstead Abbey
Newstead Abbey Park, Nottinghamshire NG15 8NA; Tel 01623 455900

Pine Lodge Gardens
Holmbush, St Austell, Cornwall PL25 3RQ; Tel 01726 735000; www.pine-lodge.co.uk

Pureland Zen Garden
North Clifton, Nottinghamshire NG23 7AP; Tel 01777 228567

Royal Botanic Gardens
Kew, Richmond, Surrey TW9 3AB; Tel 020 8332 5655; www.rbgkew.org.uk

Tatton Park
Knutsford, Cheshire, WA16 6QN Tel 01625 534400; www.tattonpark.org.uk

Tully Japanese Garden
Irish National Stud, Tully, Co. Kildare, Ireland Tel +353-45-522963; www.irish-national-stud.ie

UNITED STATES

Brooklyn Botanical Gardens
1000 Washington Ave. Brooklyn, NY 11225 Tel (718) 623-7200; www.bbg.org

Earl Burns Miller Japanese Garden
California State University, Long Beach Tel (562) 985-5930

Hakone Gardens
21000 Big Basin Way, Saratoga CA 95070 Tel (408) 741-4994; www.hakone.com

Hammond Japanese Stroll Garden, North Salem, NY 10560 Tel (914) 669-5033; www.hammondmuseum.org

The Japanese Friendship Garden
1125 N. 3rd Ave Phoenix, AZ
Tel (602) 265-3204

Huntington Botanical Gardens, 1151 Oxford Road, San Marino, CA 91108; Tel (626) 405-398

Japanese Garden, 11 Southwest Kingston Avenue, Portland, Oregon 97205 Tel (503) 223-1321; www.japanesegarden.com

The Japanese Tea Garden, Golden Gate Park, San Francisco, CA 94117

Morikami Japanese Gardens
4000 Morikami Park Road, Delray Beach, Florida 33446 Tel (561) 495-0233; www.morikami.org

Above: *Moss carpet at Sanzen-in, Ohara.*

Index

Figures in italics indicate captions

Acer (maple) 24, *32*, *41*, 57, 85, 86, *95*, 120, 140, 147, *150*, 175, 233
  A. buergerianum (Trident maple) 220, *220*
  A. cissifolium (Ivy-leaved maple) 220, *221*
  A. ginnala (Amur maple) 220
  A. japonicum (Full moon maple) 221, *221*
  A. micranthum (Komine maple) 221
  A. palmatum (Japanese maple) 25, 173, 185, *207*, 220, *220*, 221
  A.p. linearilobum 220, 221
  A.p. var. *dissectum* 221, *221*
  A. rufinerve (Redvein maple) 221
Aesculus hippocastanum (Horse chestnut) 145
ajuga 180
algae *179*, 188, 245
Althaea rosea (Hollyhock) 85, 86, 236, *236*
Amida Buddha 10, 12, 15, 43, 66, 246
Aminohashidate Peninsula *45*, 97, 140, 246
Anemone spp. 223, *223*
anemones 57, 187, 207
arbours 122, 123, 182, *182*, 183, 187
  wisteria 186, *187*, 192–3, *192*, *193*
architectural elements 30–3
Ardisia japonica (Marlberry) 225, *225*
Ashikaga shoguns 11, *11*
asobi style 51, 54
Asplenium scolopendrium (Hart's-tongue fern) 196, 233, *233*
asters 187
Atago, Mount 36
Athyrium trichomanes 233
Aucuba japonica (Japanese laurel) 225, *225*
aucubas 60, 195, 233
Augsburg Japanese garden, Germany *98*, 99
aware 246
azaleas 24, 25, 31, 38, 49, *54*, 55, *55*, *57*, 85, 86, *86*, *88*, *89*, 90, 91, *91*, *143*, 147, *160*, 160, 161, 163, 173, 185, 187, 196, 199, 207, 210, 211, *211*, 225, 239, 244

balloon flower (*Platycodon*) 86
bamboo 7, *19*, 25, 27, 31, 35, 53, 85, 86, 119, 122, 175, 185, 187, 195
  aged patina 63, 128
  courtyard gardens *59*, 60, 61, 196, 199
  in a dry garden *160*, 161, 162
  fences 35, 124–7, *125*, *126*, *127*, *128*, 140, 183, 198, 200–1, *200*, *201*, *244*, 245
beach effect *74*, 75
  cobble 151
  gravel 36, 38, *95*,
  miniature 23
  quartzite *95*
  sandy 151
besoms 238, 244–5, *245*
bluestone 72
bonsai 238
boulders 63
  large natural *81*
  replaced 17
  as stepping stones *39*
  see also rocks and boulders
boundaries 124–9, 145
boxwood 4, 88, *89*, 243
bridges 77, 80, 81, *81*, 83
  Chinese-style 28, 31, 45, 56, *146*, 148, *149*, 151
  courtyard gardens 61, 199
  in a dry garden 162, 163
  history of 132
  pond gardens *42*, 43
  stepping-stone 133, *133*
  in stroll gardens 56, *57*, *183*, 184, *185*, 187
  wattle and log 132, *132*
  wisteria 132–3
  yatsuhashi 94, 132–5
brooms 238, 244–5
Brunei Gallery roof garden, London *81*, *194*
brushes *238*
brushwood 38, *127*, *245*
Buddha 7, 34, *35*, 46, *49*, 64, *64*, 136, *136*, 140, 158, 183, 246, 247
Buddhism 6, 12, 14, 15, 20, 25, 48
  shrines 108
Buddhist Trinity 46, 247

127, *128*, 140, 183, 198, 200–1, *200*, *201*, *244*, 245
Busby, Maureen 17, *31*
Buxus (Box) 239
  B. microphylla japonica (Japanese box) 225, *225*
  B. microphyllus 128, 91
  B. sempervirens 91

Callicarpa japonica 208, 223, *223*
calligraphy scrolls 52, *52*
Camellia
  C. japonica 91, 210, *210*
  C. sasanqua 86, *90*, 91, 128, 173, 204, *208*
camellias 25, 31, 128, 140, 85, 86, *88*, 195, 160, 175, 60, 199, 207, 210, 225, 233, 243
Canadian Embassy, Tokyo 16, *27*, 250
care and maintenance 242–3, *242*
carp *45*, 57, *102*, 245
carp stone 81, 96, *98*, 156, 157, *157*, 246
cascades 99, *156*, 157, 187
cedar 25, 26
Cephalotaxus harringtonia (Japanese plum yew) 229, *229*
Cercidiphyllum japonicum (Katsura tree) 25, 221, *221*
cha-niwa tea garden 246
Chaenomeles japonica (Japanese quince) 210, *210*
Chamaecyparis
  C. obtusa (Hinoki cypress) 91, 187, 229, *229*
  C. pisifera (Sawara cypress) 230, *230*
Chelsea Flower Show, RHS *17*
cherry 25, 35, 57, 60, 85, 86, 147, 183, 184, 187, 195, 207
  blossom (*sakura*) 24, *24*, 25, 34, 35, *56*, 85, 86, 212, 213
  frames *245*
  weeping 185

Chikurin-in tea garden, near Kyoto 53
Chinese influence 9, 12–15, *12*, *13*
  architectural elements 31–2
  Buddhism 12
  Chinese style 12, 20, 23
  geomancy 14
  onset of Japanese style 12, 14
  paintings 14, 15, 65
  tea gardens and ceremonies 15
  Zen Buddhism 15
Chishaku-in, Kyoto 53
chonin (merchant class) 246
chozubachi (water basin) 51, 106, 107, *107*, *110*, 195, *197*, 246
Chrysanthemum spp. 223, *223*
chrysanthemums 25
circuit breakers 105
Claude Lorrain 23
Clematis spp. 86, 215
  C. patens 215, *215*
Clement, Gilles 39, *49*
Cleyera japonica (Japanese cleyera) 226
Cloud Island 97
"cloud pruning" 88, *89*
cobbles *37*, 68, *69*, 74, *74*, 75, *95*, 117, *117*, 151, 163, 166, *168*, 175, 176, 177, *181*, 202
concrete 73, 79, 128
Confucianism 53
Cornus kousa (Japanese flowering dogwood) 215, *215*
courtyard gardens *4*, *6*, 30, 39, 124, 140, 41, 195–5, *194*, *195*, 58–61, 196–205
  building a bamboo screen fence 200–1, *200*, *201*
  building a mound 204–5, *204*, *205*
  elements of 60–1
  garden plan 196, *196*, *197*
  history of 58–60
  how to make a courtyard garden 198–9, *198*, *199*
  laying a paving-stone path 202–3, *202*, *203*
  a modern interpretation 61
  tsubo-niwa 60
  versatility of the courtyard garden style 61
Cove Beach Island 97
cranes *15*, 22, 97, 246
crane islands (*tsurushima*) 12, 29, *29*, 44–5, 68, 154, 246
Cryptomeria (Japanese cedar) 128
  C. japonica 128, *229*, 230
cryptomerias 57, 187
Cunninghamia lanceolata (Chinese fir) *137*
cycads *135*, 245
Cycas revoluta (Sago palm) 235, *235*

Daichi-ji, near Kyoto 90
daimyo (land-owning lord) 54, 59, 246
Daisen-in, Daitokuji Temple, Kyoto 11, 27, 162

Above: *A dry garden at the Canadian Embassy in Tokyo.*

Daphne odora (Winter daphne) 226
Daphniphyllum macropodum 226, *226*
deer scarers (*shishi odoshi*) 106, 109, *110*, 112, 136–7, 247
Deutzia spp. (Japanese snowflower) 24, 85, 86, *208*, 215
  D. gracilis 215
Diospyrus kaki (Persimmon) 222
Dragon Gate Cascade, Kinkaku-ji *156*
Dragon Gate Waterfall, Tenryu-ji 80
drainage, improving 168–9, *168, 169*
dry gardens 6, 9, 11, 30, 34, 38, 39, 41, 46–9, 64, 117, 124, 143, 158–9, *158, 159*, 160–3, 187, 246, *255*
  contemporary interpretation 49
  courtyard gardens 194, *194*
  designing a dry garden 49
  drainage 168–9, *168, 169*
  edging stones 166–7, *166, 167*
  garden plan 160–1, *160, 161*
  history of 46–7
  how to make a dry garden 162–3, *162, 163*
  influence of Zen 47–8
  "no-ness" expressed in 26
  plants 49
  rocks for 69, 164–5, *164, 165*
  and roof gardens *194*
  Ryoan-ji 79, 48–9
  Ryogen-in *13, 29*, 29
  Tenju-an, Kyoto *41, 47, 116, 251*
  Zen-style 27
Dryopteris felix-mas (Robust male fern) 233
dyana (meditation) 15, 246

edging
  cobble 104, *104*
  dry garden 163
  grass 104, *105*
  of gravel paths 190
  paved 105, *105*
  for a pond 104–5
  rock 104, *104*
  timber 104–5, *105*
  water and path 128
edging stones, positioning 166–7, *166, 167*
Edo (later Tokyo) 11, *55*
Edo period (1603–1867) 10, *10, 11, 11*, 16, 31, 39, 51, 54, 55, *55*, 58, 59, 64, 66, *85*, 124, *132, 132, 146, 182*, 246
Eisai 50, 246
Eitoku, Kano *15*
Elaeagnus spp. (Silverberry) 86, 226
  E. x ebbingei 226, *226*
Enkianthus 25, 56
  E. perulatus (White enkianthus) 173, 222, *222*
Enshu, Kobori 36, 51, 90, 246
Equisetum hyemale (Small tufted mare's tail) 236, *246*
Euonymus japonicus (Japanese spindle tree) 226
Eupatorium (Hemp agrimony) (UK); Joe Pye weed (US) 224, *224*

Above: *Dry garden at Tenju-an, Kyoto*

Farfugium 60, 86, 199
  F. japonicum 236, *236*
Fatsia japonica (Japanese aralia) 227, *227*
fatsias 60, 199
fences 61, 124–6, *124, 125, 128, 129*, 187, 199
  bamboo 35, 57, 124–7, *125–8*, 140, 183, 198, *244*, 245
  building a bamboo screen fence 200–1, *200, 201*
  post and rail *128*
  rustic pole 126
  sleeve 126, *126, 127*
  timber 125, *127*
  wattle-and-daub 125
feng-shui 246
ferns *59*, 60, *82*, 86, 140, 157, 173, 175, *177*, 194, 196, 198, 199, 204, 207, 233, *233*
Ficus 86
filters 102, *103*, 245
fish *45*, 57, *102*, 187, 245
Five Dynasties (906–60) 10
flagstone 72
flower arrangements 52, *52*
Forest Isles 97
framing the view 32
Fuji-san (Mount Fuji) 32, 246
furisode (water basin) 107
fuzei (taste) 246

gates 128–9
  bamboo *4, 173*
  stooping (*naka-kuguri*) 51, 53, 128–9, *130*, 170, 172, *173*, 175, 247
  tea-path 130–1, *130, 131*
  trellis 130
gateways *129, 182*
geomancy 14, 24, 246
Ginkgo biloba (Maidenhair tree) 222, *222*
ginkgos 116
gniess 69
Go-shintai (home of the gods) 22, 246

Golden Pavilion, Kyoto (Kinkaku-ji) *4*, 11, *11, 98, 136*
granite 68, 69, *69*, 73, *73*, 77, 79, *118, 120*, 163, 166
grasses 57, *59*, 80, 84, 187, 223, 245
  ornamental 155
gravel 63, 76–7, *76, 181*, 245
  choosing 79
  and drainage 168, *168*, 169
  key elements 78
  raked *4*, 36, 48, 60, 78, *78, 118*, 158, *158, 160*, 162, 191, *191*, 199, *240*, 241, *241*, 244
  red *61*
  suggesting water 7, 12, 22, 27, 158, *158*, 163, 166, 176
  see also paths, gravel
Great Buddha Temple, Nara *35*
grit 118
  coarse 76–7
  fine 76
  raked 76, 244
  sourcing 77
ground cover 84, *84*
gyo (semi-formal pattern) 120, *121*, 247

hako-zukuri pruning technique 244
Hampton Court Flower Show *198*
hand tools 238–41, 243
  weeding 238, *238*
header pool 157
Heale House, Salisbury, Wiltshire *122, 132*
hedges *19, 34*, 35, 25, 86, *86*, 124, 128,
Heian period (785–1184) 9–12, 14, 17, 23, 24, 31, 43, *43*, 44, 55, 58, 94, *95*, 118, 124, *149*, 246
Heian shrine, Kyoto *43, 45, 146, 154*
Hemerocallis (Day lily) 236, *236*
Hiei, Mount 30, 32
Hiei-san mountain 246

hoes 238
hoggin 79
hojo (abbot's quarters) *30*, 47, 246
Hokkaido 24
Hokusai, Katsushika *10*
Honshu 24, 97, 140
Horai, Mount (Horai-san) 29, *29*, 36, *49*, 68, *70*, 149
Horai Island *13*, 20, 22, 246
Hosen-in *19*, 94
Hosta 207, 236–7, *237*
Houttuynia cordata (Chameleon houttuynia) 237, *237*
Huntington Botanical Gardens, San Marino, Los Angeles *4, 39, 96, 126, 143*, 253
hurdles, willow and hazel 126
Hydrangea spp. 24, *25*, 85, 86, 187, 207, 218, *218*
  H. macrophylla 24, 218

Iemitsu, shogun 16
Ieyasu Tokugawa *54*, 55
Ilex
  I. crenata (Japanese bush holly) 91, 227, *227*
  I. integra (Japanese tree holly) 227
  I. rotunda (Japanese tree holly) 227
Indian sandstone 72–3
Interpreting a garden 36
Ipomoea (Morning glory) 86, 218, *218*
Iris spp. 24, 25, 43, 45, *54*, 57, 85, 86, 94, 125, 132, 184, 207, 219
  I. ensata (Japanese water iris) 134, 185, 219, *219*
  I. laevigata 219, *219*
islands 23, *45*, 57, 94, 97, 143, 146, 147, 150, 151
  constructing a pine island 154–5, *154, 155*
Isui-en, Nara 32
Italian gardens 23

Japan 16, 19, 20
Japanese maple *4*
Ji (Chinese capital) 12
Joeji-in, near Yamaguchi 46
juniper 88, 243
Juniperus chinensis (Chinese juniper) 90, 91, 230, *230*

Kamakura 11, 26
Kamakura period (1185–1392) 10, 11, 26, 43, 55, 118, 246
Kame-shima see turtle islands
Kameido *10*
kami (gods) 12, 22, 246
Kamigano, Kyoto *37*
Shinto shrines *4*
Kansetsu, Hashimoto *7*
Karaku-en, Okayama *4*
kare taki (dry cascades) 82
kare-sansui (dry landscape garden) 11, 27, 46, 68, 196, 244, 246
Karlsruhe Japanese Garden, Germany *20, 34, 85*, 248
kasuga (temple-style lanterns) *137*, 140

INDEX 251

Katsura Detached Palace, Kyoto 11, 42, 122
Kenrokuen Garden, Honshu *238*
Kerria japonica (Jew's mallow) 24, 85, 147, 210, *210*
Kew Gardens, Surrey *159*
Kikuzakura (Chrysanthemum cherry) *212*
Kinkaku-ji: Dragon gate cascade *156*
koan (the writing of riddles) 26, 246
Kodaiji Temple, Kyoto *61*
kodai rokkaku stone lantern *140*
koi carp 45, *57*, *102*, 245
Konchi-in, Nanzen-ji, Kyoto *14, 15*, 66, 249
Koraku-en, Okayama *65*
Korea 12, 22
Koto-in *118*
Kyoto (Heian Kyo) 10, 11, 12, 14, 24, 26, 50, 55, 84, 94, 124, 140–1, 246
Kyushu 24

Land of Paradise Garden 12
lanterns 4, 15, 34, *36*, 37, 39, *45*, *50*, 51–2, *56*, 57, 61, *86*, 97, *131*, 136, *137*, 138, *138*, 139, 140, *140*, *147*, 163, 170–1, *170*, *173*, 175, 182–3, *184*, 194, 198, 199, 204
 oribe *61*, 140
 setting a lantern 178–9, *178, 179*
laver stone 176
leaf blowers 238
Lespedeza (Bush clover) 24, 86
 L. bicolor (Shrubby lespedeza) 224, *224*
lichens *72*
lighting 138–41
Ligustrum japonicum (Japanese privet) 227
Lilium (Lily) 207, 237, *242*
limestone 68, 72, 73
Linnaeus, Carl 208
log rolls 104–5, *105*
logs, concrete 119, 192
lotus (*Nelumbo*) 25, 86, 97, *139*
 blossom 25, 86
 bud 139

machiya (smaller town houses) 59, 60, 246
Mackintosh, Charles Rennie 17
Magnolia spp. 37, 207, 210, 211, *211*
 M. grandiflora (Evergreen magnolia) 228
Mahonia japonica (Japanese mahonia) 199, 228, *228*
maple *see* Acer
Mappo (Buddhist age of "ending law") 24, 246
marble *75*, 79
Masuno, Shunmyo *16*
Matsuo Shrine, Kyoto *67*
Matsushima 45, 246
Matsushima Bay 97
Matteuccia struthopteris (Ostrich fern) 233, *233*
Meadow Isle 97
Meiji restoration 55, 246

Above: *The Zen garden at Tenju-an, Kyoto*

millstone grit 72
millstones 35, *43*, 51, 56, 120, *184*, 246
Minamoto 11
Ming dynasty (1368–1644) 11
miscanthus 57, 223
 dwarf 154
 Miscanthus sinensis (Fountain grass; Eulalia grass) 224, *224*
Mist Island 97
mitate (recycled building materials) 56, *184*, 246
modern and Western influences 16–17
Momoyama period (1568–1603) 9, 10, 11, 140, 247
moss 29, *59*, *72*, 80, 82, *100*, *117*, 119, 120, 140, *179*, 180, *242*
 colonization by 118
 in a dry garden 46, *161*, 163
 encouraging *181*, 203, 243
 and gravel *194*
 ground cover 84
 moss carpets 60, *118*, 199, 207, 244, *249*
 mounds of 204, *204*
 and stepping stones *197*
 stone squares in a sea of moss *9, 84*
Motsu-ji, Hiraizumi, Iwate 42, *42*, 43, *100*
mound, building a 204–5, *204, 205*
mountains 20, 22
Murin-an 55, *57*
Muromachi period (1393–1568) 9, 10, 11, *11*, 24, 31, 43, 51, 55, 64, 140, 247
Musa (Hardy banana) 237
Mystic Isles 10, 11, 12, *13*, 14, 20, 22, *27*, 29, *29*, 36, *48*, *49*, 66, 97, 246

naka-kuguri (stooping gate) 128–9, 130, 247
Nandina domestica (Sacred bamboo) 91, 173, 199, 222, *222*, 233

Nansen-ji *48, 52*
Nanzen-in temple, Kyoto *125*
Nara 10, 50, 65
Nara period (712–94) 10, 12, 31, 94, 247
nature 23, 34, 63
Nelumbo (lotus) 25, 86, 97, *139*
 N. nucifera 219, *219*
Newstead Abbey: Japanese garden 94
nigiriguchi (small entrance to tea house) 129, 130, 131, 247
Nijo Castle, Kyoto 11, 64, *133*, *137*, 97
 Seiryu tea garden 55, *109*
niwaki 243
no-da-te (informal tea ceremony) 51, 247
"no-ness" 15, 26

o-karikomi (topiary) 86, *86*, 88, *88*, 89, 90–1, *90*, *91*, 238, 243, 247
 authentic styles 88
 azaleas 88, *88*
 in a dry garden 160
 Kobori Enshu 90
 Mirei Shigemori 91
 Sanzen-in *10*
 square forms 91
 stroll gardens 55–6
 suitable plants 91
 when to clip 90
Ogawa (aka Ujei) 23
Ohara *106*
Onoclea sensibilis 233
Ophiopogon
 O. graminifolius 204
 O. japonica 198
 O. japonicus (Japanese Mondo grass) 84, *177*, 180, *205*, 237, *237*
ophiopogon, dwarf 204
Oribe, Furuta 51, 140
oribe lantern *61*, 140
orientation 144
Osaka 50
Osmanthus 86, 160, 243

 O. burkwoodii 91
 O. delavayi 91
 O. fragrans (Tea olive) 228, *228*
 O. heterophyllus 91
outbuildings 145

paddlestones 75, *75*
Paeonia suffruticosa (Tree peony) 216, *216*
pagodas 6, 34, 37, 39, 136, *136*, *137*, 183, 247
paintings
 Chinese 14, 15, 65, 162
 Japanese 35, 37, 47, 65,
paling, chestnut 126
Parc André Citroën, Paris 39, *39*, 49
paths
 drainage 118
 edging gravel paths 117
 gravel *117*, 118, 120, 151, 186, *186*
 making 190–1, *190, 191*
 history of 116–18
 informal and formal styles 118
 key considerations 119
 laying a paving-stone path 202–3, *202, 203*
 mixed-stone *4*, 121
 paving and cobbling 118
 random paving stones *118*
 sand *54*, 118
 stroll garden *4*, 54, 56, 57, 182, *182*, *183*, 186, 187
 strolling 147, 187
 styles 120–1
 tea (*roji*) 15, 27, 51, *52*, *53*, 118–19, *139*, 170–1, *171*, 172, 187, 245, 247
 weaving 184
 width of 118–19
 see also stepping stones
Paulownia tomentosa (Foxglove tree) 211, *211*
pavilions 31
paving 72–3, 143, 199
 laying a paving-stone path 202–3, *202, 203*
 manmade alternatives 72
 random 72
 reclaimed stones 72
 types of natural stone for paving 72–3, *72, 73*
peach blossom 24, 25, *56*, 212, 213
pebbles 29, *72*, 74, *74*, 75, *75*, 81, 95
P'eng-lai island (later Horai) 20
Peng-lai (Mount Horai) 247
peonies (*Paeonia*) 85, 86, 207
Photinia 88, 128, 160
 P. glabra 91, 228, *228*
Phyllostachys
 P. aurea (Fishpole bamboo; Golden bamboo) 234
 P. aureosulcata (Yellow-groove bamboo) 234
 P. edulis (Moso bamboo) 234
 P. nigra (Black bamboo) *160*, 161, 234
 P. nigra henonis 196
 P. vivax (Vivax bamboo; Chinese timber) 234

Pieris 86, 88
  P. japonica (Japanese Andromeda) 91, 228
pillars 32, *32*, 33, *43*, *122*, *171*
pine 25, 27, 29, 31, 35, 38, *39*, 57, 85, 86, 88, 94, 97, 140, 146, 147, 154, *159*, 162, 163, 187, 195, 196, 229
  binding of *244*
  pruning a dwarf pine 243
pine islands 45, *45*, 148
  constructing 154–5, *154*, *155*
Pinus
  P. densiflora (Japanese red pine) 173, 185, 196, 230–1, *231*
  P.d. umbraculifera (dwarf Japanese red pine) 198, 204, 243
  P. parviflora (Japanese white pine) 231, *231*
  P. thunbergii (Japanese black pine) *85*, *116*, 149, 154, *155*, 161, 173, 185, 231, *231*, *253*
plan 144–5, *144*, *145*
  checklist for your plan 144–5
  what to include 144
plant directory 206–37
  autumn flowers 223–4
  autumn foliage 220–2
  bamboo 234
  evergreen 225–8
  evergreen trees & conifers 229–32
  ferns 233
  how plants are named 208
  how to use the plant directory 209
  late spring & summer trees, shrubs & climbers 215–17
  palms 235
  spring blossom 212–14
  spring trees & shrubs 210–11
  summer flowers 218–19
  other plants of interest 236–7
planting 87, *87*
  styles 86
plants
  and courtyard gardens 195
  hardiness 256
  how they are named 208
  Japan's natural flora 85, *85*
  in pond gardens 147
  seasonal variety 85–6
  significance of 7
  and streams 95
  in stroll gardens 183
  symbolic 85
  through the seasons 86
Platycodon grandiflorus (Balloon flower) 224
platycodons 86, 187, 207
Pleioblastus
  P. humilis (Dwarf bamboo) 234, *234*
  P. pygmaeus (Pygmy bamboo) 234
plum (*Prunus mume*) 57, 85, *161*, 187, 212, *212*
  blossom *19*, 24, 25, *56*, 86, 212
  plum, spring (*Prunus* spp.) 161
Podocarpus 128
  P. macrophyllus (Maki) 231, *231*

Polystichum setiferum (Soft shield fern) 196, 204, 233, *233*
pond gardens 6, 41, 42–5, 146–7, *146*, *147*
  following natural forms 44
  garden plan: a pond garden 148–9, *148*, *149*
  history of 42
  how to make a pond garden 150–1
  key considerations 43
  later pond gardens 43–4
  Motsu-ji 42–3, *42*
  pine islands 45
  planning a pond garden 45
  reading around the subject 45
  turtle and crane islands 44–5
ponds 12, 23, 31, 85, *94*, 97, 122
  butyl-lined 43, *74*, 75, 102–5, *102*, *103*, *105*, 154, 156, 188–9, *188*, *189*
  clay-lined 43, 150, 152–6, *152*, *153*, 188
  creating edges for 104–5
  key elements 97
  lanterns in *140*
  liners 97, 105
  making a pond with a flexible liner 188–9, *188*, *189*
  naturalistic outlines 34
  sacred 22
  in a stroll garden 57, 182, *183*, 186, 187
pools, "dry" 77
Poussin, Nicolas 23
pruning 243
  dwarf pine 243
  saws 239, *239*
  shears *4*
Prunus
  P. 'Amanogawa' 214, *214*
  P. laurocerasus (Cherry laurel) 91
  P. lusitanica (Portugal laurel) 91
  P. mume (Japanese plum, Japanese apricot) 86, 212, *212*, *247*
  P. persica (peach) 16–17, 213
  P. sargentii 214, *214*

P. serrulata (Japanese cherry) 213
P. subhirtella pendula (Weeping cherry) 185
P. 'Shirofugen' 214, *214*
P. 'Tai Haku' 214, *214*
P. 'Ukon' 214, *214*
P. x yedoensis (Yoshino cherry) 213, *213*
Pseudosasa japonica (Arrow bamboo) 234
pumps 57, 95, 96, 99, 102, 103, *103*, *108*, 109, *110*, 112, *112*, 113, 151, 156, *157*, 175, 176, 187
Pure Land Paradise 10, *247*
Pureland Zen garden, Nottinghamshire 147

Qing dynasty (1644–1911) 11
quartz 77, 79
quartzite 61, 95
Quercus (oak) 128

Raikyu-ji, Takahashi 88, 90, 36
rakes 238, 240–1, *241*
raking patterns 78, *78*, 79, *79*
reeds 94
reliefs, carved *136*
reservoir construction 112–13, *112*
residual current devices (RCDs) 105
Rhapis excelsa (Miniature fan palm) 235
Rheinaue Japanese Garden, Germany *42*, *117*, *254*
Rhododendron spp. (azaleas) 211, *211*
rhododendrons 37, 210
Rikyu, Sen no 11, 51, 116, 107, 247
Rinka (rural monks) 26
rocks
  alternatives 38
  by ponds and waterfalls 146
  courtyard gardens *58*, 60, 61, *61*, 194, 196, 198, 199
  in a dry garden 158, *158*, *159*
  grouping 36, 43, 48, *48*

Above: *Japanese black pines in the Huntington Botanical Gardens*

planting to contrast with their outline 89
in pond garden 151
positioning 164–5, *164*, *165*
in stroll gardens 56
rocks and boulders 20, 22, 26, 31, 63, 64–71
  Chinese style *12*
  choosing 68–9
  creating a rock garden 65–6
  in dry water gardens *4*, 11
  making rock groupings 66–7
  manmade alternatives 69
  moving rocks and boulders 70–1
  replaced 17, *26*
  representing Mystic Isles 27
  rocks for dry gardens 69
  rocks for water features 68–9
  sacred 22
  significance of 7
  sources of natural rock 69
  spiritual qualities and symbolism 64–5
  using rocks in the Japanese garden 67
  weathered stone 68
Rocky Islet 97
rocky islets 148, *149*
Rocky Mountains 16
roji (tea path) 15, 51, *52*, *53*, 59, 128, *131*, *139*, 170, 172, 187, 245, 247
roji-mon (entrance gate to tea garden or *roji*) 128, 247
roof gardens 61, *194*
roofs
  reed and bamboo 53
  sweeping *124*
  tiled *50*
roses, wild 24
Ryoan-ji, Kyoto 11, 17, 27, 47–9, 66, *66*, 68, 79, 90, 106, 160, 247
Ryogen-in, Kyoto *4*, *13*, 29, *29*, *60*

Saiho-ji (Moss Temple), Kyoto *9*, 11, *42*, 80, 132
St Mawgan Japanese Garden, Cornwall *7*, *80*, *248*
Sakai 50
Sakuteiki 6, 10, 17, 23, 82, 97, 44, 45, 156, 247
samurai (soldiers) 11, 31, 51, 52, 58, 247
sand
  choosing 79
  cones *4*, *37*
  courtyard gardens *58*, *60*, 196, 198
  expressing "no-ness" 26
  fine *76*
  raked 20, *30*, *47*, *48*, 56, *66*, 76, 78, 82, 158, 169, *204*, *240*, 241
  sharp 118, 181, *181*
  sourcing 77
  suggesting water 7, 11, 22, 48, *48*, 64, *80*, 120, 158, *160*
sandstone 68, 72, 73
Sanzen-in, Ohara 10, *59*, *84*, 90, 107, *143*, 249

Sanzon, Mount 68
scalpings 79
schist 68, 69
Sciadopitys verticillata (Japanese umbrella pine) 232, *232*
screens 60, 127–8, 129, *198*, 199
sculptures 136, *136*
scythes 238
seasons 24–5
secateurs (pruners) *4*, 238–9, *239*, 243
sedges (*Carex*) *82*, 132, 140, 157, 173, 175, *177*, 207
Seiryu tea garden, Nijo Castle *109*
Sento, Imperial Palace of, Kyoto: Wisteria Court 58
Sesshu, Toya *13*, 46–7, 247
setts
  driveway 73
  granite *63, 72*, 117, 120
  Indian sandstone 73
shakkei ("borrowed landscape") 19, 30, *30*, 32, 54, 90, 140, *160*, 182, 186, 187, 243, 247
shears 239, *239*, 243
shibumi (minimalist Edo aesthetic) 54, 247
Shigemori, Mirei *16*, 17, 22, *38*, *61*, *67*, *80*, 91, *91*, *95*, *158*, *194*, 247
shiki-no-himorogi (sacred precincts) 22, 247
Shikibu, Murasaki: *The Tales of Genji* 22, 24, 42, 45, 246
shime (binding of artefacts with rice straw ropes) 22, 247
Shimusen, Mount 12, *49*, 68
shin (formal pattern) 120, *121*, 247
shinden ("sleeping hall") 31, 247
Shinto 14, 19, 20, 22–3, 247
shrines 37, 108
Shisendo, Kyoto *46*, *54*, 79, 244
Shoden-ji, Kyoto *30*, 49, 90, 160
shoguns (military dictators) 11, *11*, 16, 33, 129, 247
shoin architecture 31, 32, 33, 247
Shonagon, Sei: *The Pillow Book* 24, 45
shorelines, miniature 23
shrines *37*, *108,* 138,
shrubs 120
  deciduous flowering 60
  clipped 34, 35, 36, 55–6, 57, 64, 86, *99*, 182, 199
  evergreen 25, *25*, 35, 36, 60, 82, 86, *99*, *147*, 163, 199, 225–8
shukkei (miniature landscapes) 60–1, 196, 199
Shumisen, Mount 158, 247
sickles 238
Silver Pavilion (Ginkakuji), Kyoto 11, *59*, *106*, *240*
Site of Reversible Destiny, Gifu, Japan 22, *245*
slate 68, 69, *69*, 73, *73*, 75, 77, *77*
sleeve fences 126, *126*, *127*, 247
sliding doors (*shoji*) 32, 123
"snow flowers" 20

so (informal pattern) 120, *121*, 247
soan (rustic architecture of tea houses) 31, 247
Song dynasty (960–1279) 10, 11, 14
Sophora japonica (Japanese pagoda tree) 216, *216*
  weeping sophora *242*
sori-hashi (Chinese-style bridge) 132
Sotatsu, Tawaraya 22
sotomon (covered outer gateway) 170
spillstone 99
Spiraea nipponica (Nippon spiraea) 216, *216*
spiraeas 85, 86, 147
spirits *26*, 64, 97
statues 136, 183
steel: edging gravel paths 117
stepping stones *4*, *17*, 31, 39, *43*, *58*, 69, 72, *72*, *73*, 77, 116–17, 119, 120, *121*, *97*, *147*, 163, 175, 180–1, *180*, *181*, 182, 186, 187, 196, *197*, 199
  laying 180–1, *180*, *181*
steps, stone 184
Stewartia pseudocamellia (Japanese stewartia) 216, *216*, 222
stones
  aged patina 63
  chippings 77
  correct placing of 23
  positioning edging stones 166–7, *166*, *167*
  streams running over 95
  weathered 68
streams 20, 23, 31, 35, 94, *94*, *95*, 102, *122*
  arranging the elements of 98–9
  boulder 67
  building a meandering stream 100–1, *100*
  dry 7, 80–3, 158, 162, 163
  garden 23
  key elements 95
  liners 98, 99

meandering 12, 80, 94, *95*, *98*, 100–1, *100*, 147, *44*, 148, *148*
  mountain 55
  preformed stream units 99
  steep rocky 19
  stream effect 74
  in stroll gardens 56–7, 187
stroll gardens 6, 11, 39, 41, 43, 54–5, 123, 182–3, *182*, *183*, 184–93
  designing a stroll garden 57
  garden plan 184–5, *184*, *185*
  history of 54–5
  how to make a stroll garden 186–7, *186*, *187*
  Katsura Detached Palace, Kyoto 11, 122
  key considerations 57
  Koraku-en, Okayama 65
  making a gravel path 190–1, *190*, *191*
  making a pond with a flexible liner 188–9, *188*, *189*
  making a wisteria arbour 192–3, *192*, *193*
  rocks and topiary 55–6
  the route to the tea house 57
  streams 56–7
  Syoko-ho-en, Kyoto *137*
  viewing points 56
stupas 136, 108
styles of Japanese gardens 6
Styrax japonicus (Japanese snowbell) 217, 222
sui-kinkutsu (water echo-chamber) 137, 111, *111*
Sumeru 247
sweet peas (*Lathyrus odorata*) 86
sycamore (*Acer*) 145
Syoko-ho-en, near Kyoto *4*, *23*, *137*

tama-mono pruning technique 244
Tang dynasty (618–906) 10, 14
tatami (woven rush matting) *32*, 33, 52, 53, 60, 122, 247

Tatton Park, Cheshire: Japanese Garden 37
Taxus 145, 243
  T. baccata 91
  T. cuspidata (Japanese yew) 91, 232, *232*
tea ceremony (*cha-noyu*) 11, 33, 50, *51*, 52, 53, *170*, 176, *197*, 246
tea gardens *4*, 6, 9, 11, 15, 36, 39, 41, 50–3, 143, 170–1, *170*, *171*, 172–81
  arranging a *tsukubai* 176–7, *176*, *177*
  construction of the tea house 52
  design 128
  the features of a tea garden 52–3
  flexibility of 53
  garden plan 172–3, *172*, *173*
  history of 50–1
  how to make a tea garden 174–5, *174*, *175*
  lanterns in 138, *138*, *139*
  laying stepping stones 180–1, *180*, *181*
  in miniature 53
  planting 86
  RHS Chelsea Flower Show 17
  Seiryu, Nijo Castle *109*
  setting a lantern 178–9, *178*, *179*
  the tea garden ritual 51–2
  and wells 137
  Zen-style 27
tea houses 11, 15, 27, *27*, 31–2, 122–3, 170, *170*, *171*, *182*
  design and construction 52, 53, 122
  interiors 52, 123, *123*
  Saiho-ji Moss Temple, Kyoto *9*
  and stroll gardens 57, 187
  Toji-in, Kyoto 33, *33*
Tenju-an, Kyoto *44*
  dry garden *41*, *47*, *116*, *251*
  pond garden *150*
  stepping-stone bridge *133*
  Zen garden *28*, *252*
Tenryu-ji 11, *56*, 80, 132
Thuja plicata (Western red cedar) 91
Thujopsis dolabrata (Japanese elkhorn cypress) 232
tiles 48, 79, 163, 166
  clay *76*
  roof *84*, 120
  terracotta pantiles 124
Tofuku-ji, Kyoto *16*, *22*, *30*, *38*, *160*, *61*, *78*, *80*, *84*, 91, *91*, *124*, *58*
Toji-in tea houses, Kyoto 33, *33*
tokonoma (alcove in a tea house) 32, 33, 52, *52*, 123, 247
Tokugawa shogunate 11, 16, 54, 55
tools *see* hand tools
topiary *see* o-karikomi
Torii gates 20
  Karlsruhe Japanese Garden, Germany *20*, *34*, *248*
Trachycarpus fortunei 235, *235*

Above: *The author working in his Shropshire garden.*

trees 22, *26*, *35*, *138,* 145
  evergreen 82, 187
  supports 245, *245*
Tricyrtis (Toad lily) 57, 86, 187, 224, *224*
trimmers 238
tsubo-niwa (courtyard garden) 60, 126, 196, 247
tsubos see courtyard gardens
Tsuga (Hemlock) 232, *232*
tsukubai (low basin and lantern) 50, 51, 52, 102, 106–8, 111, *109, 110*, 131, 140, 171, *173, 174*, 175, *175*, 178, 180, 233, 247
  arranging a *tsukubai* 176–7, *176, 177*
Tsuru-shima see Crane island
Tully Japanese Garden, Ireland 25, *146, 157, 166,* 187
turfing 145
turtle islands (*kameshima*) 12, 29, *29*, 44–5, 68, *143*, 154, *155*, 247
  Konchi-in, Nanzen-ji, Kyoto *14, 249*
  making 148, *149*
turtles 20, 22, 29, 80, 97, 247

Ulmus parvifolia (Chinese elm) 217
  U p. 'Yatsubusa' 217, *217*

understanding the Japanese garden 34–36
  natural and manmade elements 37
  rocks and water 34
  utilities 144–5, *144*

verandas 31, 32, *32*, 48, 51, *94, 107*, 109, 117, *138, 171, 174,* 195
viewing points 145

wabi-sabi ("withered loneliness") 34, 51, 247
waiting booths (*koshikake*) 53, 172, 175, 187
walls 124, *124,* 163
  oil and clay 48, 66
water
  dry 41, 80–1,
  imitating the flow of 79
  in the Japanese garden 94
  significance of 7
  suggesting see under gravel; sand
  see also ponds; streams; waterfalls
water basins 4, 15, *35,* 106–9, 50, 51, 61, *106, 107, 108, 109, 110,* 112, *129, 131,* 136, *139, 140, 170,* 170, 171, *174,* 175,

176, 177, *177*, 182, 187, 194, 195, *197*, 198, 199, 204, 247
water features, rocks for 68–9
water lilies (*nymphaea*) 97
water mill 137
watercourse, preparing the 98–9, *98, 99*
waterfall stone 156
waterfalls 15, *15*, 23, 68–9, 94, 96, *96*, 98, *98*, 102, 146
  building a waterfall 156–7, *157*
  dry 4, 80–3, *81, 82*, 158, 162, 163
  in a pond garden 150, 151
  Rheinaue Garden, Germany 42
  St Mawgan Japanese Garden, Cornwall 7
  in a stroll garden 184, *185,* 187
weeding 244
wells 137
wind tunnels 145
Wisteria spp. *10*, 24, 25, 85, 86, *122,* 132, 133, 183, 187, *207,* 217, *217*
  arbour 186, *187*, 192–3, *192, 193*
  W. floribunda 133, 185, 192, *192*

wood
  aged patina 63
  edging gravel paths 117
  preservatives 201
Wright, Frank Lloyd 17

yarimizu (meandering stream) 94
yatsuhashi (zigzag bridge) 94, 132, 134–5, 247
yew see *Taxus*
yin-yang 14, 246
York stone 72
Yoshimasa, shogun 33
Yuan (Mongol) dynasty (1279–1368) 11

Zazen (meditation) 26
Zen Buddhism 7, 11, *13*, 15, 17, 19, 26–9, 47–8, 50, 53, 78, *136,* 178, 247
Zen gardens
  dry gardens 26–7, *27*, 47–8, 163
  with raked waves 29, *29*
  tea gardens 27
  Tenju-an, Kyoto 252
Zen monks 7, 15, 19, 26, *27*, 48, 64, 80, 116, 244
zoyza grass 84
Zuiho-in Temple, Kyoto 240

Acknowledgements

Author's acknowledgements
In the making of this book I would specially like to thank David Greatorex and Roger Midgley, for their enthusiasm and dedication in building the project sequences; Anna Laflin for her beautiful drawings and for her help with the designs; and my wife Anne for her support and tolerance for all the disruptions to our garden.

As well as all the location owners mentioned in the following section, I would like to thank Masahiro Takaishi, creator of the Japanese garden in Holland Park, who showed me around and gave me lessons in pruning. Also to Marc Keane who kindly included me in his group of volunteers, weeding and tidying the wonderful gardens of Hakusa-sonso. Thanks to Gunter Nitschke for his stimulating hours of discussions on the philosophies of Zen and gardens over coffee in Kyoto, and for directing me to the most interesting sites. A special thanks to Egami and his wife Hiromi who took me to all kinds of wonderful places and showed me some of the Ways of Tea, and the intricacies of tea-house architecture. Thanks also to Joho Ozeki for his hospitality at the Jiko-in Zen Temple in Nara; and Venetia Stanley-Smith for introducing us to the private gardens of Ohara as well as her encouragement and useful introductions, and to her husband Tadashi, a few of whose photographs adorn the pages of this book.

Publisher's acknowledgements
The publisher would like to thank the following for kindly allowing photography to take place in their gardens: Stella Hore of the Japanese Garden and Bonsai Nursery, St Mawgan, Cornwall; Frances Rasch at Heale Garden and Plant Centre, Salisbury, Wiltshire; the Japanese-style roof, Brunei Gallery, School of Oriental and African Studies, London; the Royal Botanic Gardens in Kew, London; Newstead Abbey, Newstead Abbey Park, Nottinghamshire; the Pureland Zen Garden, Nottinghamshire; the Tully Japanese Garden, courtesy of The Irish National Stud Co., Tully, Co. Kildare, Ireland; Helmut Kern at Stadt Karlsruhe, Karlsruhe, Germany; Stadt Augsburg (Augsburg Botanic Garden) in Germany; the Bonn Japanese Garden in Rheinaue Park, Nordrhein-Westfalen, Germany; Lisa Blackburn at The Huntington Library, Art Collections and Botanical Gardens, San Marino CA 91108; Kazuo Tamura of Tatsumura Silk Company for his garden of Syoko-ho-en; and to the other temples and gardens in Japan who kindly gave us permission to take photographs: Byodo-in, Hakusa sonso, the Heian Shrine, Honen-in, Isui-en, Kinkaku-ji, Koetsu-ji, Konchi-in, Koto-in, Murin-an, Nanzen-ji, Nigo Caste, Ryogen-in, Sanzen-in, Shoden-ji, Tenju-an, Tofuku-Ji and Toji-in.

The majority of the photographs in this book were taken by Alex Ramsay, with images of materials and equipment taken by Peter Anderson. A large selection were provided from Charles Chesshire's collection. Thanks also to Peter Busby, who very kindly gave us access to the late Maureen Busby's extensive photographic record of garden projects. All photographs are © Anness Publishing Ltd unless stated otherwise. The photograph on p31 (© Anness Publishing) shows Maureen Busby's 'Shizen' Japanese garden at Chelsea Flower Show 2004.

The publisher would like to thank the following for allowing their photographs to be reproduced (t = top; b = bottom; c = centre; r = right; l = left) **Alamy Images**: p35b (Takashi Yamaguchi), p39b (Paul Shawcross), p60t (Photo Japan), p61t (Photo Japan), p73tm (John Glover), p76b (Iain Masterton), p85b (Jon Arnold), p86b (John Glover), p109t (VisualJapan), p109bl (Claire Takacs), p110r (John Glover), p111t (Paolo Neri), p121tr (John Lander), p189b (Juniors Bildarchiv), 195b (Andrew Holt), p198t (Aflo Co. Ltd), p214tr (Rob Whitworth), p214br (Neil Holmes), p215t (Simon Colmer and Abby Rex), p240tl (Christian Kober), p242tr (Ulana Switucha), p243t (Ulana Switucha); **The Bridgeman Art Library**: p10b (Leeds Museums and Galleries UK), 13b (Tokyo National Museum, Japan), p15t (Tokyo Fuji Art Museum, Tokyo, Japan); **Harpur Garden Images**: p47tr; **istock**: p73tl (Maurice van der Velden), p73tr (Daniel González Acuna), p94 (Pierre Yu), p114–115 (Michael Irwin), p114 (Martin Mette); **Peter Busby**: p37t, p58t, p61bl, 134t, p144t, p145t, p145b, p158t; **Charles Chesshire**: p11b, p12t, p12b, p16t, p20, p22t, p26t, p26b, 27tl, 27b, p37b, p38t, p38b, p41, p42t, p42br, p46t, p48b, p53t, p53b, p54t, p56tl, p58b, p59t, p59br, p61br, p65t, p66b, p67, p70bl, p88t, p95t, p95b, p96t, p100b, p111bl, p111bm, p111br, p128t, p128b, p129t, p132t, 135b, p149br, p174t, p182t, p195t, p211br, p215m, p215b, p217b, p219bl, p220bl, p220br, p221bl, p222br, p224bl, p226tr, p242tr, p245bl; **Corbis**: p121tm (M. Yamashita), p213tl (Mark Bolton), p238b (M. Yamashita), p242b (B.S.P.I), p245t (M. Yamashita); **Getty**: p121tl (Kaz Chiba), p129t (Umon Fukushima), p242tl (B. Tanaka); **Karlsruhe Japanese Garden**: p6, p19, p24t, p25b, p85b; **Tadashi Kajiyana** p24b, p212bl, p218tr; **Werner Forman Archive**: p22b (Burke Collection, New York).

Plant hardiness

Each of the plants in the Plant Directory has been given a plant hardiness rating for European readers (see text below) and a zone range for readers in the United States (see map and zone categories below).

So, when applied to the United States, plant entries in this book have been given zone numbers, and these zones relate to their hardiness. The zonal system used, shown below, was developed by the Agricultural Research Service of the U.S. Department of Agriculture (USDA). According to this system, there are 11 zones, based on the average annual minimum temperature in a particular geographical zone. When a range of zones is given for a plant, the smaller number indicates the northernmost zone in which a plant can survive the winter, and the higher number gives the most southerly area in which it will perform consistently.

This is not a hard and fast system, but simply a rough indicator, as many factors other than temperature also play an important part where hardiness is concerned. These factors include altitude, wind exposure, proximity to water, soil type, the presence of snow or existence of shade, night temperature, and the amount of water received by a plant. Factors such as these can easily alter a plant's hardiness by as much as two zones.

HARDINESS RATINGS

Frost tender Plant may be damaged by temperatures below 5°C (41°F).
Half hardy Plant can withstand temperatures down to 0°C (32°F).
Frost hardy Plant can withstand temperatures down to -5°C (23°F).
Fully hardy Plant can withstand temperatures down to -15°C (5°F).

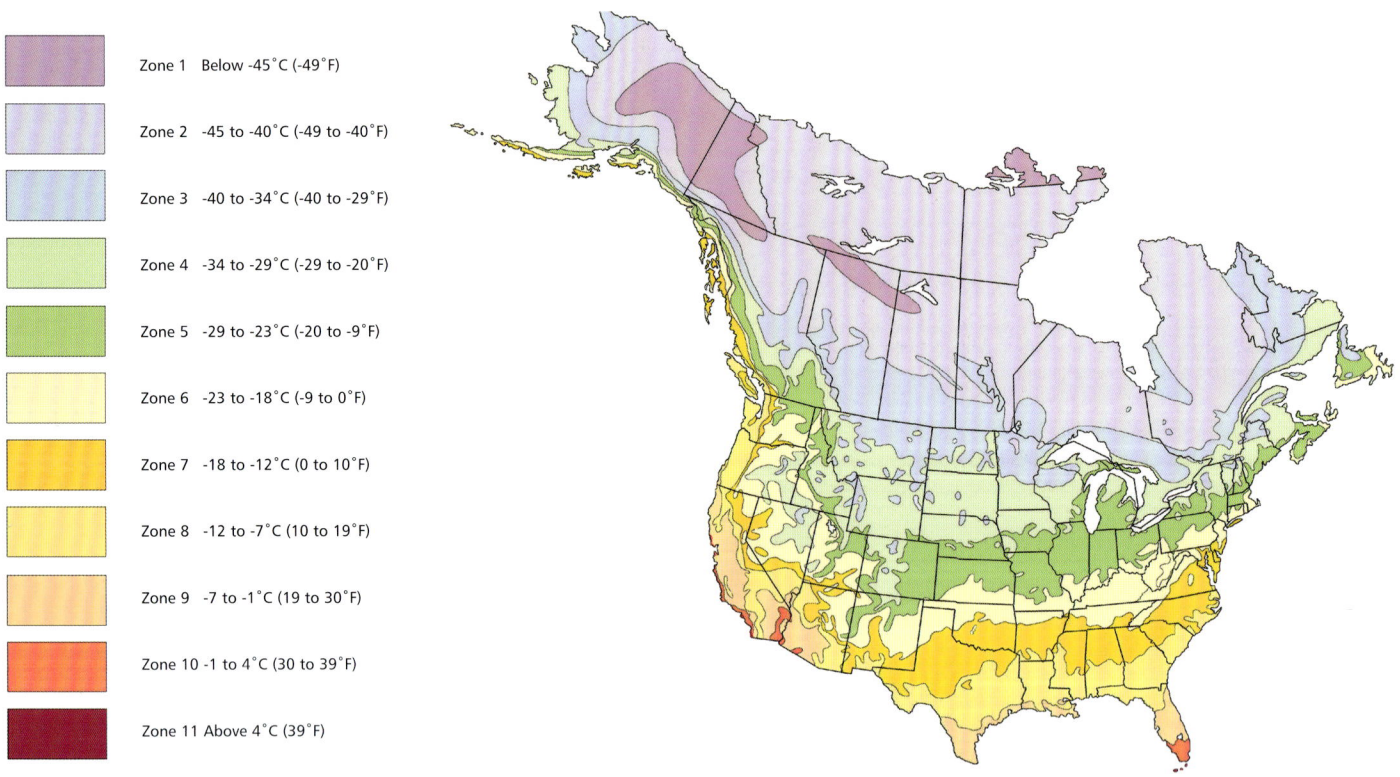

Zone 1 Below -45°C (-49°F)
Zone 2 -45 to -40°C (-49 to -40°F)
Zone 3 -40 to -34°C (-40 to -29°F)
Zone 4 -34 to -29°C (-29 to -20°F)
Zone 5 -29 to -23°C (-20 to -9°F)
Zone 6 -23 to -18°C (-9 to 0°F)
Zone 7 -18 to -12°C (0 to 10°F)
Zone 8 -12 to -7°C (10 to 19°F)
Zone 9 -7 to -1°C (19 to 30°F)
Zone 10 -1 to 4°C (30 to 39°F)
Zone 11 Above 4°C (39°F)

ETHICAL TRADING POLICY

At Anness Publishing we believe that business should be conducted in an ethical and ecologically sustainable way, with a proper regard to the replacement of the natural resources we employ.

As a publisher, we use a lot of wood pulp to make high-quality paper for printing, and that wood commonly comes from spruce trees. We are therefore currently growing more than 750,000 trees in three Scottish forest plantations: Berrymoss (130 hectares/320 acres), West Touxhill (125 hectares/305 acres) and Deveron Forest (75 hectares/185 acres). The forests we manage contain more than 3.5 times the number of trees employed each year in making paper for the books we manufacture.

Because of this ongoing programme, you, as our customer, have the reassurance of knowing that a tree is being cultivated on your behalf to replace the materials that were used to make the book that you are holding.

Our forestry programme is run in accordance with the UK Woodland Assurance Scheme (UKWAS) and will be certified by the Forest Stewardship Council (FSC), an organization that promotes responsible management of the world's forests. Certification ensures forests are managed in an environmentally sustainable and socially responsible way. For more information, go to www.annesspublishing.com/trees